Praise for *Discovering Ou*

"A moving, inspiring, easy-to-read testimony to the pure goodness of God. By posing pertinent questions, Trevor Hudson takes us into the transforming, healing presence of God. Individuals and groups desiring to grow in grace and go deeper into God could benefit enormously from applying themselves to this profound and powerful book."

Joyce Huggett, author of *The Joy of Listening to God*

"I met Trevor Hudson one sunny day in his home country, South Africa. The moment I met him I knew him to be a profoundly spiritual person, and our lengthy conversation that day confirmed my initial impression. Trevor Hudson is one of South Africa's contemporary spiritual masters. The book in your hands contains the wisdom of a gentle pastor guiding each of us into a deeper walk with a God who heals. If I had one person I'd choose to be a pastor to my children, it would be Trevor Hudson."

Scot McKnight, author of *Jesus Creed* and blogger at www.beliefnet.com

"I consider Trevor Hudson to be a wonderful friend. He must be because even after my wife started using one of his books (instead of mine) for a college course she was teaching on spiritual formation, I still like him. And she's certain to begin using *Discovering Our Spiritual Identity*, because I can hardly imagine a better resource for Christ-following; like the author, it is practical and profound."

Gary W. Moon, M.Div., Ph.D., vice president, Richmont Graduate University, and author of *Apprenticeship with Jesus*

"From his long-time pastoral heart and skills, Trevor invites us to be shepherded and strengthened with practices that immerse us in God and lead us into Christlikeness."

Jan Johnson, spiritual director and author of *Invitation to the Jesus Life* and *Spiritual Disciplines Companion*

"To those who have already discovered him, Trevor Hudson is a much-loved and trusted spiritual guide who is known for his practical books on the Christian spiritual journey. Organized around sixteen signposts toward a renewed spirituality that is centered in Jesus, *Discovering Our Spiritual Identity* presents a series of what he calls 'holy experiments'—time-tested practices that hold the potential of transforming hearts and minds, attention and awareness, willing and doing. Don't just read this book; take the time to live it, to make space in your life for these experiments to gain a foothold. It will leave you forever changed."

David G. Benner, author of *The Gift of Being Yourself*

formatio

TRADITION. EXPERIENCE.
TRANSFORMATION.

Formatio books from InterVarsity Press follow the rich tradition of the church in the journey of spiritual formation. These books are not merely about being informed, but about being transformed by Christ and conformed to his image. Formatio stands in InterVarsity Press's evangelical publishing tradition by integrating God's Word with spiritual practice and by prompting readers to move from inward change to outward witness. InterVarsity Press uses the chambered nautilus for Formatio, a symbol of spiritual formation because of its continual spiral journey outward as it moves from its center. We believe that each of us is made with a deep desire to be in God's presence. Formatio books help us to fulfill our deepest desires and to become our true selves in light of God's grace.

TREVOR HUDSON

FOREWORD BY DALLAS WILLARD

DISCOVERING OUR

SPIRITUAL IDENTITY

Practices for God's Beloved

IVP Books

An imprint of InterVarsity Press
Downers Grove, Illinois

InterVarsity Press
P.O. Box 1400, Downers Grove, IL 60515-1426
World Wide Web: www.ivpress.com
E-mail: email@ivpress.com

InterVarsity Press® is the book-publishing division of InterVarsity Christian Fellowship/USA®, a movement of students and faculty active on campus at hundreds of universities, colleges and schools of nursing in the United States of America, and a member movement of the International Fellowship of Evangelical Students. For information about local and regional activities, write Public Relations Dept., InterVarsity Christian Fellowship/USA, 6400 Schroeder Rd., P.O. Box 7895, Madison, WI 53707-7895, or visit the IVCF website at <www.intervarsity.org>.

Design: Cindy Kiple
Images: Jaime Monfort/Getty Images

ISBN 978-0-8308-1092-5

Printed in the United States of America ∞

Library of Congress Cataloging-in-Publication Data

Hudson, Trevor, 1951-
Discovering our spiritual identity: practices for God's beloved/
Trevor Hudson; foreword by Dallas Willard.
p. cm.
Includes bibliographical references (p.   ).
ISBN 978-0-8308-1092-5 (pbk.: alk. paper)
1. Spiritual life—Christianity. I. Title.
BV4501.3.H82184 2010

2010024969

P	22	21	20	19	18	17	16	15	14	13	12	11	10	9	8	7	6	5
Y	29	28	27	26	25	24	23	22	21	20	19	18	17	16	15			

CONTENTS

FOREWORD

IN THIS BOOK, TREVOR HUDSON states with utter simplicity and clarity the profound truths of Jesus Christ, about how we can live well and beautifully, no matter what our circumstances. Chapter by chapter, he takes the fundamental aspects of the life of faith in Jesus, the Master of Life, and spells them out in vivid language and practical procedures: finding our identity, hearing and speaking with God, speaking for God, the stewardship of our daily work and play, approaching our death and the world beyond, and living now as an apprentice of Jesus in the kingdom of God.

He draws constantly on his rich and fruitful experience as a pastor, retreat leader and counselor, but also on a broad and deep knowledge of the history and writings of Christ's people through the ages. But this is done in a way that makes every treasure of his knowledge completely accessible. He gives us a gentle but honest book by revealing his own struggles, personally and in the wounded context of contemporary South Africa, where Christ still leads his followers in radiant triumph.

Trevor Hudson provides a profound and intensely practical guidebook to life as God intends it to be. It will be of great benefit both to individuals and to study groups.

Dallas Willard
Department of Philosophy
University of Southern California

INTRODUCTION

ONE DAY, DURING MY SIXTEENTH YEAR, I became a Christ-follower. That gracious word of invitation, " Follow me," rooted in a great love that had sought me from my very beginnings, burned its way into my heart and evoked both desire and response. Since that moment of new beginnings I have been exploring how to live out within the context of my daily life my spiritual identity as God's beloved. This search has connected me with the lives of many other seeking pilgrims along the Way. In recent years I have come to recognize this common seeking as a widespread yearning in the hearts of men and women for a vital and real spirituality.

Spirituality is a slippery word. Some are suspicious in its presence. For those whose daily lives revolve around frantic timetables of preparing breakfast, getting children to school on time, holding down a stressful eight-to-five job, paying monthly accounts and cleaning the house, the word sounds somewhat strange and impractical. It suggests another world of inactivity, passivity and uninterrupted silences. For those whose lives have been scarred by the wounds of suffering and oppression, the term often suggests escapism, indifference and non-involvement. Indeed the word needs definition. Therefore let me clarify the specifically Christian sense in which I shall be using the word: *Spirituality is being intentional about the development of those Christ-shaped convictions, attitudes and actions through which our identity as God's beloved is formed and given personal expression within our everyday lives.*

Amidst this widespread yearning for a vital and real spirituality there is need for careful discernment. Many expressions of spirituality making the rounds within contemporary Christian congregations can only be described as foreign to the biblical tradition and unrelated to the spirit of the crucified and risen Lord. Often they are obsessively concerned with personal needs and reflect minimal concern for those who suffer. Alternatively, a spirituality of social struggle and involvement is frequently endorsed which avoids the biblical imperative for personal conversion and transformation. Such endorsement falls victim to the dangerous illusion that we can build a more just, equitable and compassionate society while we remain the same and continue life as usual.

Signposts

In this workbook I offer sixteen signposts toward the development of a renewed spirituality that is centered in the life of Jesus, our ever-present Savior and Lord, faithful to the treasures of the diverse streams within the Christian tradition, accessible to the people living next door, interwoven with those practical concerns that constitute daily living, and also deeply related to those human struggles taking place on the streets. I write neither as an academic theologian nor as an expert in the study of spirituality. The words that follow found their birth amidst the daily tasks of washing dishes and raising children, the vocational commitments of breaking bread, supporting and encouraging people along the Way, and the continual crises of a turbulent nation struggling to reconstruct itself. Within these tasks, commitments and crises, I have struggled, often unsuccessfully, to live out my identity as God's beloved. This workbook is shaped by these struggles.

This workbook is for ordinary people who seek to follow Christ within the pressures, problems and pain of everyday life. Some may be hesitantly embarking on the first steps of the pilgrimage of faith. Some may be well-seasoned travelers requiring fresh resources for the journey. Some may be discouraged and weary pilgrims almost about to pull off the road. Some may be disillusioned by the crass spirituality that passes for much Christian practice today and wanting to explore an alternative route. Wherever you may find yourself along the Way, a real and vital spirituality always stretches toward the transforming of our personal lives and of the societies in which we live, work and play.

Discovering Our Spiritual Identity: Practices for God's Beloved aims to help you experience this spirituality of personal and social transformation. Thankfully, as we seek to become more intentional in our Christ-following, we receive a gracious gift. Jesus himself, in the power of his Spirit, emerges from the pages of the Gospel, steps into our lives, and becomes an empowering and transforming presence. We discover how Christ can be our living teacher today as he was for those who discarded their nets and followed him by the Sea of Galilee. As we fall into step with him, within the beloved community, he shows us his way to live and provides us with strength to follow. Most wonderful of all, we discover that we are not alone.

Using This Book

Let me describe the elements of each chapter and how you can use them.

SIGNPOST

This is a summary description of the chapter content. You may like to take some time to think about the signpost and wonder about its connections with your life and faith before you proceed any further.

READING

Each chapter consists of several pages reflecting on the chapter theme. I hope that you will read each chapter as an open invitation to imagine yourself living your life as Jesus lived his. This does not mean trying to copy his Palestinian life with its sandals and robes. Nor does it mean always asking yourself, *What would Jesus do now?* The WWJD question keeps the relevance of Jesus' teaching and guidance at an external level of our lives. Rather, may I suggest, ask *how* Jesus would do it if he was in your situation. The HWJDI question takes us on a much deeper journey of inner and outer transformation—the transforming of our seeing and listening, of our hearts and minds, of our attention and awareness, of our willing and our doing. How to go on this journey forms the substance of what follows next.

HOLY EXPERIMENTS

These are practices to try on your own interspersed within the reading. I hope that you will take time to engage practically with these exercises. Discovering our spiritual identity as God's beloved demands more than using our imagination—it requires a relentless participation in actions designed to bring our minds and bodies into a vigorous interaction with the life-transforming Christ. Without this intentional partnership, the New Testament ideals surrounding our spiritual identity remain empty words on paper. Only those who take practical, down-to-earth measures to act with Christ know what it means to truly live as God's beloved. As you enter into the suggested holy experiments spread throughout this book, your everyday life will come alive with God's immediacy and power. There is space provided to write in these pages where it is needed. You may also want to use a journal to record your journey through these exercises.

Some of the chapters have several experiments. Take your time working through them. You may need more than a week to go through each chapter.

FOLLOWING THE SIGNPOST TOGETHER

There are discussion questions designed to be used in a small group or with a spiritual friend or mentor. The questions assume that you have begun to engage with some of the issues and holy experiments discussed in the chapter you have just read. It is in sharing our experiences of the holy experiments that we will discover a more vital and real spirituality.

REFLECTION QUESTIONS

Here and there you will also find boxed questions, with space to write as needed. These questions give you an opportunity to pause and reflect on the material as you read.

In Closing

Over eighteen centuries ago, St Ireneaus penned this rather provocative sentence: "The glory of God is a human being fully alive." Whatever else these words mean, this insight underlines what discovering our spiritual identity is all about. It is about aliveness—coming alive to the wonder of our belovedness in God's eyes, discerning the depth and sacredness of ordinary life, alerting ourselves to the hidden tentacles of evil within and around us, becoming more aware of those closest to us, responding to the suffering of our neighbor. Above all, it is about waking up to the always available presence of the crucified and risen Christ, alive and at large throughout the world, who invites us to be his followers wherever we are. Should the Spirit of God breathe this aliveness into your everyday life, I will be deeply grateful.

1

DRAWING A PICTURE OF GOD

The Signpost

THERE IS A PICTURE OF GOD drawn inside each of our hearts and minds. This picture, formed over the years through various influences, significantly shapes the way we live our daily lives. As we reflect on our ideas about God, we are invited to enter a redrawing process in which we gain a clearer view of who God truly is.

Holy Experiment

Knowing God through knowing Jesus

Reading

"What is your picture of God?"

The question surprised me. I was sitting in the plainly furnished study of a close friend and mentor. Over the years his listening presence, at critical moments in my own pilgrimage, had been a gracious gift. In the previous thirty minutes I had sought to describe those patterns of behavior that were leaving me bedraggled in spirit, weary in body and withdrawn in relationship. When I had finished speaking, he remained silent for a while, almost as if he were listening to his own heart. Then came the surprising question.

At first the question seemed unrelated and irrelevant to the concerns I had expressed. What did my view of God have to do with crowded days, an over-scheduled

appointment book and strenuous efforts to achieve and accomplish? Surely, I thought to myself, all that was needed was some practical counsel regarding time management and realistic goal setting. However, the question communicated my companion's clear conviction that the way we live is profoundly shaped by our picture of God.

William Temple, that great Anglican minister and spiritual leader, once rather provocatively observed that if people live with a wrong view of God, the more religious they become, the worse the consequences will be, and eventually it would be better for them to be atheists.

In each of our hearts and minds there is drawn our picture of God. Formed over the years through our interaction with parent figures, church representatives and our surrounding culture, it significantly influences the way we live our daily lives. Listening perceptively to the description of my drained condition, my friend had offered a spiritual diagnosis. My picture of God needed to be critically examined. There was a connection between my schedule, driven lifestyle and view of God.

For the first time in my life, I stopped to think about my image of God. Yes, I did feel that I needed to earn God's grace. Yes, I did believe I had to achieve his affirmation. Yes, I did sense that God would withdraw his blessings if I did not measure up. Gradually it dawned on me that I had come to view God as a somewhat passive spectator, sitting in the balcony of my life, whose applause would only come in response to satisfactory performance. A dysfunctional picture of God, I was discovering, had expressed itself in a dysfunctional way of living.

A DYSFUNCTIONAL PICTURE OF GOD, I WAS DISCOVERING, HAD EXPRESSED ITSELF IN A DYSFUNCTIONAL WAY OF LIVING.

When distortions creep into our picture of God, their negative effects reverberate throughout our lives. Consider some commonly held views of God, together with their usual consequences. Those who view God as an impersonal force tend toward a cold and vague relationship with him. Those who see God as a heavenly tyrant, intent on hammering anyone who wanders outside his laws, seldom abandon themselves with joy to the purposes of his kingdom. Those who imagine God to be a scrupulous bookkeeper, determined to maintain up-to-date accounts of every personal sin and shortcoming, rarely acknowledge their inner contradictions and struggles in his presence. Those who regard God as a divine candy machine (just say a prayer and you can get what you want) inevitably end up in disillusionment. Since, as author-philosopher Dallas Willard has pointed out, we live at the mercy of our ideas, we would be wise to reflect carefully on those that we have about God.

Our picture of God can be redrawn. It happened for Cardinal Basil Hume, archbishop of Westminster and well-known spiritual guide, and is illustrated in an amusing story he tells about himself. On a speaking tour of the United States, he shared how he had been raised by a good but severe mother. Constantly she would say to him, "If I see you, my son, stealing an apple from my pantry, I'll punish you." Then she would add quickly, "If you take an apple and I don't see you, Almighty God will see you, and he will punish you." It doesn't take much imagination to catch a glimpse of the harsh picture of God these words sketched in young Basil's mind! As his Christian experience matured however, his picture of God gradually changed. Eventually he had come to realize, the cardinal testified, that God might have said to him, "My son, why don't you take two?"

GOD IS A BOUNDLESS MYSTERY

James Houston writes:

> Awe encourages us to think of God as a transcendent presence: someone outside and beyond our own small concerns and our own vulnerable lives. Awe opens us up to the possi-

I invite you to begin immediately. For a few brief moments lay this book aside and ponder your current image of God. Try to be as honest as you can. Do you believe that God wants to relate with you personally and individually? Do you feel that God is for or against you? When life goes wrong, do you assume that God is punishing you? As you reflect on these questions, note any negative components in your God picture. Can you remember where these came from? How do these negative components affect your relationship with God and your life in his service?

bility of living always on the brink of mystery. Awe helps us to be truly alive, fully open to new possibilities we had not envisaged before.[1]

This redrawing process begins in the scriptural affirmation that God is a boundless Mystery. This does not mean that he is a giant puzzle to be fathomed out. It simply means that there is no one else like him. When the word *holy* (meaning to be separate, to be different) is used to describe God, it indicates this sense of wholly otherness. Indeed, if ever we think that we have finally got God all worked out, then we can be sure that we are wrong. As a professor-friend would keep reminding me in my know-it-all student days: "Trevor, when

you are in the presence of the real God you either shut up or fall on your face."

We are often uncomfortable and uneasy in the presence of mystery. We struggle to be involved with an ungraspable God. We feel safer when faith is confined within dogmatic formulations and tidy theories. Then we can tame God, bring him under control and manage his workings in our world. But these attempts to control and manage cost us dearly. Our sense of wonder is exiled, our faith begins suffocating from thick layers of dull familiarity and easy answers, and our lives are emptied of surprise.

In any true picture of God there will always be room for mystery. Acknowledging God in this way gets us to take off our shoes in his presence. We begin living on tiptoe. Our lives are touched with a renewed sense of awe.

IN ANY TRUE PICTURE OF GOD THERE WILL ALWAYS BE ROOM FOR MYSTERY.

GOD IS CHRISTLIKE

The bottom line of the Christian faith is the amazing claim that God has stepped into human history in the person of Jesus. In Jesus, God comes close and shows us his face. The boundless Mystery is not something vague and woolly, but Someone personal. Listen to Paul's confident exclamation about Jesus in the midst of his carefully worded theological letter to the Colossians: "he is the image of the invisible God. . . . For in him all the fullness of God was pleased to dwell" (Colossians 1:15, 19).

[If we want to get our picture of God clearer, we must look in the direction of Jesus. Through word and deed, dying and rising, Jesus introduces us to what God is really like.] In a famous remark, Archbishop Michael Ramsey teases out the staggering implications of this claim: "God is Christlike and in Him is no un-Christlikeness at all."[2] Dare we take this seriously? Every idea and assumption that we have about

---

IN THE SAME WAY, THE GOD WHOM WE SEE IN JESUS ALWAYS LOVES. LIKE THE SHINING SUN, HIS LOVE NEVER CEASES.

God must be measured against the person of Jesus. If they are contradicted by what we have come to know about God through Jesus, they need to be relinquished. If not, then they can safely be included in our God picture.

This is what letter-writer John does when he puts forward his picture of God for our consideration. In the opening sentences of his first letter he reminds his readers that he writes from the perspective of one who had known the company of Jesus firsthand. On this basis he concludes a few chapters later that "God is love" (1 John 4:16). Notice that he does not say that God *has* love, but rather that God *is* love. This is the very essence of who the Holy One is: extravagantly, sacrificially, passionately loving. And since this is his essential nature, this is what God is always doing—loving you and me.

Popular Catholic writer John Powell illustrates from nature the meaning of this truth for our lives. He suggests that we compare God's love to the sun. It is the nature of the sun always to give off warmth and light. The sun always shines, always radiates its warmth and light. There is no way in which the sun can act against its essential nature. Nor is there any way in which we can stop it from shining. We can allow its light to fill our senses and make us warm; alternatively, we can separate ourselves from its rays by putting up an umbrella or going indoors. But whatever we may do, we know that the sun itself does not change.[3]

In the same way, the God whom we see in Jesus always loves. Like the shining sun, his love never ceases. We have the freedom to open ourselves to this love and be transformed by it, or we can separate ourselves from it. But we cannot stop him from sending out continuously the warm rays of his love. At the heart of the boundless Mystery there is a blazing love that has created us, searches for us every moment and desires to bring us, along with all creation, into wholeness.

JESUS IN WORD AND DEED

The words of Jesus direct us constantly toward this faithful divine Lover. Consider the parable of the prodigal son: here is God who is recklessly in love with you and me, forgiving us freely before we have properly repented and clothing us with gracious acceptance even before we have had our baths.

The deeds of Jesus wrap flesh around his words. Throughout his life he consistently reached out in friendship to those around him. In his company, people from all walks of life felt accepted and welcomed. Whether it was a well-to-do public official like Zacchaeus, lepers living in forced isolation or children simply wanting a lap to sit on, everyone seemed at home in his presence. These people contacts often took place around mealtimes, which, in the Middle East, was a particularly intimate form of association. South African theologian Albert Nolan, reflecting on the impact these mealtimes would have had on those who sat at table with Jesus, writes: "Because Jesus was looked upon as a man of God and a prophet, they would have interpreted his gesture of friendship as God's approval of them. They were now acceptable to God."4

While in these friendships and meal-sharing moments, Jesus lives out the Holy One's all-inclusive love that enfolds each one of us, there is in his heart a distinctive sensitivity toward the most broken and vulnerable. Scan the Gospels and it becomes clear that Jesus invests a large percentage of his time in those who are suffering. Frequently he is to be found in the company of the sick, the mentally tormented, the poor and the marginalized. His example reminds me of the caring mother who, when asked by a friend which of her three children she loved most, replied that she loved them all equally. Her friend refused to accept this answer and pressed for an answer to her question. For a few seconds the mother became quiet and then firmly responded: "Okay, I love them all the same, but when one of them struggles and is in trouble, then my heart goes out to that child the most."

JESUS CRUCIFIED

The dying Jesus takes us deeply into the sacred mystery of God's passionate heart. Take some time to fix your eyes on this broken man nailed to the tree. Remember that he is the image of the invisible God, the One in whom God was pleased to dwell. The tortured, ravaged figure strips our talk about God's love of its empty clichés and familiar sentimentality. As we stand at the foot of the cross we catch a glimpse of how God in Christ absorbs the very worst we can do, bears it sacrificially in his own body and then responds with life-giving forgiveness. The welcome-home scene of the wayward son is not too good to be true. It is as real as broken flesh and a pierced side.

Visitors to the Notre Dame chapel in Paris tell me that the front altar is flanked by two impressive statues. One is the statue of the "prodigal father" embracing his returning son. This is the story that Jesus *told*. The other statue is Mother Mary holding the figure of her crucified Son. This is the story that Jesus *lived*. The story that he lived convinces us that the story he told is true. We are the beloved sons and daughters of the Father. All is forgiven. We can come home.

GOD, WE GRADUALLY REALIZE, NOT ONLY UNDERSTANDS OUR PAIN, BUT SHARES IT. THE SUFFERING GOD, NAILED TO THE TREE, PARTICIPATES IN OUR SUFFERING.

Contemplate once more the crucified Christ figure hanging on the cross. Trying to comprehend the meaning of what we see stretches our capacity for understanding to its limits. God, we gradually realize, not only understands our pain, but shares it. The suffering God, nailed to the tree, participates in our suffering. It is this truth that keeps the light of faith flickering in the darkened hearts of the grieving, that renews hope in the oppressed, that empowers loving in hearts that have been betrayed and broken.

I have just learned this again from the spontaneous testimony of a courageous and grieving mother. As I write these paragraphs I'm leading a forty-eight-hour silent retreat for first-time retreatants. Moments ago I spent time listening to the prayer experience of this mother whose nineteen-year-old son died in a car accident. Her suffering is immeasurable and goes far beyond the comfort of the human word. She has been kneeling in a darkened chapel before a stark crucifix. She tells me simply, "I can face tomorrow. I know God knows and suffers with me."

JESUS RISEN AND ALIVE

But the story of Jesus' life is not yet over. On the third day his disciples and women friends find the tomb empty. Then follow the resurrection appearances through which Jesus demonstrates the death-defeating power of God's love. The lives of the disciples are completely turned around. They realize that the love that Jesus proclaimed, the love that he lived, the love that he was, can never be defeated by the powers of evil and darkness. This is the key to understanding the message of the resurrection. Easter Sunday morning is a joyful celebration of the power of God's love and its unquenchable capacity to bring life out of death.

Much testimony today is given to the "power of God." Constantly the impression is created that whenever God's power is at work, life works out successfully and prosperously. Reflecting on these testimonies, I sometimes wonder what these words mean for those who suffer—for the teenager dying of cancer, for the parents receiving the news that their newborn child is severely brain-damaged, for the families of the thousands of people murdered in our country every year. What do these words about God's power communicate about the kind of God we worship, especially when those speaking often appear well dressed, well fed and well off? Clearly our understanding of God's power requires biblical revision.

Look closely at the resurrection figure of Jesus in the Gospels. Notice that he continues to bear in his resurrected body the wounds of crucifixion. I am reminded of an ancient legend that describes how the devil tried to enter heaven by pretending to be the risen Christ. Accompanied by his throng of demons disguised as angels of light, he stood at the gates of heaven shouting aloud: "Lift up ye heads, O ye gates; and be ye lift up, ye everlasting doors; and the King of glory shall come in." The angels of heaven responded with the refrain of the psalms: "Who is the King of glory?" Then the devil gave himself away. Opening his arms he answered: "I am." In this act of arrogance he showed the angels his outstretched hands. *There were no nail imprints.* The angels of heaven refused to let him in.

Through those wounds written into his resurrection body, Jesus gives us an immeasurably rich symbol for glimpsing the ever-present power of God's love. Plumbing its depths we see that suffering and evil are real, love often gets crucified, and people do get hurt. That is the non-negotiable reality of the world that we share. Nevertheless (and that is a good resurrection word), the strong love of God always has the final word. Nothing can hold it back from working out its purposes. Not only

> THE STRONG LOVE OF GOD ALWAYS HAS THE FINAL WORD. NOTHING CAN HOLD IT BACK FROM WORKING OUT ITS PURPOSES.

does the Holy One experience our suffering as though it were his own, he is also relentlessly seeking to bring light and life where there seems to be only darkness and

Holy Experiment

KNOWING GOD THROUGH KNOWING JESUS

Write the word God *below. Brainstorm your immediate responses to this word. Record all these under the word* God. *Now write the word* Jesus *on a sheet of paper. What immediate responses to this word do you have? Record them. Compare your lists and pray over them. What do you note about your image of God?*

_____

_____

_____

_____

_____

_____

_____

_____

_____

death. When this happens for us, even in a small way, we experience a "little Easter."

JUST ABOUT ANY TIME WE ARE SURPRISED WITH NEW POSSIBILITIES FOR LIFE AND HEALING IN THE MIDST OF BROKENNESS AND DECAY, THERE IS A LITTLE EASTER THAT GIVES US A GLIMPSE OF THE RESURRECTION POWER OF GOD'S LOVE.

I recall a sudden reversal of all that I had hoped for in a vocational sense. For almost ten years I had cherished a dream of beginning a small missionary congregation within the inner city. However, after years of exploration it seemed best to those in my church's hierarchy that permission not be granted for this endeavor. When I received the news, it was a painful moment. I felt that I had reached a kind of vocational cul-de-sac. Slowly I realized that I needed to relinquish an image of myself as a radical pioneer in congregational renewal. Simultaneously with this letting-go occurring there came a surprise opportunity for me to join a pastoral team that would give space in which I could foster people's spirituality in individual and small group settings. For three years this is what I did, with a real sense of fulfillment. Looking back now I see this new vocational beginning as a little Easter.

When courage is given for the despairing heart to keep living through the pain, that is a little Easter. When listening friendship enables the timid and withdrawn soul to slowly open up, that is a little Easter. When inner pain causes the self-reliant and self-sufficient to ask for help from beyond themselves, that is a little Easter. When a forgiving spirit empowers an oppressed people to reconcile with their oppressors for the sake of building a new nation, such as we witnessed during our time of nation-

Following the Signpost Together

1. Share the major negative components of your present God picture. Where were these learned in the past?

2. Michael Ramsey makes the statement that "God is Christ-like and in Him is no un-Christlikeness at all." How do you respond to this comment?

3. What would it mean for you to begin redrawing your picture of God? How would this affect your everyday way of life?

4. When did you first become aware of God's personal love for you?

5. When have you experienced "a little Easter"?

al transition in South Africa, that is a little Easter. Just about any time we are surprised with new possibilities for life and healing in the midst of brokenness and decay, there is a little Easter that gives us a glimpse of the resurrection power of God's love made manifest in the crucified and risen Jesus.

I have come to learn that the God whose face I see in Jesus speaks to each one of us by name, and whispers, "You are loved just as you are. I am Abba, your heavenly parent, who welcomes you with open arms when you come home to me. Your presence is deeply desired at the family table of my friendship. When you hurt my other children through your actions and words I get angry, though my anger will never stop me from loving you. On the cross I died so that you would know the full extent of my offer of forgiveness. Your suffering is my suffering. Your grief is my grief. In your darkness and pain I want you to know that I'm constantly seeking to bring about for you another little Easter. This is how much I love you." When our hearts and minds are touched by this great love we are ready to explore the adventure of the spiritual life.

2

DISCOVERING WHO WE ARE

The Signpost

THE SEARCH FOR IDENTITY threads its way throughout our lives. In this quest the incarnate Christ meets us right where we are. Throughout his earthly ministry, Jesus received his identity from the Father. The Beloved Son reveals to us our own belovedness, so that from this place of inner security we may invest ourselves in seeking God's will and helping others discover how beloved they are.

Holy Experiment

The beloved charter

Relating to others as beloved

Reading

When the moment arrives to step down from active pastoring, I will be immensely grateful if, among the many whom I have pastored, there are a handful of men and women who say, "My pastor helped me to discover who I really am. He opened my eyes to my own infinite worth and immense potential as a dearly beloved child of God."

This ministry focus finds its roots in my own testimony. For some reason, in my early adulthood days, I found it extremely difficult to accept that God delighted in me. I knew about God's love in theoretical terms, but there seemed to be a yawning chasm between the knowledge in my head and the experience of my heart. However, a little miracle has been taking place within me. Knowing myself to be beloved of God is slowly becoming more than intellectual conviction; it is gently developing into the core truth of my everyday existence. This is the message I most want to communicate— the marvelous news that, at the heart of the universe, there is a divine Lover who longs for every one of us to wake up to the amazing truth of our belovedness.

I know well, from personal experience, the deadening effects of not knowing who and whose we are. When we are uncertain about our true identity, the inferiority disease spreads throughout our lives. We think thoughts and mouth phrases like: "I am no good." "I can't do anything right." "I'm no use to anyone." "I'll never be able to do it." "I can't accept myself." And the list goes on. We struggle to believe that God has unique purposes for our earthly sojourn and instead become paralyzed by a haunting sense of insignificance that leaves us feeling isolated. Little wonder that, when we see ourselves wrongly, we often end up in the muddy pit of worthlessness with its attendant despair.

In his searching autobiography, Frederick Buechner, the widely read American writer and respected Presbyterian pastor, illustrates movingly the life-destroying consequences that often occur when we feel worthless. One Saturday morning, as the sun was rising, Frederick and his brother, Jamie, woke up excited. Their parents had promised to take them to watch football. Since the rest of the family was still sleeping, the brothers decided to stay in their room and amuse themselves with an old roulette wheel. While they played together, they noticed their father quietly open the bedroom door and look in. After a while, he disappeared and closed the door behind him. Some time later, there was a piercing scream from downstairs. Looking out of their window, the boys saw their father lying outstretched on the gravel driveway. Blue smoke drifted from the open garage door into the crisp autumn day. Their father had gassed himself. Frederick Buechner writes:

> It was not for several days that a note was found. It was written in pencil on the last page of *Gone with the Wind*, which had been published that year, 1936, and it was addressed to

WHEN WE SEE OURSELVES WRONGLY, WE OFTEN END UP IN THE MUDDY PIT OF WORTHLESSNESS WITH ITS ATTENDANT DESPAIR.

> my mother. "I adore and love you," it said, "and *am no good*. . . . Give Freddy my watch. Give Jamie my pearl pin. I give you all my love."[1]

As a pastor, discovering what it means to be unconditionally loved, I want to help others expose the phrase "I am no good" as a cruel and vicious lie.

Alternatively, in our uncertainty about our identity, we go to the opposite extreme. We climb lofty pedestals and manufacture glittering façades of ourselves as successful, competent and adequate. Behind these masks we hide our feelings of vulnerability and inadequacy. Nothing scares us more than public failure or weakness. We over-identify with our strengths, struggle to accept any limitation and believe that we can do all things. People around us, especially those with whom we have close contact, complain that they do not feel close to us. They tell us we are aloof, distant and cold. The pedestal, we find out, becomes a very lonely place.

Men, especially, are prone to climb pedestals. When asked to address a men's breakfast gathering on a subject of my own choice. I decided on the title "The Subject Men Don't Talk About," and took as my text the words of Paul, "My grace is sufficient for you, for power is made perfect in weakness" (2 Corinthians 12:9). For just under forty-five minutes I explored the various ways in which we try to cover up our weaknesses and wounds. I was struck by the quiet attentiveness of the men. Afterward, an outwardly confident and well-dressed young man strode up to the speaker's podium and said with a smile, "You've been reading my mail. Can we get together sometime to talk?"

INVITED TO BE THE BELOVED SONS AND DAUGHTERS OF ABBA FATHER, WE FALL PREY TO DECEIVING VOICES THAT TELL LIES AND HALF-TRUTHS ABOUT WHO WE ARE.

The two extremes seem worlds apart, yet both are expressions of self-rejection and bring tragic consequences to our relationship with the Holy One. Invited to be the beloved sons and daughters of Abba Father, we fall prey to deceiving voices that tell lies and half-truths about who we are. Believing these untruths, we adopt patterns of living that impoverish the soul, cripple relationships and block the glory of God from shining through us. Lost among the many who wander along this well-traveled road, we fail to stand apart from the crowd and become our own person—the person God intends us to be. Tragically, we miss the mark that God sets for our lives.

OUR SEARCH FOR IDENTITY

Given the crucial importance of knowing who we are, it is not surprising that the identity quest threads its way throughout our lives. Usually we search for answers in any one of three possible directions: looking inward, looking toward others and looking toward achievement.

Looking inward. Some people embark on a lengthy inward journey, often with the skilled help of a trained counselor or therapist. Along this therapeutic route we seek the truth of our identity within, and often end up defining ourselves solely in categories of temperament and personality, or perhaps more negatively in terms of personal addictions and conflicts. While the psychological labels we use to describe ourselves may give certain comfort, they do not reveal the full story about who we are.

In saying this, I do not wish to negate the critical importance of looking within. Without getting to know ourselves and where we have come from, it is doubtful whether we will grow toward fuller personal maturity. Nor do I wish to downplay the valuable insights that modern psychology can provide in helping our progression in the godly challenge of self-knowledge. I have received immense benefit from speaking with those who are professionally trained to accompany people on their inner journeys. I simply believe that a purely inward, psychological approach diminishes the unfathomable mystery of who we truly are.

Looking toward others. Our sense of who we are can become determined by whatever family or friends or colleagues say about us. Whenever this happens, our lives can degenerate into a series of desperate attempts to please, to perform and to be popular. While others certainly play a significant part in what makes you you and me me the cost of conforming to their expectations and scripts can be great. We fail to find our own voice, live a second-hand existence and in the end forfeit our true identity. Moreover, we end up living on an emotional seesaw: when others speak well of us we are up, and when they don't we are down.

I am not offering cold clinical observations; I am also confessing. Too often in my work as a pastor I have looked toward others to validate my own personal worth. This tendency renders me vulnerable to that hazardous temptation of trying to be all things to all people. Succumbing, as I frequently do, suffocates the spirit, thins the soul and wearies the body. I find myself disconnected from my depths, living from the outside in and breathlessly running around trying to meet impossible expectations. In these moments of estrangement and tiredness, my own spiritual abyss looms dangerously close.

Looking toward achievement. It is often said of someone clearly intent on climbing the success ladder, "That person is really trying to make a name for himself!" Readily we assume automatic relationship between accomplishment and an inner assurance of significance. However, this connection can-

---

Where do you look for your sense of identity? Thinking about the way we live usually yields crucial clues about our answers. Reflect for a few moments on your everyday conversations and activities:

- Do you sometimes reduce the profound mystery of who you are to a psychological label?

- Is the way you think and act controlled by the approval and disapproval of those around you?

- Are you constantly preoccupied with the pursuit of success, with the desire to achieve greater status and position?

The time used to uncover answers to these questions would be well spent. Your reflections may help to clarify the basis of your present identity.

not be accepted uncritically. For what happens when you fail, or find yourself in a position where you are no longer able to achieve? And what do you say to a person who experiences only inward emptiness upon an occasion of outstanding success?

Certainly, peak moments of attainment must be celebrated—receiving a long-awaited promotion, completing a university degree, winning an important match, securing a carefully planned business deal. These special times need to be savored. Still, there is a critical difference between striving to achieve "to make a name for oneself" and the kind of carefree achievement characteristic of someone already secure in who they are. Accomplishments and achievements are an integral part of the fulfilled life, but they need to flow from a personal center already assured of its identity; otherwise experiences such as unemployment, retrenchment, retirement and forced rest, when they come, will devastate us.

JESUS' IDENTITY

In our quest for identity, the crucified and risen Christ meets us right where we are. Like us, he also needed to know who he was. He was not immune to the human quest for identity. Reflecting on the insistence of the four Gospels in this regard, Anglican theologian Thomas Smail observes: "Jesus needed, not once, but again and again at each stage of his mission and each crisis in his living and dying, a freshly confirmed knowledge of his own identity."[2] However, in stark contrast to ourselves, when Jesus needed to know who he was, he listened to his Father's voice, trusted that voice and claimed its truth for his own life.

Recall that decisive moment when Jesus is baptized in the River Jordan by his cousin John. Thirty formative years of hidden preparation have come to an end; his public ministry is about to begin. As Jesus emerges from the water, he hears a voice from heaven. Gospel writers Matthew, Mark and Luke all draw our attention to what he hears:

> This is my Son, the Beloved, with whom I am well pleased. (Matthew 3:17)

> You are my Son, the Beloved; with you I am well pleased. (Mark 1:11)

> You are my Son, the Beloved; with you I am well pleased. (Luke 3:22)

The point is clear: Jesus receives his identity from beyond himself; he is the Beloved of God upon whom the delight and the Spirit of the Father rest.

Aware of his belovedness, Jesus sets forth to accomplish the will of his Father. However, his sense of identity requires both subsequent confirmation from beyond and ongoing affirmation from himself. Confirmation comes in the mountaintop transfiguration encounter; speaking from the cloud, in familiar words that echo those spoken at his baptism, the Father assures Jesus of his belovedness (see Matthew 17:5). Days later, in the darkness of Calvary, Jesus receives strength in personally affirming his relationship with Abba. "Father," he cries out loudly, "into your hands I commend my spirit" (Luke 23:46).

Throughout his earthly ministry, Jesus finds his identity and confidence in his relationship with Abba Father. Little wonder that when the evil one attempts to thwart

Jesus' ministry, the starting point of attack is the casting of doubt upon his identity as the beloved: "The devil said to him, 'If you are the Son of God . . .'" (Luke 4:3).

Jesus underlines how important it is for us to know who we are. Because of his inward assurance that he is the Beloved of God, he is consistently his own person, able to pour himself out in extravagant self-giving, and is finally free to lay his life down in complete self-surrender upon the cross. Secure in his interactive relationship with Abba Father, he resists the wilderness temptations to forge an identity based on the illusions of success, popularity or power. Not once throughout his life does he need to prove himself, win the approval of contemporaries or be involved in any manipulative power games. Knowing who he is, Jesus invests himself single-mindedly in the realization of his Father's kingdom vision for our broken world.

BELOVED OF GOD

But, do I hear you wondering, *how do these past events connect with my own struggle for identity?* I suggest that they connect deeply. Jesus, the Beloved of God, reveals the truth of our own belovedness. Notice how this repeatedly occurs in his gospel encounters: sharing a meal with those rejected and marginalized, responding to the desperate cry of a blind beggar by the roadside, requesting the company of an unscrupulous tax collector, refusing to condemn a woman caught in the act of adultery (see, for example, Matthew 9:10; Mark 10:46-52; Luke 19:1-10; John 7:53–8:11). In each encounter, Jesus communicates through his words and deeds the message: You are beloved. Indeed, his entire public ministry

enfleshes the astonishing words spoken shortly before his death: "As the Father has loved me, so I have loved you" (John 15:9).

> **KNOWING WHO HE IS, JESUS INVESTS HIMSELF SINGLE-MINDEDLY IN THE REALIZATION OF HIS FATHER'S KINGDOM VISION FOR OUR BROKEN WORLD.**

In these and other gospel encounters we glimpse in Jesus' tender compassion the Father's ever-present love streaming toward you and me. No matter what we have done, how disastrously we have failed or into what distant country we have wandered, God wants us to know that we are loved. Archbishop Desmond Tutu captures this good news vividly:

> We don't need to prove ourselves to God. We don't have to do anything at all, to be acceptable to him. That is what Jesus came to say, and for that he got killed. He came to say, "Hey, you don't have to earn God's love. It is not a matter for human achievement. You exist because God loves you already. You are a child of divine love."[3]

Explore this mystery-laden truth carefully. Jesus, uniquely the Beloved Son, attests to your and my infinite value as a child of God. From all eternity it has been God's purpose that everyone discover their belovedness in the Beloved, for this is truly who we are: beloved children of the Most High. In exuberant theological language, the apostle Paul celebrates the wonder of this gospel conviction when he writes that the Holy One "destined us for adoption as his children through Jesus Christ, according to the good pleasure of his will, to the praise of his glorious grace that he freely bestowed on us in the Beloved" (Ephesians 1:5-6).

WRESTLING WITH THE QUESTION OF HIS OWN IDENTITY, THOMAS MERTON ONCE DESCRIBED HIMSELF: "I AM ONE LOVED BY CHRIST."

In their reflections about the identity quest, well-known Christ-followers from diverse backgrounds affirm the truth of our belovedness. Asked if he could summarize the essence of his beliefs after a lifetime of theological exploration, theologian Karl Barth answered with the words of a childhood hymn: "Jesus loves me, this I know, for the Bible tells me so."[4] Responding to a journalist friend's request that he write a book especially crafted for the secular-minded, Henri Nouwen stated: "Fred, all I want to say to you is 'You are the Beloved,' and all I hope is that you can hear these words as spoken to you with all the tenderness and force that love can hold. My only desire is to make these words reverberate in every corner of your being— 'You are the Beloved.'"[5]

Does the truth of your belovedness reverberate through your being? For many years, the mystery of my belovedness remained primarily an intellectual conviction. From the pages of the Bible I would gratefully affirm that I was beloved of God and redeemed by Jesus Christ. One of my earliest Scripture memory verses confirmed this truth of faith: "For God so loved the world that he gave his only Son, so that everyone who believes in him may not perish but may have eternal life" (John 3:16).

By contrast, my everyday behavior, my constant looking toward others for approval, kept reminding me that this biblical truth still needed to bridge that massive crevasse between head and heart. Too often my behavior denied my belief. Theory needed to be translated into the language of the heart.

More than twenty years of pastoral ministry in diverse settings has convinced me that numerous people lack a deeply felt confidence of their belovedness. I remember conducting a weekend preaching mission in a congregation widely known for its liveliness and charismatic expression. Using the biblical passage of Jesus' baptism as the focus for my message, I shared simply the good news of our belovedness. As the service ended I offered an opportunity for those unsure of their belovedness to come forward. To my surprise almost half of those present, many of them churchgoers of long standing, walked toward the altar for personal counsel and prayer.

The reasons underlying this struggle to experience inwardly our belovedness can sometimes be uncovered. Explanations may range from distant memories of childhood abuse and conditional acceptance or present-day voices that constantly undermine and ridicule, to dehumanizing socioeconomic realities that mock the gospel's proclamation about every human creature being a cherished child of God. Tragedy can also make it very hard for us to believe that we are loved by God.

The ringing testimony of Christ-followers from all walks of life, however, affirms that these negative memories, voices and conditions can be disempowered from expressing the final word on who we are. Three practical and interrelated exercises help in the process whereby we appropriate our belovedness more deeply.

THE BELOVED CHARTER

Throughout the Scriptures, there are numerous verses that underline the fact of our belovedness. When joined together to form what I like to call "a personal beloved charter," they can induce us to see ourselves through the eyes of the Holy One and to feel about ourselves the way God feels. With hearts and minds we begin to grasp that every one of us represents God's unfolding creation; that the Holy One is continuously attentive to what we are experiencing; and that there are eternal purposes that God has for our lives. Carefully creating such a charter, committing it to memory through regular repetition, in the faith that the Spirit of God is whispering these words in our hidden depths, is one way of recovering the truth of who we are. To give you some idea of what a beloved charter could look like, here is one I have formulated in recent years:

> Trevor, you are my beloved child in whom I delight. You did not choose Me but I chose you. You are my friend. I formed your inward parts and knitted you together in your mother's womb. You are fearfully and wonderfully made, made a little lower than the angels, and crowned with glory and honor. You have been created in Christ Jesus for good works which I have already prepared to be your way of life. When you pass

> through the waters, I will be with you; and through the rivers, they shall not overwhelm you; when you walk through fire you shall not be burned and the flame shall not consume you. You are precious in my sight, and honored, and I love you. I know all your longings; your sighing is not hidden from Me. Nothing will ever be able to separate you from my love in Christ Jesus, your Lord. Abide in my love.

Allowing words and images like these to percolate within indicates our willingness to let God be God in our lives, affects the way we see ourselves and alerts our hearts to the divine Whisper telling us who we are—not that we will always be able wholeheartedly to receive the truth of our belovedness. Listening to our personal beloved charter may surface strong feelings of resistance, ranging from boredom and dull familiarity to sheer disbelief.

This resistance should not surprise us. It is an integral part of any growing, intimate relationship. Noticing these interior indicators of resistance, befriending them without judgment and exploring their possible sources with a trusted spiritual companion can often pave the way for our beloved charter to reach hitherto untouched depths of our inner beings.

I am awed at times by how the Spirit presses home the message of a beloved charter into our hearts. I once counseled at length a woman and mother of three small children. Drained by the constant demands of motherhood and housekeeping, and her husband's frequent absence, she was struggling with feelings of worthlessness and inferiority. She felt (to use her own descrip-

Holy Experiment

BELOVED CHARTER

Experiment with the creation of your own beloved charter. Look up those verses that are expressive for you of the way God values our lives. Write these verses down at random. When your list is complete, arrange your verses into a meaningful personal charter. It need not be lengthy—five or six sentences are sufficient. With time, it may change and develop as different verses attract your attention. For the next month, on a daily basis, set aside about ten minutes to be alone. Picture the risen Christ sitting alongside you, speaking these words to you. Bid the indwelling Spirit to press home the message of your own belovedness. Notice your own inner responses and share them with the Holy One.

tive phrase) "like the handle of the broom I use to sweep the floors." Together we spoke about the importance of seeing ourselves through the eyes of the Divine Lover, and I suggested that she create a beloved charter which she could paste on her bathroom mirror.

Two weeks later, we met again at the church office. I sensed a quiet joy and a renewed commitment to her everyday tasks. I enquired about her source of obvious new vitality. She showed me the charter that she had put together and then recounted the contents of a vivid dream:

Two days after I began praying with my Beloved Charter, I had a powerful dream. I dreamt that I was a lifeless paper doll lying discarded in a rubbish bin. Suddenly a strong hand reached down—it seemed like the hand of Christ—and lifted me upwards. As I was raised from the bin I slowly began to come alive. When I woke up I knew that God was resurrecting me into a completely new way of life.

LEARNING TO LOVE OURSELVES

Learning to love ourselves, as God continually does, further realizes the truth of our belovedness. Unfortunately, many people of faith interpret this suggestion as a contradiction of the gospel way, a subtle disguise for selfishness and narcissism. Invariably, when I introduce the importance of taking care of ourselves there is someone who responds: "But surely this is being self-centered? Did Jesus not teach us to put others first, deny ourselves and take up our cross?" This was precisely my own response when, in a dark time of severe depression and weary disillusionment, a wise spiritual mentor challenged my lifestyle and outlined a startling revision of my priorities. "Put your relationship with God first," he suggested, "and then before family, work and community commitments, put yourself next."

Gradually I have come to appreciate the wisdom in my mentor's challenge. When we neglect and undervalue ourselves we tend to do the same to those with whom we interact. However, once we learn to treat ourselves as dearly beloved of Christ, the freer we become to give ourselves away in sacrificial service, and to do so without resentment and heaviness of spirit. Having love for ourselves, we can then forget ourselves, direct our attention toward others and respond to their needs. Self-love and other-love are deeply bound together. Could this be the reason why Jesus reaffirmed the centuries-old Levitical command given to the Hebrew people as binding upon his own followers: "You shall love your neighbor as yourself" (Matthew 22:39)?

How do we care for ourselves practically? Usually, it involves giving honest attention to the various aspects of our inner and outer lives, taking time to listen to our needs, longings and unresolved struggles. With regard to the latter, we can be daring enough to ask for help, seek support and allow others to serve us. With the insight of those who know us well, we can acknowledge our gifts and abilities, and perhaps investigate means of developing them further. Where we have gone wrong, we can open our hearts to the mercy of the Crucified One, learn to forgive ourselves and make amends toward those whom we have wronged. We can explore ways of restoring energy and strength to our souls and bodies, particularly in times of stressful and demanding work.

Dr. Mamphela Ramphele is one of the courageous spirits of recent history. In her published autobiography she tells the story of her personal and political growth. Over-

> **"PUT YOUR RELATIONSHIP WITH GOD FIRST, AND THEN BEFORE FAMILY, WORK AND COMMUNITY COMMITMENTS, PUT YOURSELF NEXT."**

coming numerous constraints in the pursuit of her ideals, including detention and a banning order, she has come to occupy an influential place in contemporary South Africa. However, her immersion in the human struggles of our time cost her dearly. In 1990, she began to experience considerable inner tension as she tried to balance the demands of single parenthood and social activism. In the midst of her breakdown, her spiritual director persuaded her to spend a few days in silent retreat. Reflecting on her learnings from this difficult time, Dr. Ramphele quotes the injunctions of St. Bernard of Clairvaux to a new pope:

> So then in order that your humanity may be entire and complete, let your bosom, which receives all, find room for yourself also. So remember to restore yourself to yourself. . . . As an ordinary mortal I have an even greater need to "restore myself to myself"! There is no other option for the sake of my sanity. I have to stop more frequently and smell the flowers.[6]

RELATING TO OTHERS AS BELOVED OF GOD

Relating to others as beloved of God is the third way in which our own awareness of belovedness can be strengthened. Being the beloved is not a private trip. Rather, it encourages us to acknowledge our joint belonging in the human family, reach out in real relationship toward our neighbor, and bring God's blessing wherever we go. Mysteriously, it is as we see others as brothers and sisters and affirm our common belovedness that there grows within our hearts a fuller appreciation of just how much we are loved by God. John, the disciple whom Jesus loved, alludes to this mystery in his letter to the early Christ-followers: "Beloved . . . if we love one another, God lives in us, and his love is perfected in us" (1 John 4:11-12).

Christ, our ever-present Mentor, wants to teach us how to help others claim their belovedness. Pursue his footsteps from the beginning of his gospel ministry until its end. See him bless the children. Watch him listen to the Samaritan woman. Listen as he affirms his disciples. Watch him feed the hungry. Notice him befriend the rejected. Wherever he went, people knew they were valued. Today he requests that we relate to others as he would if he were in our place. He does not leave us to do this unaided. Should we intentionally obey his wishes, in dependence on his indwelling

---

Holy Experiment

SEEING OTHERS AS BELOVED

Think of the person you are most likely to meet next. She or he may be your spouse, a close friend, a working colleague or a complete stranger. Ponder the holy mystery of who they truly are. Like yourself, this person is unconditionally loved and accepted by God in Jesus Christ. As you prepare to meet him or her, ask the Holy One to help you affirm their belovedness. You can communicate this affirmation by the active way in which you listen, through attitudes expressive of courtesy and respect, or by some specific helpful action. Later, you may want to reflect on your encounter and consider whether it drew you closer to the divine Lover.

Spirit, we can count on him showing us how best to bear the beams of his love toward those we meet.

A story about a businessman and manager of a medium-sized manufacturing plant illustrates how the Spirit guides us in our care of one another. Jack Smith, in the midst of an intense labor conflict, went into his office, sat down and said to himself, "I'm not running this business well and I don't know what to do. I guess I can either get drunk or I can pray." He thought a little longer and then reflected quietly, "If I get drunk I'll have a hangover and nothing will change. However, if I pray and nothing comes of it, I can always get drunk later." With this tiny seed of faith he put his head down on his hands and cried out, "Okay, Lord, I can't run this business any longer. What should I do?"

He was quiet for a few moments. Almost immediately an answer came to mind. That thought offers an excellent description of agape love in both personal and social terms: "Create the conditions whereby each individual can develop to the maximum of his or her potential within the opportunities at hand." For several months, he mulled over this insight in his prayer times. Gradually, several practical ways of implementing this principle emerged, be-

ginning with the rule "to serve those whom you expect to serve you." What emerged not only made good business sense or merely enabled Jack to relate to his employees as beloved of God, it also connected him more deeply to the God of love and the blessing of his own belovedness.[7]

Recovery of life at its best begins when we experience ourselves to be the beloved children of God. Only then can we safely embark on the perilous inward journey, to face our inner shadows and darkness, secure in the knowledge that nothing we uncover can ever render us unlovable to God. Conscious of our belovedness, we can reach out to others with a fresh transparency, honestly acknowledging our real thoughts and feelings since we are no long-

RECOVERY OF LIFE AT ITS BEST BEGINS WHEN WE EXPERIENCE OURSELVES TO BE THE BELOVED CHILDREN OF GOD.

er dependent on their approval or imprisoned by their expectations. With our personal worth no longer bound to achievement, we are free either to succeed or to fail. We begin to taste "the freedom of the glory of the children of God" (Romans 8:21).

Following the Signpost Together

1. Go around and allow each person to introduce themselves to the group without referring to their family status, present job or any position they may hold. Talk about how this felt.

2. Where do you tend to find your sense of identity?

3. Describe your experience or lack thereof of being loved and accepted by God in Christ.

4. Share the passage from Scripture that most enables you to experience your beloved-ness.

5. In what way do you need "to restore yourself to yourself"?

6. Describe one memorable experience of unconditional love. What did the other person do to make you feel beloved?

3

DEVELOPING A
CHRISTIAN MEMORY

The Signpost

RABBI ABRAHAM JOSHUA HERSHEL WRITES: "Much of what the Bible demands can be comprised in one word, *Remember*."[1] Christian faith is grounded in remembrance—we are called to remember God's presence in the gospel life of Jesus, in our personal stories and in our daily lives.

Holy Experiment

Remembering Jesus in the Gospels

Remembering our personal stories

Remembering the present day

Reading

Seldom has one sentence imprinted itself so powerfully on my mind. Written by that remarkable rabbi Abraham Joshua Hershel, the thirteen words have signposted the direction of my faith journey ever since I first read them. As I learned to follow this particular signpost, my awareness of the Holy One's active presence throughout my life has been considerably strengthened. The sentence reads: "Much of what the Bible demands can be comprised in one word, *Remember*."

Why dwell on the past? Surely if we take the rabbi's words seriously, will we not be avoiding the challenges that face us in the present? Is not remembering a time-wasting activity that actually limits responsible participation in the immediate business of everyday life? Is it not more important to forget the past, live in the present and plan for the future?

A pastor friend of mine would strongly disagree. Recently over a cup of coffee, he described for me an evening out with his wife. It was their seventh wedding anniversary and, celebrating the occasion with an act of reckless generosity, he took his wife to a rather exclusive French restaurant. Lingering over their candlelit supper they were able to talk together, uninterruptedly and leisurely, for over three hours. Aware that their relationship had felt the strains of parenting three young children, lack of quality time together and the demands of conflicting work schedules, I expressed the hope that it had been a renewing time for them both. My friend's response intrigued me. "Yes, we spent the evening remembering. Between the courses of our meal we shared memories of our relationship together, joyful and painful." And then, pausing for a moment as if he were inwardly registering a freshly birthed awareness, he continued, "And you know, it's been a long time since I have felt so grateful and close in my marriage."

A few years ago I shared in a somewhat similar experience with my father. At that time, my dad was living out his final days in a frail care center many hundreds of miles from where I lived with my family. For the past four years he had struggled with the devastating effects of Alzheimer's disease, including the loss of his memory. As I sat holding his hand during what could have been my last visit, my mind went back over the years and I began remembering some of the things he had done for me. I remembered the times he had come to watch me play rugby. I remembered how he would fan me to sleep on hot summer nights. I remembered how he would put his arms around my shoulder, even as an adult, and remind me of his daily prayers for me. Sitting there with him I felt the tears well up behind my eyes—tears of appreciation and profound gratitude. Even though

he could not speak or recognize me, I felt close to and deeply connected with him.

Can you see what begins to happen when we take time to remember? All of us carry memories within our hearts, and when they are recalled we enter into a mysterious journey. The past breathes again, in such a way that the present is injected with new life. Previously hidden significance bursts into conscious awareness. Suddenly, we see clearly what we could not see before. Locked-up feelings find their freedom and, in their appropriate expression, bring renewed vitality and aliveness. Our sense of who we are and to whom we belong is nourished and sustained. These are just a few of the deep things that happen when we look back upon the way we have come.

THE BIBLE AND MEMORY

Biblical writers affirm this understanding of memory. Engraved on their hearts was the conviction that God had made his loving presence known in their own history. When curious Israelite children desired to know more about God they were seldom taught abstract precepts. Memories were shared with them. They were told stories of the Lord their God who had brought their parents out of Egypt, led them through the wilderness, made water flow from flint rock, fed them manna in the wilderness, and protected them from scorpions and poisonous snakes. For people of the Covenant, remembering was no cop-out. Remembering God's loving presence active in their past made that presence real within the present. No wonder the answering prayer of the psalmist echoes with the cry, "I remember you, O Lord."

Christian faith likewise is grounded in

remembrance. Students of early church history remind us that within the early Christian communities the first obligation of the apostle involved making the faithful remember what they had received. The new Christ-follower needed to develop a Christian memory. Such a memory found its primary focus in the story of Jesus. Entering into the memory of his words and deeds, dying and rising, they were led into the inexhaustible, loving heart of that Holy Mystery who had enfolded their lives from their very beginnings. The command of Jesus in connection with the breaking of bread applied to the whole of their lives: "Do this in remembrance of me."

REMEMBERING JESUS IN THE GOSPELS

Developing a Christian memory that is centered on Jesus requires personal engagement with the Gospels. Without them it would be nearly impossible for us to know Jesus and, through him, the character and nature of God. This is why the Gospels are so very important. Reflecting on his reasons for recording the deeds of Jesus, Gospel-writer John explains: "But these are written so that you may come to believe that Jesus is the Messiah" (John 20:31). Almost every line in his book, and in those of Matthew, Mark and Luke, has the power to lead its readers into an enriched relationship with Jesus, provided these books are read carefully and with a sense of expectant encounter. Knowing this to be true, saints throughout the centuries have encouraged Christ-followers to constantly meditate on the figure of Jesus as he is revealed in the Gospels.

I have sought to take this counsel seriously in my own pilgrimage and have often offered it to other pilgrims. Frequently in my work as a pastor I meet people who, while they may be tired of religion, yearn for a firsthand relationship with the Holy One that will empower their lives with a fresh sense of vision. They are hungry for a living spirituality. Reflecting on my conversations with these seekers after God, I've noticed a remarkable similarity in the

SAINTS THROUGHOUT THE CENTURIES HAVE ENCOURAGED CHRIST-FOLLOWERS TO CONSTANTLY MEDITATE ON THE FIGURE OF JESUS AS HE IS REVEALED IN THE GOSPELS.

yearnings expressed. How do I come to know God? How can I deepen my friendship with him? How does God want me to live my life together with him? Usually I respond with one sentence: *Keep company with Jesus in the Gospels.*

Establishing a basic habit of devotional Gospel reading fosters the information of a Christian memory. As we follow Jesus through the pages of the Gospels we are reminded of what God is like and how we can live in partnership with him. Upon this memory the Holy Spirit acts, causing Jesus to become for us a living presence and making us mindful of his wishes for our daily lives. Thus, as we can see, gradually developing a Christian memory around the person of Jesus, growing in relationship with God, and practical everyday discipleship all go hand in hand. Joseph Girzone describes these links well when he writes: "That is why a precise understanding of Jesus is so important for us, so we can share

Holy Experiment

REMEMBERING JESUS IN THE GOSPELS

Choose one Gospel with which you would like to journey over the next year. If undecided about which one, I would suggest the shortest—the Gospel according to Mark. Most scholars agree that Mark's is the basic Gospel, preceding the other three. Set time aside, an hour or so, to read the Gospel through in one sitting. This will give you some sense of its overall continuity and predominant emphases. After you have done this, try on as regular a basis as possible to read from its pages a short passage. As you read, keep company with Jesus. Try to understand his feelings about God, notice the way he relates to people, listen to the message he brings, explore his views about material things and watch what he does. Consider always what meaning all this would hold for you if you were to live your life as Jesus would, if he were in your place.

His vision of God and His understanding of human nature and frame for ourselves our own relationship with God within the context of the rest of His creation."[2]

REMEMBERING OUR PERSONAL STORIES

Another dimension of Christian memory is the remembering of our own personal stories. This practice happens in the biblical faith that "in him we live and move and have our being" (Acts 17:28). Life is continuously lived in God's creative, loving presence. Our lives are never secular. They are sacred journeys in which God is constantly involved, always seeking to disclose his gracious word and passionate love.

OUR LIVES ARE NEVER SECULAR.

From our very beginnings our lives have been divinely enfolded. Such is the conviction expressed in the psalmist's cry of wonder: "For it was you who formed my inward parts; you knit me together in my mother's womb" (Psalm 139:13).

In the early stages of my Christ-following pilgrimage I did not fully realize this. My impression was that God had only become part of my life when I turned to him at the time of my conversion. But as my understanding of God slowly developed, I recognized that the Holy One had been present throughout my life, continuously loving me and inviting me to accept his friendship. When this finally became clear I began remembering my own personal history with the specific purpose of discerning God's ever-present participation within it. Now, if asked to share my faith story, I would begin by speaking about my earliest memories of warmth and kindness. Through experiences like these, God had been working in my life long before I first became aware of him. This is what Paul helps Timothy to grasp when he writes: "I am reminded of your sincere faith, a faith that lived first in your grandmother Lois and your mother Eunice and now, I am sure, lives in you" (2 Timothy 1:5).

Mary, mother of Jesus, mentors us in this task of remembering. Crammed into her life are the contrasting experiences of expectation and disappointment, ordinariness and upheaval, joy and fear. Growing up in the uncomplicated plainness of Palestinian village life, she falls in love with a young, upright Jewish man, Joseph. Wedding arrangements are set in joyful motion. However, a sudden angelic visitation turns Mary's life upside down. If willing, she will bear a child who will be called Son of God. Her trembling consent throws the engagement into the trauma of mistrust and suspicion. Only a dream in the middle of the night restores to the relationship the commitment of Joseph.

Events surrounding the eventual divine birth are wearying and chaotic: traveling seventy miles on a donkey's back from Nazareth to Bethlehem, struggling vainly to locate a motel room for rest and renewal, giving birth in the messiness of a stable shed, receiving visits from rich wise men and poor shepherds bringing gifts of worship, hearing news of a hit squad's intention to kill all boys under the age of two. Hidden among these experiences there is a still moment, overlooked by many, but noticed by Luke. Without overstatement or exaggeration the moment is recorded for us: "Mary treasured all these words and pondered them in her heart" (Luke 2:19). Engaging faithfully in the ancient practice of her people, Mary is both the faithful Israelite and our symbol for the remembering life.

Certainly the cold recall of the computer, the mechanical reproduction of the photographic mind is not what Mary was about. Developing a Christian memory is a matter of the faith-soaked heart. We begin from a stance of faith. The Holy One has always been with us, even when we were unaware of his presence. Knowing this, we then recall significant experiences and reflect on them, pondering upon how God has been present within them.

One of the most practical ways of following Mary's example involves the writing of a spiritual autobiography. A lengthy book is not what I have in mind! One can begin by putting down on paper all that has been given over the years. As Paul re-

DEVELOPING A CHRISTIAN MEMORY IS A MATTER OF THE FAITH-SOAKED HEART.

minds us: "What do you have that you did not receive?" (1 Corinthians 4:7). Reflecting on your life journey, include people who have touched your life with kindness, opportunities that have crossed your path for growth, talents and abilities that have enriched your life and brought blessing to others. See in all these gifts the generous love of the One who is the giver of all good things. The Giver is present in the gift. When your list is completed, offer to God your heart's response of joyful gratitude and appreciation.

A second stage of our spiritual autobiography relates to *the pain that we have known*. Not all memories are joyful. For six weeks in 1978 I had the privilege of sharing in the life of the Church of the Saviour, a small ecumenical congregation in inner-city Washington, D.C., now finding expression through numerous faith communities scattered throughout the city. I remember one lunch date with Gordon Cosby, the church's cofounder and pastor. Forty years of servant ministry had instilled in my lunch companion a profound pastoral wisdom. Together we were reflecting on the challenges of preaching within the contemporary urban context. "Never forget," he said thoughtfully, "each time you stand up to preach, each person in your congregation is sitting next to a pool of tears."

In our spiritual autobiographies, how do we connect memories of painful suffering with the presence of God? I remember a dear friend and colleague asking this question some years ago. On a bleak winter's night, June 17, 1992, over forty unsuspecting inhabitants of Boipatong were brutally and senselessly murdered. Shock waves triggered by the massacre rippled throughout South Africa. The extent of the barbarism was horrendous: a heavily pregnant woman hacked to death, a nine-month-old baby stabbed, and a number of elderly persons mutilated beyond descrip-

Holy Experiment

REMEMBERING OUR PERSONAL STORIES

Stage one: Set aside a few hours spread over a period of several days. Begin by making a random list of those key moments in your life when the Holy One seemed particularly close; moments when your life was touched by a sacred sense of awe and wonder and gratitude. Memories could range from a powerful awareness of life's utter giftedness, from witnessing the birth of a baby to an answered prayer for yourself or a loved one. Limit your list to about ten such memories. Next to these experiences describe the feelings you had during them. Feelings of deep joy and wholeness are usually a sign of God's presence. Celebrate these experiences as sacraments of God's self-giving love, especially shared with you.

Holy Experiment

REMEMBERING OUR PERSONAL STORIES

Stage two: Make notes in your spiritual autobiography of memories of past pain. Pay particular attention to those feelings associated with each painful memory. Gently connect those memories with the ever-present suffering love of the crucified and risen Lord. Keep the cross before you. Commute for however long seems appropriate between the painful memory and the crucified Jesus. There is always a cross in the anguished heart of God.

tion. At the memorial service, my friend preached. After recalling the events of that fateful night he pointed the worshipers to a gaunt, hollow-eyed figure nailed to a cross, mouth wide open as if screaming in agony, and said simply, "God weeps and suffers silently with you."

Each one of us sits beside a pool of tears. These pools reflect those memories that are hard to bear. Whatever they are—childhood abuse, relationship betrayal, parental neglect, unfair tragedy—these memories are an integral part of our spiritual autobiographies. Often we try to push aside these wounds from the past. When stirred in conversation, we say to each other, "Let's talk about something more positive." But painful memories pushed under the carpets of our consciousness cripple

EACH ONE OF US SITS BESIDE A POOL OF TEARS.

our capacities to live and love fully. "Forgetting the past," writes Henri Nouwen, "is like turning our most intimate teacher against us."[3]

Recalling past pain can be quite traumatic. Often those we love the most hurt us the most, and it is usually extremely difficult to face up to these wounds. Besides writing out our experiences of pain, it may be necessary to find a professional person, such as a qualified counselor or therapist, to be our "wailing wall." At different stages of our lives we all need a human wailing wall—a person who can sit with us alongside our pool of tears as an embodiment of God's compassion and comfort.

This remembering of past pain takes place with a hopeful heart. Christ, the crucified One who both understands and shares our suffering, lives beyond crucifixion. His living presence is constantly at work in every painful memory from the past, seeking all the time to bring forth another little Easter. This resurrection power

of God's love cancels the power of hurtful memories to pronounce the final word about our lives. Exposing our painful past to the light of the risen Lord is therefore absolutely crucial. Through the power of his crucified love, Christ can bring healing for the wounded child within, can strengthen the betrayed heart to give itself away again, can restore confidence in the conquest of death.

The third stage involves *writing down those ways in which God has used you to bring light and hope into the lives of others.* For some this part of the spiritual autobiography could prove difficult to do. Some may feel they are being vain and conceited. Yet keeping track of positive

Holy Experiment

REMEMBERING OUR PERSONAL STORIES

Stage three: Ask the Lord to bring to mind moments when you have been a bearer of his loving presence. Write them down, no matter how insignificant they may seem. Often the small gesture of love and kindness can carry a meaning far greater than what seems outwardly apparent. When your list is completed, give thanks to God for the privilege of being his copartner in his ongoing work in his world today.

things done for others can help us experience the joy of sharing in a living partnership with God.

Writing a spiritual autobiography is a holy experiment in remembering. Through our participation in this experiment, our experience of the Holy One is immeasurably enriched. By noticing how God has been with us in the past, our present awareness of his companionship is deepened. By discerning those divine invitations that have been offered, our spirits are sensitized to God's initiatives as they come to us now. By reflecting on those times when God has used us, our willingness to risk ourselves in his service today is increased. Undoubtedly there exists an intimate connection between this kind of remembering and growing into an authentic spirituality.

REMEMBERING THE PRESENT DAY

Daily reflection constitutes one other crucial dimension of developing a Christian memory. Through its practice we keep our remembering up to date. No day is empty of God's presence. In the people we meet, the tasks we do, the difficulties we face—and in our responses to them—God is continually trying to catch our attention and give us fresh glimpses of his loving presence. Pausing for a few quiet moments before we fall asleep creates the space needed to reflect on how God has been with us over the past twelve hours or so, and how we have responded.

It was just over twenty years ago that I first began to practice a form of daily reflection. The doors had closed on my hoped-for vocational future and I was needing to make some critical decisions.

Not wanting to hurry into premature choices, I decided to do the Spiritual Exercises of St. Ignatius within the context of

OFTEN THE SMALL GESTURE OF LOVE AND KINDNESS CAN CARRY A MEANING FAR GREATER THAN WHAT SEEMS OUTWARDLY APPARENT.

my daily life. Finding my way to a little monastery in the back streets of Johannesburg, I asked one of the monks if he would lead me through this program of biblically based, Christ-centered meditations. Very kindly he agreed. In our first interview together he spelled out the required time commitments. For the following nine-month period I would need to set aside an hour each morning before work for prayer around the Scriptures, and in the evening spend about ten minutes doing "an examen of consciousness." I had no idea what this strange-sounding phrase meant. Patiently my newfound monk friend explained what this would involve. I can still remember the rough outline of his answer:

> Before you go to bed, look over the day and see where you need to be thankful. Ask the Spirit of God to show you what he wants you to see. Ask him also to reveal where he has been present in your life throughout the day, either in you or in others, and what he has been asking of you. Reflect upon your moods during the day. See if there is any underlying attitude that needs conversion. Ask the Lord for forgiveness for those moments when you did not respond to his love. And in closing, think

Holy Experiment

REMEMBERING THE PRESENT DAY

In the pursuit of an authentic spirituality, words count for very little, and practice means everything. Therefore you may want to experiment with the examen immediately. It will not take you longer than about ten minutes. Place yourself consciously in God's presence, asking for his light as you review the past few hours. Then ponder the following questions, which summarize the major emphases of the examen: What have I to be thankful for? What strong moods have I experienced, and what attitudes lie beneath them? For what do I need to ask forgiveness? For what do I need God's help and guidance tomorrow? When you have completed this small experiment, you have just done your first examen of consciousness!

about the following day and ask God for whatever help and guidance you need.

For the following nine months I practiced the examen of consciousness. It became the highlight of the entire Ignatian adventure. More than anything else that I did during that time, it sharpened my sensitivity to the nudges and promptings of the Spirit. I began to discern where God was leading me. Since the completion of the Exercises, I have continued practicing

the examen at the end of each day.[4] It doesn't take longer than five to ten minutes and continues to keep me in tune with the presence and leading of God in different aspects of my everyday life. I have also learned that one can take the basic principles of the examen and apply them to any period of time—the preceding hour, day, week or year. Indeed, following the guidelines of the examen can become a built-in way of life.

"Chosen before the world began" is a recurring biblical phrase to which I constantly return. It describes our earliest beginnings in the loving heart of God. There each of us knew the indescribable joy of being God's delight and desire. Imprinted on our hearts and buried beneath layers of consciousness is this primal memory. Remembering God's loving presence in Jesus Christ, in our own personal stories and in our daily lives signposts the way toward that memory hidden in our hearts.

Following the Signpost Together

1. Go around the group and ask what have become known as the four Quaker questions. Think back over your life during the ages of seven and eleven, and then share:

   - Where did you live during this time, and who were family for you?

   - How was your home heated?

   - Where did you look for personal warmth and affection?

   - When was the first time in your life that God became more than a word?

2. What has been one of your most significant spiritual experiences?

3. How have you experienced the presence of God in tough times?

4. Read aloud Psalm 139:1-18. Identify a phrase that strikes you in light of your own experience of God over the years. Share this phrase and talk about its meaning for you.

4

RECEIVING THE KINGDOM

The Signpost

THE GOOD NEWS OF JESUS is the availability of the kingdom of God. The nature of this kingdom is defined by the nature of the King; it is wherever the loving will of the Father effectively reigns. We receive the gift of the kingdom with the open hands of repentance and faith.

Holy Experiment

Turning toward Jesus

Opening clenched fists

Reading

It was a nerve-racking moment. I had resigned from secular employment and offered myself as a candidate for the ordained ministry. The first requirement involved passing an oral examination before the annual Synod. Examining me was a bishop well known for his direct and stern approach. His first question seemed simple enough.

"Tell me, Mr. Hudson," asked the bishop, "what was the central message of Jesus?"

"Forgiveness of sins, sir!" I shot back immediately.

"No," responded the bishop matter-of-factly.

"Peace on earth, sir," I tried again, re-membering a line from the chorus of the heavenly host that startled sleepy shepherds in the middle of the night.

"No," said the bishop again, as my face, I'm sure, began to redden.

By this time I thought it would be best for me to give up trying and I said so. Leaning over his desk the bishop caught my eyes in his solid gaze and said, "I want you to never, never forget that the main message of Jesus was, 'The kingdom of God is at hand.'"

THE NATURE OF THE KINGDOM

The bishop was right. While I had certainly described aspects of the kingdom, I had overlooked the key description used by Jesus to proclaim his message. Recall that dramatic curtain-opening moment of his public ministry when Jesus came to Galilee. Almost thirty years of hidden preparation lay behind him. Eventually, as he emerges from his struggle with the devil in the wilderness, Jesus embarks on his life's work. Mark summarizes the essence of his inaugural sermon in one explosive phrase, "The kingdom of God is at hand" (Mark 1:15 KJV).

What do we make of this statement? To begin with, our thinking about it must be shaped primarily by our picture of God. After all, it is his kingdom. Jesus, as we have seen, discloses God as an infinitely caring father who runs down the road and welcomes home a wayward child with a big hug. Therefore, whatever else it may be, the kingdom is wherever the loving will of the Father effectively reigns. It is an eternal kind of life characterized by the presence of grace and mercy and powerful little Easters. Entering into its orbit, as that prodigal son did, is all about coming home to ourselves, being reunited with family, and learning to live again as a beloved daughter and son of the King.

Jesus is this kingdom in the flesh. This is made clear in his response to his critics after he had delivered a person from the dark forces of evil. He answers them: "But if it is by the Spirit of God that I cast out demons, then the kingdom of God has come to you" (Matthew 12:28). Wherever Jesus ministered in word and deed the loving will of the Father effectively reigned. When he healed the sick, that was the kingdom of God. When he forgave sins, that was the kingdom of God. When he shared meals with the outcasts and outsiders of his day, that was the kingdom of God. Hence while God's kingdom has been in existence right from the very beginning of creation, in the person of Jesus it became clearly visible and was made available to all. Through him the kingdom of God was indeed at hand.

And it is at hand for us. We don't need to wait for the kingdom until we are dead. Our lives can be touched today by its power of resurrection. We can begin learning

---

THE KINGDOM IS WHEREVER THE LOVING WILL OF THE FATHER EFFECTIVELY REIGNS.

---

immediately what it means to live within its presence. Like the earliest disciples we can experience its gradual transformation of our everyday lives. Like them we can discover how to bear its reality into those situations where it is seemingly absent. But first we must receive it. We cannot give to others what we do not possess. The good news is that through the crucified and risen Jesus' presence throughout the world the kingdom is available as a sheer gift. "Do not be afraid, little flock," says Jesus, "for it is your Father's good pleasure to give you the kingdom" (Luke 12:32).

CLENCHED FISTS OR OPEN HANDS

Gifts are received with open hands. It is the same with the offer of God's kingdom. Recently I reflected with a dear friend on her beginnings upon the Christian way. At the conclusion of a usual Sunday worship service the officiating pastor extended an invitation. All worshipers were asked to clench their hands into tightly balled fists. Evidently this was not unusual for this congregation. However, on this particular morning things seemed different for my friend. The liturgy came alive, and she profoundly experienced a sense of God's searching love. She sat in the silence, clenched fists resting on her lap. Finally worshipers were invited, should it be their desire, to express their response to God by unclenching their fists. My friend described the moment simply: "Somehow I stopped resisting and slowly opened my hands to God."

CLENCHED FISTS DISTANCE US FROM THE INTIMACY AND FRIENDSHIP THAT GOD DESIRES TO SHARE WITH US. THEY SUGGEST THAT WE WANT TO KEEP CHRIST OUTSIDE OF OUR LIVES WHERE HIS TRANSFORMING INFLUENCE CAN BE KEPT AT ARM'S LENGTH.

We live either with clenched fists or open hands. These radically opposed images symbolize two contrasting ways in which we can relate to the Holy One. Tightly closed hands indicate our refusal to be part of his kingdom of "righteousness and peace and joy in the Holy Spirit" (Romans 14:17). We want rather to live our lives on our terms and according to our own wills. Clenched fists distance us from the intimacy and friendship that God desires to share with us. They suggest that we want to keep Christ outside of our lives where his transforming influence can be kept at arm's length. To put it abruptly—clenched fists say no to God and the gift of his kingdom.

Open hands say yes. Taking the hand stretched out toward us in Christ, open hands express our heart's desire to receive all that God longs to give. They make visible our inward willingness to let God be God in our lives, and to let him lead and guide us. Hands opened in this way toward the Holy One are simultaneously opened to those around us. They speak of our willingness to be vulnerable, to give and to receive, to come home and to be part of the family that is the kingdom of God. Open hands connect with friend and neighbor.

Only hands opened by repentance and belief can receive this gift of the kingdom. "The kingdom of God has come near," proclaims Jesus and so his listeners are urged to "repent, and believe in the good news" (Mark 1:15). Contained in this response are two frequently misunderstood verbs. Many associate "repent" only with negative images of gloomy preachers threatening their listeners with grim warnings of pending doom. Meanwhile "believe," in the minds of some, has been tragically shrunk to mean mere intellectual assent to creedal statements. And in this sense, as John Wesley has reminded us, "the devil also believes in God." Both verbs must be reclaimed with their rich biblical meanings.

THE OPEN HAND OF REPENTANCE

Repentance is the translation of the Greek word *metanoia*, which essentially implies a change in our way of thinking, a turning back or return. It does not mean putting ourselves down, being preoccupied with our sinfulness or feeling sorry for ourselves. Neither is it aimed at earning acceptance, deserving forgiveness or achieving God's

Holy Experiment

TURNING TOWARD JESUS

Meditate for a few moments on Mary's "turning moment." Notice that she turns as she is, in her grief and pain and tears. But it is a turning toward life. One of the central meanings of repentance is turning toward Jesus, as we are, and accepting the gifts of the kingdom that he freely offers us.

favor. True repentance involves the complete turnabout of our mind and outlook that turns us in a new direction, changes our distorted attitudes and gives our lives a new center from which a new kind of life begins emerging.

Repentance turns us in a new direction. Mary's experience in the garden of the resurrection provides a striking picture of this truth. She is standing outside the tomb where the body of Jesus had been laid, obviously overcome by her grief. While standing there in the garden she is joined by Another. Initially she thinks that her companion is the gardener. And then the stranger speaks one simple word: "Mary." She recognizes the voice. It was that same voice that several months earlier had assured her of her belovedness and worth. In describing her immediate response, Gospel-writer John gives us a beautiful picture of genuine repentance: "She turned toward him and cried out" (John 20:16 NIV).

Such turning is never a once-and-for-all experience. Conversion always continues. Hence repentance becomes a way of life—a lifelong process of turning toward the Holy One that happens one day at a time. Anthony, the well-known desert father from the fourth century, is reported to have

once said, "Every morning again I say to myself, today I start."

Repentance changes our distorted attitudes. Over the years we acquire literally hundreds of different attitudes, many of which block us from living free and joyful lives. Turning toward Jesus allows him the opportunity to change those attitudes that are diseased. Over time he imparts to us a new vision and fresh understanding of our lives. Joseph Girzone spells out these changes of attitude and perception in fuller detail:

> We think differently about God. We think differently about material things. We think differently about ourselves and others. We think differently about rich people and poor people. We see God's creation and everything in it as sacred. Given the time God will eventually transform our whole life.[1]

One of the first changes that God brought about within my own life was in my attitude toward words. Before turning toward Christ, words were not that important to me. Often I would use them casually and without much thought. Gently God seemed to impress on my mind that words were more than words. I began to think differently about them. I began to see them as carriers of life and light as well as death and darkness. To this day this I continue learning to see words as one of the most important ways in which we can share in the ministry of the kingdom.

WITH THEOLOGIAN WILLIAM TEMPLE WE REALIZE THAT THERE "IS ONLY ONE SIN, AND IT IS CHARACTERISTIC OF THE WHOLE WORLD. IT IS THE SELF-WILL WHICH PREFERS 'MY' WAY TO GOD'S—WHICH PUTS 'ME' IN THE CENTRE WHERE ONLY GOD IS [SHOULD BE] IN PLACE."[2]

Repentance gives our lives a new center from which a new kind of life begins emerging. From early childhood onward our lives are dominated by an assumption that "I am the center of the universe and everything else must revolve around my wishes, my desires, my interests and my needs." We become imprisoned in this cell of self-centeredness and unable in our own strength to break free. The essence of apartheid, the legacy from which we in South Africa are still seeking to untangle ourselves as a nation, was legalized self-interest. Its consequences bankrupted the soul of a nation.

When we are given a glimpse of the possibilities of what our lives could become if they were part of the kingdom, we reconsider the center of our lives. Turning toward the Holy One, our lives are able to slip over into a new center and enter a new way of life. Not only are we born again, we begin to live again.

Establishing this new personal center does not happen without struggle. When we put God at the hub of our lives, we find ourselves exposed to the blazing light of his self-giving love. Touched by these rays we see more clearly the dark and hidden depths of our self-centeredness. We realize how much this sin condition has permeated our past actions and behaviors. And we see how much it has hurt others—especially those closest to us. While these insights make us more conscious of just how much God really forgives us, they also, if our repentance is to be real, lead us to want to make amends so far as we can. This process demands courage and wisdom. We do not become new people overnight.

Turning toward Christ introduces into our lives a new inner battle. I discovered this very soon after my initial conversion. There was, I learned, a deeply ingrained part of me that still wanted to be at the center, to be in control, to do it my way. Then there was also that part of me that really wanted to live from my new center in God. This battle continues to rage to this day.

The consequences of our selfishness reveal themselves all around us. Consider how self-centered behavior prevents the giving of ourselves, sabotages intimate relationships and ruins the life of those groups to which we belong. Reflect on how the social consequences of this assumption work themselves out in the structural evils of our time.

Camouflaged amidst a variety of self-centered attitudes and behaviors, my sin condition continues trying to regain the upper hand over my life. Its disguises range from impatience in traffic snarl-ups or withdrawal when my needs are not met to sometimes presumptuously believing that I can meet everyone else's needs without giving time to my own. Often I lose the battle and get discouraged. But I'm learning to return gently to Christ who never leaves me, to open my life again to his gifts of acceptance and mercy, to confess my failures and continue on the Way. Repentance, in other words, is becoming a way of life that keeps me open to grace.

THE OPEN HAND OF BELIEF

Belief opens the other hand to receive God's gift of the kingdom. To believe, in the New Testament sense of the word, involves clear content, risky surrender and persistent effort. It means affirming something very particular about Jesus, entrusting ourselves to him and steadfastly learning from him how to live. Holding these components of believing together in creative tension keeps Christian belief from deteriorating into sheer fuzziness. I want therefore very carefully to tease out what is meant by each of these interwoven threads.

To believe means affirming something very particular about Jesus. For almost twenty-five years I have wrestled with Jesus' question "Who do you say that I am?" During this time I have frequently sought to keep company with Jesus in the Gospels. I have come to see Jesus as the most alive, aware and responsive human being that ever lived. I have come to recognize his dying as revealing love's response in the face of evil. I have come to realize that something most extraordinary must have taken place after the crucifixion in order to transform those frightened and grieving disciples into bold witnesses willing to die for their beliefs. I have found it most reasonable to accept the biblical explanation accounting for this transformation: this man, Jesus, was both fully human and God come in the flesh, was tortured and killed, was resurrected from death and is among us now in the power of his Spirit, making available God's gracious kingdom as he did for his earliest disciples.

When we talk about believing in Jesus there is certain content to it. Believing in him we come to believe particular things about him. This was the experience of the early disciples in the New Testament and, as I have tried to illustrate from my own pilgrimage, can be our experience today. As these men lived in the company of Jesus they came to understand him in a particular way. From their Old Testament heritage they were able to find words to describe this understanding. New Testament scholar Donald English points out that Jesus was someone about whom they were able to say Son of Man, Lord, Savior, Emmanuel, Word of Life. These titles were all ways through which the disciples could affirm their bottom-line belief—the belief that in Jesus, God had stepped into human history.[3] Or as Jesus himself put it: "Whoever has seen me has seen the Father. . . . Do you not believe that I am in the Father and the Father is in me?" (John 14:9-10).

To believe involves entrusting ourselves to the crucified and risen Christ. I have learned most about this experience of surrender through friends recovering from al-

Holy Experiment

OPENING CLENCHED FISTS

Wherever you may be sitting right now, make yourself comfortable and place both your hands on your lap. Curl up your fingers into tightly closed fists. Imagine that in these tightly clenched hands you are holding on to everything that is important for you—your life, your loved ones, your work, your possessions, your hopes and dreams for the future. Feel the tension build up from your hands and spread throughout your body. Now hear the words of Christ as if they were coming from a deep place within you: "The kingdom of God is available; repent and believe the good news." As you are able, allow your response to find expression in the slow opening of your hands. May you know the joy of receiving the kingdom!

cohol abuse. I remember a middle-aged father and husband's testimony. Celebrating his tenth anniversary of sobriety and sanity, he recounted the painful devastation his drinking habits had caused. A hushed congregation listened intently as he described his personal history of denial and delusion, of how he had arrogantly assumed that he could be the center of his own life. Gesturing toward the candlelit altar upon which stood a stark wooden cross, his concluding words revealed the radical and ongoing process of real trusting:

> Ten years ago I found myself at the end of my rope. At an evening service in this church I came forward and knelt there at the altar and looked long and hard at that cross. I said to God, "I've tried to take your place in my life and have made a total mess. I ask for your forgiveness and surrender myself and my future to you. Show me how to live with you at the center." And I've prayed these words almost every day since.

This testimony reveals the intimate link between repentance and belief. These two hands open together to receive the gift of the kingdom. If repentance turns our eyes toward the Holy One, believing relinquishes our lives into his loving hands. If repentance transforms our distorted attitudes, believing trusts that it is God who is at work. If repentance gives a new center to our lives, believing surrenders the old and yields ourselves to Christ who now becomes our Lord. And like repentance, entrusting ourselves to God in these ways is never a one-off experience. Shifting from a self-centered lifestyle into a God-centered way of life takes a lifetime.

"I don't find it easy to believe like this," you may be saying under your breath. Don't force yourself. Genuine belief seldom comes quickly or without struggle. Over the years, I have been encouraged in this learning process by developing a more mature Christian memory, honestly facing my inability to overcome my sin condition on my own and simply asking God to help me to trust him. When I am able to recognize that God is like Jesus, that his kingdom is truly available and that he is able to do within my life what I cannot, a fresh capacity to surrender myself into his hands is released within me.

To believe means steadfastly learning from Jesus how to live. Entrusting ourselves to him, we believe that he, more than anyone else who has ever lived, knows how to live. To believe in Jesus therefore involves learning how to live our lives in the kingdom as he did when he walked the roads of Palestine. This does not mean trying to copy the historical life of Jesus. That would lead us into the most deadly forms of legalism. Rather it means committing ourselves to Christ, immersing ourselves in his example and teaching as it comes to us in the four Gospels, and learning from him how to put into practice what we see there. We do not attempt this relying on our own strength. Our commitment, Jesus has

> ENTRUSTING OURSELVES TO GOD IN THESE WAYS IS NEVER A ONE-OFF EXPERIENCE. SHIFTING FROM A SELF-CENTERED LIFESTYLE INTO A GOD-CENTERED WAY OF LIFE TAKES A LIFETIME.

promised us, will bring his constant presence into our everyday lives as a living and tangible reality. "Those who love me will keep my word, and my Father will love them, and we will come to them and make our home with them" (John 14:23).

Following the Signpost Together

1. Write the phrase "the kingdom of God" on a sheet of paper. Brainstorm your understandings of this phrase and write them down.

2. Have you ever opened your hands to the gift of the kingdom? How did this first take place in your life?

3. Describe one change that God seems to have brought about in your life since you first turned toward him.

4. Share one way in which the sin condition manifests itself in your present way of life.

5. What has helped you to entrust yourself more deeply to Christ?

6. Talk about your experience with the exercise outlined at the close of the chapter.

5

BELONGING TO THE
FAMILY OF GOD

The Signpost

WE CANNOT BE CHRIST-FOLLOWERS ALONE. This becomes clear from the moment we decide to follow Jesus along the conversion road. When we open our lives to him, he enters with arms around his brothers and sisters. As we uncurl our clenched fists to receive the kingdom's gifts, they are touched by the hands of others. Without option we discover ourselves situated within a new family, the family of God.

Holy Experiment

Spiritual friendship

Reading

Without others it is doubtful whether I would ever have started on the Christ-following journey, let alone remained on it. A friend first introduced me to Jesus and his message, I made my initial public commitment within a gathered community of worshipers, I was nurtured in my new faith among a local congregation, and I received guidance for the way ahead through the pages of an ancient book authored by fellow pilgrims thousands of years ago. Saying yes to Jesus, I discovered, involved saying yes to his family, both visible and invisible.

We cannot become the persons God wants us to be without experiencing divine and human relationships. Genuine repentance and belief in Christ almost always immerse the disciple into a life together with others.

WHAT ABOUT THE CHURCH?
People all around us are questioning the church. Some years ago, emblazoned across the T-shirt of a young woman pictured on *Time* magazine's front cover were words that echoed a widespread disenchantment. "Jesus yes," the slogan shouted, "the church no." Asked about the meaning church holds for her, a high-profile South African activist responded: "It tends to contain and

limit my quest for wholeness, rather than liberating me from myself and freeing me to be a better person."[1] In my own context, I have often listened to an absent church member's angry accusation—"the church doesn't care."

Underlying these critical comments are understandable sentiments. Those with whom we are brought together are not always nice people. Reflected in their lives are self-centered attitudes and behaviors with which we all struggle. When personally disillusioned I remind myself that the main problem of the church is that people are often like me. Instead of consoling, understanding and loving those around us, we demand to be consoled, understood and loved. The sin condition is universal. Paul the apostle writes: "For there is no distinction, since all have sinned and fall short of the glory of God" (Romans 3:22-23).

However, the kingdom of God is never a private banquet. Deciding to follow Christ locates us amidst fellow followers. Replay leisurely that curtain-opening moment in the ministry of Jesus besides the Sea of Galilee. Immediately upon proclaiming the kingdom's availability, Simon and Andrew are invited into discipleship. Leaving their nets they follow Jesus into an unchosen network of human relationships. Before long their lives are interwoven with James and John, whom Jesus has also called (Mark 1:16-20). Christ-following, these disciples would testify, is anchored in community.

This relational reality shaped significantly the convictions of the infant New Testament congregations. In the company of Jesus, their leaders experienced with one another a depth of fellowship they had not known before. Their life together provided

GENUINE REPENTANCE AND BELIEF IN CHRIST ALMOST ALWAYS IMMERSE THE DISCIPLE INTO A LIFE TOGETHER WITH OTHERS.

those nutrients necessary for personal transformation and growth in generous loving. They were convinced that the ongoing creation of a similar community would be an indispensable goal for their ministry efforts. Confirming this conviction in the opening lines of his pastoral letter, John exclaims: "we declare to you what we have seen and heard so that you also may have fellowship with us; and truly our fellowship is with the Father and with his Son Jesus Christ" (1 John 1:3).

Now we can understand why we read little in the New Testament about individual spiritual formation. The biblical language for growing in Christ is interdependent language. Gospel life is life together. Affirming this interdependence in our growth into wholeness is the recurring scriptural phrase *one another*. Repeatedly we are encouraged to accept one another, serve one another, bear one another's burdens, care for one another (Romans 15:7; John 15:12; 13:14).

THE KINGDOM OF GOD IS NEVER A PRIVATE BANQUET.

Within community, God is known, Christ takes shape, and the Spirit burns with transforming power. Within community, we gradually become the people God wants us to be. Authentic faith therefore

Pause for a few moments and ask yourself: What are my feelings about being placed among other disciples? How seriously have I invested myself in this family whose foundation is Abba's all-inclusive, self-giving love in Jesus? What are my plans for a greater sharing in God's household? Indeed, how am I going to make real my belonging within the community?

intentionally integrates the Christ-follower into community.

CONNECTING WITH THE GREAT CLOUD OF WITNESSES

African pilgrims constantly affirm the eternal dimensions of community. Mmutlanyane Mogoba, once a prisoner on Robben Island and a deeply respected leader within the South African church, explains:

The departed person in Africa is not dead and removed from this life, but rather continues to be consciously affirmed in the family as the values, wisdom and example of that person are incorporated into the family. The African is thus able to understand the Bible in a manner that Westernised people never will. . . . We understand the reality of a person being surrounded by a great cloud of witnesses who have lived and departed this world.[2]

In those faith-empowering opening lines of his twelfth chapter the writer to the Hebrews exclaims: "Therefore, since we are surrounded by so great a cloud of witnesses . . . let us run with perseverance the race that is set before us" (Hebrews 12:1).

Nowadays scant attention is paid to these unseen companions seeking to encourage us along the Way. Disconnection characterizes our links with departed Christ-followers. Restricting the experience of God's community within the present day costs us dearly. It estranges us from our spiritual inheritance, promotes tunnel-vision discipleship and shrivels up the soul. Witness the thirst among many contemporary Christ-followers for a richer, more expansive, life-giving relationship with the living God.

A legendary story encourages a vital connection with our ancestors in the faith. Once upon a time, the water of life, seeking to make itself known on the face of the earth, bubbled up in an artesian well and began to flow freely and strongly. The thirsty thronged to the well and drank gratefully its life-giving water. However, it was not long before decisions were made to fence the well, charge entrance fees and make elaborate laws as to who could come to the well. Soon the well was the protected property of the elite and powerful. Angry and offended by these decisions, the water stopped flowing and began to bubble up elsewhere. Those who owned the first well were so consumed by bureaucracy and legislative paperwork they did not notice that the water had gone elsewhere. They continued selling nonexistent water and few people noticed that its life-giving power was gone. Sadly, the same fate overtook the new artesian well. Again the water of life sought another place—and this process has been repeatedly going on throughout recorded history.

Discerning those past places and people where the water of God's Spirit has brought nourishment invigorates our own lives. This is not an exercise in nostalgia. Neither do we worship our ancestors. It is about renewing family bonds, unpacking bequeathed treasures, enlarging our perspective of Christ-following beyond modern fads and finding clues to where the water of life is flowing these days. It is about rediscovering the heroes of our faith, getting to know them and learning what they can teach us. Surely this is why some branches of the family of God set aside specific days to remember the lives of certain women and men who have lived passionately for Christ and his kingdom.

In this regard I give thankful testimony. During the early years of my Christ-following pilgrimage, there was minimal connection with the great minds and hearts from the past. I had little feeling for those who had born bold witness for Christ after the New Testament era. My faith heroes were, without exception, contemporary. Gratefully, while preparing for the pastoral ministry, my attention was directed toward those wells from which life-giving water had once flowed. Soaking myself in these long-ago streams, I found my passion for God refreshed and deepened.

The first stream to which I was drawn flowed through the Egyptian deserts. During the fourth and fifth centuries, numerous Christ-followers, in their quest for a transforming experience of God, abandoned their ancient cities for the solitude of the desert. Around them, desert communities began forming. Such was their contagious witness that thousands of seekers flocked to these desert fathers and mothers, as they were called, for counsel and direction. Reflecting on their lives and sayings immeasurably enriched my under-

> DISCERNING THOSE PAST PLACES AND PEOPLE WHERE THE WATER OF GOD'S SPIRIT HAS BROUGHT NOURISHMENT INVIGORATES OUR OWN LIVES.

standing of the Christ-focused life. While I knew that the desert option could never be considered literally normative for discipleship, it became clear that without "desert moments" of solitude and silence there would always be in my pilgrimage a certain superficiality and lack of depth. Encouraged by their example, I began exploring for myself the experience of silent retreat, something that was quite foreign to my own faith tradition.

Where does one begin connecting with this "great cloud of witnesses"? I would respond simply. Every Christ-follower stands in one faith tradition or another—Catholic, liturgical, evangelical, Reformed, Pentecostal, Orthodox. Discover where, when and how in your own particular tradition the water of life initially flowed. Befriend those God-drenched women and men. Identify the passions and practices that shaped their inner and outer lives. Discern those emphases, obscured perhaps by our modern prejudices and obsessions, which need to be freshly discovered for an authentic discipleship today. Finally, experiment in small ways with those treasures that you discover.

COMMUNITY IN YOUR LOCAL CONGREGATION

God's gift of community is grounded within the relationship network of the local congregation. Community remains an abstract ideal unless it finds expression in real relationships. Singing "We are one in the Spirit" without embarking on the adventure of knowing and being known makes little sense. Christian community—fellowship—involves real-life people relating through the Holy One who enfolds our individual lives and provides our common meeting point.

Consider briefly the rich content of the familiar biblical word *fellowship*. Its strong meanings have been weakened almost beyond recognition. Mention the word to friends and colleagues and they will associate it with church committees, meetings, teas and meals all held, of course, in the fellowship hall! The importance of such events is not to be underrated, but they do not demonstrate the rich realities to which the word points. *Koinonia,* the Greek equivalent for "fellowship," refers to life-sharing with God and one another at the deepest levels. Using the human body as a model for relationships within the church, Paul captures vividly the potential richness of this life-sharing: "If one member suffers, all suffer together with it; if one member is honored, all rejoice together with it" (1 Corinthians 12:26).

Participation within the general activities of the local congregation does not automatically bring about this kind of life-sharing. Church membership can often be nominal. Recently this was underlined afresh for me. Over an after-service cup of coffee I was chatting with a long-time member of our congregation. For over ten years this person has worshiped regularly, worked on committees, served at church functions. Yet he described his church experience in these words: "I feel a stranger at church. I don't feel I belong."

Some form of small group involvement within the wider congregation seems crucial if genuine life-sharing is to occur. Such practice has solid biblical support. Describing the life of the early Christian community, Luke specifically observes that they assembled in both temple *and* home (Acts 2:46). These home gatherings suggest small companies of Christ-followers banding together for mutual encouragement, care and celebration. In his spiritual direction to the Hebrews the author raises the question of ongoing conversion and recommends the way ahead in two sentences: "And let us consider how we may spur one another on toward love and good deeds. Let us not give up meeting together, as some are in the habit of doing, but let us encourage one another" (Hebrews 10:24-25 NIV).

Establishing small groups requires caution. Not all facilitate healthy life-sharing. Some inhibit fellowship through authoritarian leadership, legalistic attitudes and conformist pressures. Consequently, these groups fail to create a safe, spacious and sacred space for self-disclosure and honest conversation. Group life must be thoughtfully structured if it is going to realize its life-sharing purposes.

I find the simple approach of a neighborhood gospel-sharing group appealing.[3] When everyone has been welcomed, the group coordinator invites a spontaneous affirmation of Christ's presence among his people. "Will one or two please thank our Lord Jesus for being with us?" The Gospel passage is introduced, and group members, especially those with differing versions of the text, are asked to read it aloud, leisurely and prayerfully. In the third step, participants are encouraged to select a gospel word or phrase that strikes them personally, read it aloud slowly three times and then listen attentively as others speak. In between individual contributions, short periods of silence are observed to allow the words and phrases to echo in the hearts of those present. After everyone has spoken, the coordinator announces a clearly defined period of silence: "Let us now be silent together for five minutes as we allow God to speak to us." Following this communal silence, opportunity is given to all members to share, *without* comment from the group, what they have heard in their hearts and how they intend to live their gospel word or phrase during the coming week. During this time there is also a report back regarding the past week's joys and struggles of living the gospel. Finally, the group closes with shared prayer and the Lord's Prayer.

Recently I asked a professional woman, married with three young children, seriously desiring a God-yielded life, what weekly participation in a gospel-sharing group over a period of almost two years had meant for her. Her carefully phrased, written-out response personalizes the faith-building, life-transforming possibilities made available when we intentionally follow Christ together:

> My gospel sharing group has helped me develop a first-hand relationship with God. It has initiated me into the value of actively listening to God and neighbor. I find myself more open to the struggles of others than ever before. I am learning to view my daily life through the eyes of Christ. In my efforts to follow him I feel less isolated. I know that others are bearing me up in their thoughts and prayers.

BUILDING FAITHFUL FRIENDSHIPS

Remember how Jesus, after inviting his disciples into intimate friendship with himself, commissions them in pairs (Luke 10:1-8)? Faithful friendship lies at the very heart of the gospel. To use a delightful

Holy Experiment

SPIRITUAL FRIENDSHIP

Ask God to lead you to someone with whom you can walk along the conversion road. Look around your circle of present acquaintances, those with whom you already interact at church or at work. Is there anyone who stands out as a possible companion on the Way? During this time of praying and looking, keep the channels of communication open between yourself and those closest to you. It is important that they do not feel threatened by your choice of faithful friend. For this reason it may be wise to choose a friend of the same sex. Once you have settled on a choice, the next step involves the risk of asking the person concerned whether he or she is open to the possibility of meeting regularly. This initial request needs to be clear, straightforward and direct.

Quaker phrase, those early students of Jesus were "a society of friends." Christ-following, we learn from them, happens together, two by two. While we are most certainly responsible for our own growth in discipleship, we do not mature into the people God wants us to be without the gifts that real friendship provides. One-to-one support, encouragement and care is absolutely essential if our faith is to be kept strong and growing.

But do we seek to find them? In the competitive, frantic, fast-lane scurry of everyday life, we seldom carve out time and space for life-sharing friendship. It is highly unlikely that you will drift into this kind of friendship. Begin to pray specifically about this.

I remember the first time I found myself on the receiving end of such a request from a colleague in ministry. "Trevor," he asked, "how would you feel about us getting together on a monthly basis over a cup of coffee to share with each other something of our lives and faith?" I felt comfortable with

his request and we have been meeting now for several years. The friendship we feel for each other is deeply mutual; we refrain from moralizing, we share personal joys and struggles, and we promise to pray for each other. I do not seek to be his counselor or spiritual director; neither does he seek to fulfill these roles in my life. Our purpose is far more modest—we are seeking to be friends along the Way.

Becoming faithful friends is an adventure into personal vulnerability. It is not always easy. Often there are misunderstandings, disappointments and unmet expectations. Like any real adventure, the outcome is seldom a foregone conclusion. However, when we are with someone who accepts us as we are, listens attentively to what we share and is committed to mutual interaction, courage is given for the first steps in this life-sharing enterprise.

Of all the God-given gifts provided to encourage us on the Christ-following way, few equal the presence of faithful friends.

Without faithful friendship we block the road to wholeness, fail to become all that God intends and risk losing our way. Without pilgrim companions the Christ-light can sometimes go out. Faithful friendship is God's disguised way of befriending us with his encouraging, life-enriching presence. "For where two or three are gathered in my name, I am there among them" (Matthew 18:20).

Belonging signposts the route toward becoming. An African proverb affirms scriptural wisdom when it says: "A person becomes a person through other people." There can be no I without you. Becoming truly human embraces the risks of life-sharing. Growing into fuller Christlikeness requires community. Little wonder, therefore, that upon entering our yielded lives the Christ of grace comes with arms around his brothers and sisters.

Following the Signpost Together

1. Write the word *church* on a sheet of paper. Brainstorm your immediate responses.

2. "We cannot be Christ-followers alone." Discuss your thoughts regarding this statement.

3. Discuss your sense of connection with the great spiritual heroes of the past.

4. How do you feel about the importance of "faithful friendship" for the spiritual journey?

5. End your time of group-sharing with a time of gospel-sharing. Select a passage from the Gospels, such as Matthew 11:28-80, and build a time of gospel-sharing around it using the steps outlined in the chapter.

6

BECOMING HOLY,
BECOMING OURSELVES

The Signpost

THE GOD PORTRAYED IN SCRIPTURES is the Holy One who wills holiness for each of us. God is set apart and unique in his immense, self-giving love, yet in Jesus God's holiness is given a human face. Through turning toward Christ, yielding ourselves to his transforming Spirit and following him into his practices, we enter into the freedom of growing into our true selves and becoming the people that God wants us to be.

Holy Experiment

Solitude and silence

A desert day

Suffering with a neighbor

Reading

He was different. That is the only explanation I can offer for my school friend's faith-forming influence on my life. In his life I sensed qualities of depth, realness and compassion which were missing from my own and for which I longed. As we walked home together from school one afternoon, these longings formed themselves into a searching question that was to launch me out on my own spiritual journey: "How can I experience what makes your life different?"

Biblical writers would say that there was a holiness about my friend. Holiness is not mentioned much these days. The word tastes strange on our lips, sounds odd in casual conversations and appears sidelined in much current Christian literature. This is surprising since in the Scriptures God is the Holy One who wills holiness for each of us. Writing to scattered pilgrims, Peter quotes an ancient text that underlines this divine imperative: "You shall be holy, for I am holy" (1 Peter 1:16).

Recently I was part of a large group who were asked to brainstorm their spontaneous associations with the word *holiness*. Written-up feedback on the overhead projector reflected the ambivalent feelings many have concerning the concept. In the lengthy list were words like "guilt," "perfection," "faultless," "a sense of failure," "angelic," "monks and nuns." In many people's minds, holiness seems associated with an over-scrupulous, straight-laced and ethereal lifestyle lacking any attractiveness, vitality and joy. Clearly there is a need for a biblical perspective on the subject, a flesh-and-blood vision of what holiness looks like and, most importantly, a practical understanding of how we can grow into holiness.

Biblical revelation suggests that the single most important word to describe God is *holy*. Attending a Communion service recently, I was struck again by the strange beauty of the Eucharistic chant: "Holy, holy, holy; God of power and might; heaven and earth are full of your glory." The Hebrew word for "holy," *qodosh*, emphasizes that God is essentially different. Engagement with the living God immerses us in a boundless Mystery. There is really no one else like God. Holiness testifies to this sense of difference.

So in Hosea God declares: "for I am God and no mortal, the Holy One in your midst" (Hosea 11:9).

But what is this essential difference? Recall our earlier reflections upon the picture of God given us in Scripture. Mystery is not the final word spoken about God. New Testament faith declares the utter Christlikeness of God. At the heart of the Holy Mystery there is an immense and outrageous love that gives us life, accepts us as we are, draws us forward into wholeness and will never let us go. The fire of God's holiness is the fire of blazing love. God is

BIBLICAL REVELATION SUGGESTS THAT THE SINGLE MOST IMPORTANT WORD TO DESCRIBE GOD IS *HOLY*.

set apart from us by self-giving love. Donald McCullough describes succinctly this essential difference: "God is holy because he loves, and loves because he is holy. The Wholly Other is wholly for us."[1]

THE HUMAN FACE OF HOLINESS

Jesus, the Holy Servant, as Luke twice describes him in his Gospel, joins heaven and earth together, gives holiness a human face, and offers insight regarding its shape in our daily lives. Notice, therefore, the three deeply interwoven threads of holy living as the figure of Jesus emerges from the pages of the Gospels.

First, throughout his earthly life Jesus is his own person. He is the same person inside and outside, never wears masks, and is always his real and true self. By his example he sets us free from any form of carbon-copy holiness that would seek to diminish

RATHER, TO BE HOLY IN A CHRISTLIKE WAY IS IN FACT TO BECOME MORE TRULY OURSELVES.

our individuality. Rather, to be holy in a Christlike way is in fact to become more truly ourselves. Holiness has little in common with pharisaic rule keeping, stuffy churchiness or sterile ritual. But it has everything to do, if we take the example of Jesus seriously, with the glorious freedom of growing into our true selves and becoming the people that God wants us to be.

A delightful Hasidic tale reinforces this truth. When Rabbi Zusya arrived in heaven, as the legend goes, he was anxious about the degree of his holiness. He wondered whether God was going to reprimand him. He imagined God angrily cross-questioning him about his way of life: "Tell me, why did you not become like Moses or Solomon or David?" When God approached the rabbi, however, the question was altogether different. "Tell me," asked God quietly, "why did you not become Rabbi Zusya?"

Second, Jesus mingles easily with people from all social strata. He enjoys socializing over a good meal at dinner parties and constantly has time for little children. Outcasts

---

GOSPEL HOLINESS TOUCHES OTHERS WITH COMPASSION AND CARE. TO BECOME HOLY, THE CHRISTLIKE WAY, IS TO BECOME INCREASINGLY LESS SELF-CENTERED AND MORE CONCERNED ABOUT THE NEEDS AROUND US.

---

feel relaxed and at ease in his company, while those who have messed up their lives seem to sense that they are unconditionally accepted. His relationships are consistently characterized by awareness, insight and responsiveness: noticing a man hiding in a tree, seeing into the painful entanglements of a woman aching for intimacy, hearing the anguished cry of a blind beggar above the din of a noisy crowd. Gospel holiness touch-

es others with compassion and care. To become holy, the Christlike way, is to become increasingly less self-centered and more concerned about the needs around us.

Third, at the center of Jesus' life there is a devoted closeness with the Holy One whom he experiences directly as Abba and whose kingdom is his dearest passion. This intimate friendship between Jesus and his Father is the holy hub of his entire life. The Gospel records indicate that Jesus was concerned with only one thing: to do the will of the Father. Consider again his recorded words: "Very truly, I tell you, the Son can do nothing on his own, but only what he sees the Father doing; for whatever the Father does, the Son does likewise" (John 5:19). "The word that you hear is not mine, but is from the Father who sent me" (John 14:24). Without nurturing our intimacy with the Holy One, holiness remains out of reach. Holy men and women are those for whom God comes first.

TRANSFORMED BY HIS SPIRIT

How do we come to share in the holiness of Christ? There are two sides to the answer to this important question. On the one side we must affirm that in this holy-making process it is Christ by his Spirit who transforms us. Holiness is not a do-it-yourself job. As we turn toward Christ and entrust ourselves to him, he comes to live within us in the power of his Spirit. Remaining open and yielding to this Spirit of transformation is absolutely crucial for the serious Christ-follower. Through his loving power we are gradually transformed into our true selves, fashioned into instruments of his love and nourished in our relationship with the Holy One. Holiness is an inside work of the

Spirit, a gracious gift to those who live with open hands. Paul makes this clear when he writes these words: "And all of us, with unveiled faces, seeing the glory of the Lord as though reflected in a mirror, are being transformed into the same image from one degree of glory to another; for this comes from the Lord, the Spirit" (2 Corinthians 3:18).

Yet the moment we grasp this liberating insight we must not fall into the tragic error of saying that there is nothing we can do. Holiness does not just happen. Hence the other side of our answer must affirm our part in the holy-making process. Faith without action is dead. The spiritual journey demands a great deal of human effort. Personal transformation requires our determined and planned cooperation. We have to work at becoming all that we are meant to be. Compassion is not for the lazy and passive. Our relationship with the Holy One only grows when we take appropriate measures for this to happen. The writer to the Hebrews stresses the human side of our answer when he encourages his readers to "make every effort . . . to be holy" (Hebrews 12:14 NIV). But what are we to do? God has graciously given to us, in the life of Jesus, activities through which we can open our hearts more widely to the Spirit's transforming presence.

Often described as "disciplines for the spiritual life," these activities enable us to place our lives more consciously before God so that we can be changed.[2] I want to highlight two such activities, many times neglected and overlooked, that are crucial for an authentic expression of Christlike holiness: making space to be alone in God's presence and exposing ourselves to the suffering of others.

> BUT WHAT ARE WE TO DO? GOD HAS GRACIOUSLY GIVEN TO US, IN THE LIFE OF JESUS, ACTIVITIES THROUGH WHICH WE CAN OPEN OUR HEARTS MORE WIDELY TO THE SPIRIT'S TRANSFORMING PRESENCE.

SPACE ALONE IN GOD'S PRESENCE

Carving out space in our activity-filled lives to be alone with God is a vital ingredient of the Christ-following life. In spite of the enormous demands made on him, Jesus' life is punctuated with such spaces: retreating for forty days into the silence of the desert, spending a night alone before selecting his twelve companions, withdrawing before sunrise to a solitary place following an exhausting day's ministry, seeking the solitude of the Gethsemane garden before the Calvary victory. These moments of silence and solitude were the secret of his life. In them Jesus was able to nurture his intimate communion with Abba, replenish his resources for compassionate ministry, wrestle with that dark, tempting voice intent on enticing him into illusion, and renew his body in restful relaxation. If Jesus needed these spaces, surely our need is even greater.

Choosing to step away from human interaction, withdrawing attention from the outer world and becoming quieter and trusting that God is both graciously present and tremendously active, all have life-transforming benefits. Time is given for seeking God's mind on decisions, issues and conflicts that must be faced. Other spiritual disciplines—study, reflective reading and meditation, prayer, journaling, Sabbathresting, dream interpretation—can only be faithfully practiced provided this discipline is firmly set in place. Solitude, and the silence inside it, enables an exploration of our shadow selves which, as we have already seen, is a prerequisite for traveling along the conversion road of the kingdom. We are put in touch with all kinds of previously unrecognized thoughts and feelings—jealousy, envy, lust, revenge, anger—lurking in our subterranean depths that God wants us to own and bring to the kingdom banquet. Perhaps above all, this practice makes room for a fuller occupation of our lives by God's holy-making Spirit whose goal is our total transformation.

THIS PRACTICE MAKES ROOM FOR A FULLER OCCUPATION OF OUR LIVES BY GOD'S HOLY-MAKING SPIRIT WHOSE GOAL IS OUR TOTAL TRANSFORMATION.

I am a beginner in these matters of silence and solitude. Carving out empty spaces does not come easily for me. Recently I allowed myself to get snarled up in a whirlwind of compulsive busyness. For almost two weeks I neglected my daily discipline of sitting quietly with Scripture and journal. From early until late I juggled commitments, dashed here and there responding to crises, and raced to meet deadlines. A simple dream stopped me in my tracks: I was driving my Datsun when suddenly its rear wheels punctured, sending it careening dangerously about the road. Thankfully, as the wisdom of the Song of Songs reminds us, even as we sleep the heart keeps watch—often through these visions given in the night. The next day I put the brakes on, halted my busyness, sat myself down in an empty nearby chapel and read the inner gauges. In my journal I scribbled out my prayer:

> Lord, thank you for that warning dream. It's good to be sitting silently here again. I confess that I have been living hurriedly and distractedly. I feel out of touch with my own depths and with your indwelling Presence. I seem to be running around continuously, trying to meet everyone else's demands but not living my own life. I see now as I sit here that I am sometimes more interested in establishing my importance than in serving You. I am sorry, Lord, and want to make a fresh beginning. Help me, Lord, to discern what drives me into hurry. And as I seek to carve out in my life those empty spaces that I need, please give me your wisdom.

Does my experience in any way echo your own? We live fast, frenetic and filled lives that inwardly strangle the re-creating presence of the Spirit. We find it difficult to stop. Yet it is something we must learn to do. I still remember the first bit of advice that I received when I began learning to drive: "The first thing you need to know," said my driving instructor, "is how to stop." The same principle applies to our journey along the Way with Christ. Donald Nicholl writes: "Unless we can stop the rush and noise of daily traffic in our lives we do not have the slightest chance of hearing the call to holiness."[3]

Unfortunately, many of us keep delaying that time when we can bring our lives to a halt and stop and listen to what's going on inside of them.

Stop for a moment and consider some questions that I find immeasurably helpful in my endeavors toward a less breathless, more leisurely, evenly paced way of life. When do I catch myself hurrying? Why am I so often living in hurry mode? What patterns of greed or avoidance are revealed in my hurriedness? How can I rearrange my daily activities in order to carve out some "stopping moments" for myself?

Do not delay! Take time to stop now. A story from the Egyptian deserts drives this point home in a rather delightful way. One day a harassed and busy executive was on his way to his office when he spotted a Bedouin from the desert sitting and resting under a city park tree.

The executive stopped and asked the Bedouin, "What are you doing here?"

"Well as you can see," answered the Bedouin, "I've decided to stop for a while."

"You know that you could be earning money if you were working," said the executive.

"What would I do with it?"

"If you earned some money you could open an office."

"And then?"

"Then you could earn more money and build a factory."

"And then?"

"Then you could have your own villa at some fancy resort."

"Good, and then?"

"Then you would still have some money to put in the bank."

"Yes, and then?"

"Well, then you could stop, sit down and rest."

"But that's what I'm doing at the moment."[4]

Embarking upon steps into solitude and silence puts our feet on that pathway described by Isaiah as the "Way of Holiness" (Isaiah 35:8 NIV).

Holy Experiment

SOLITUDE AND SILENCE

Consider making a few modest commitments toward practicing solitude and silence. Here are some ideas:

- *taking time upon waking to jot down the night's dream*

- *pausing at the beginning of each new activity and reminding oneself of God's immediate presence*

- *withdrawing before work or at lunch break for fifteen minutes of silence and prayer*

- *replaying before falling asleep the day's encounters and events and noticing where God has been present in grace and blessing*

For those who struggle to be quiet on their own, joining a small group that is committed to including opportunities for silent reflection on Scripture could prove helpful.

EXPOSURE TO THE SUFFERING OF OTHERS

Any spiritual journey that removes the Christ-follower from human suffering is counterfeit and delusive. It betrays God's passionate love for every person, denies our connectedness in the human family and results in what has been described as "a false inwardness."[5] We become the person God intends, not inside a private religious zone, but within God's broken and wounded world. Becoming holy opens eyes blind to Christ's presence in suffering people, increases awareness of our neighbor's pain and draws the Christ-follower into the human struggles of the day. Jesus, the holy Servant, makes this clear. We have observed his practice of frequently punctuating his ministry life with empty spaces. These moments were never selfish or escapist. Intimacy nurtured with Abba in silence and solitude streamed outward in compassionate responsiveness.

Two Gospel sentences placed in close proximity in Mark's opening chapter powerfully portray the inward-outward journey dynamic so characteristic of Jesus' life. The first reads matter-of-factly: "Very early in the morning, while it was still dark, Jesus got up, left the house and went off to a solitary place" (Mark 1:35 NIV).

Six verses later we read: "Filled with compassion, Jesus reached out his hand

JOHN WESLEY, HUGELY INSTRUMENTAL IN THE EVANGELICAL AWAKENING DURING THE EIGHTEENTH CENTURY, WOULD CONSTANTLY INSIST: "THERE IS NO HOLINESS BUT SOCIAL HOLINESS."

and touched the man" (Mark 1:41 NIV).

Compassion is evidence of the holy life. The Christlike person formed gradually by the Spirit will be characterized by an ever-growing responsiveness and sensitivity to the pain of others. Compassion extends beyond fleeting feelings of sympathy. Compassion, in the way of Jesus, places our lives beside those in turmoil, seeks understanding of their anguish and labors with them for the sake of their wholeness. Without disciplined effort it is doubtful whether we shall touch another in this way. God infuses our hearts with divine compassion as we become more responsive.

Exposing our lives intentionally to the suffering of others is one of the practical ways of doing this. Jesus himself practiced this activity and, in his crucified and risen presence, promises to meet us wherever people are in need (Matthew 25:34-45). I learned the value of this spiritual discipline through a decade's involvement with "the pilgrimage of pain and hope." Throughout the traumatized eighties of our country's history, these pilgrimages were an integral part of our congregational life. Over one hundred young and not-so-young adults participated. The event became an instrument of lasting personal transformation.

The "pilgrimage of pain and hope" was an eight-day journey of twofold encounter. First, it was an encounter with the real faces of pain of our shattered and fragmented society. Usually the pilgrims came from backgrounds that had shielded them from the harsh realities of the South African context. Poverty, destitution and homeless-

Holy Experiment

A DESERT DAY

If you want to go deeper into solitude and silence, try planning a "desert day," in which you spend an entire day in silence and solitude. Obviously this requires careful consultation with loved ones, wise arrangements for their welfare and thoughtful plans that ensure legitimate responsibilities are well cared for. Then a suitable place to which one can retreat must be located. This could be a nearby retreat center, the grounds and facilities of your local church, or the quiet back garden of a friend's home. Structure the day itself carefully with time set aside for rest and reflection, exercise and prayer. Perhaps the day could begin with the leisurely reading of a portion of Scripture that you want to keep resounding in your depths throughout the day—a psalm, a Gospel story, a portion of a letter. Bring along a journal and write down insights that come from your engagement with the Scriptures, as well as the thoughts that pop into your mind during the silence of the day. Writing these things down tends to bring clarity and direction in our thinking. Experiencing the benefits of a desert day encourages our commitment to building "stopping moments" into our everyday lives.

ness tended to be abstractions in their experience, as they were in my own.

Second, the pilgrimage was an encounter with hope. Scattered throughout these deprived communities are those who resiliently refuse to become prisoners of hopelessness. These people had suffered and struggled for a new South Africa. Encountering these "signs of hope" challenged the pilgrims to examine their own faith responses within that historical moment. They learned that the future was open-ended and that their lives could make a creative difference in a land torn apart by division and suffering.

Reflection on experience is a critical ingredient in the pilgrimage process. Daily the pilgrims experienced a wide range of emotions, circumstances and people. Without reflection they ran the risk of losing those insights that empower those experiences to transform them. While we could plan into the pilgrimage the elements of encounter and reflection, we could not ensure the experience of transformation. However, when there was openness among the pilgrims, the Spirit transformed hearts and lives. An intern doctor reflected on this

Holy Experiment

SUFFERING WITH A NEIGHBOR

Think of someone who is suffering and whom you are able to contact. Arrange to spend time with this person. When you make personal contact, adopt the stance of a pilgrim. You are with this person not to give him advice or to try to solve his problems, but to learn from him what it is like to be in that kind of situation. Seek to listen rather than to speak. Remind yourself that the Holy One is present in the suffering of the sufferer. Do not underestimate what your simple presence may mean. After the visit, take time to reflect on it, write out your feelings and thoughts, and ask God if there is anything you need to learn from the experience.

experience: "I realized that it is not enough to be shocked or indignant at the circumstances of people who suffer. If I am to follow Christ seriously I must be prepared to give my life in sacrificial service."

Not everyone can go away on an eight-day pilgrimage. Nonetheless, we can build into our lives the discipline of planned encounter with those who suffer in our midst. We begin to practice this discipline by committing ourselves to spend some time each week with someone who suffers deeply. This person may be elderly and alone, terminally ill, severely handicapped, desperately poor or stuck in dark depression. Rather than doing things for the person, the emphasis of our time together is upon being with, actively listening and seeking understanding. As we give ourselves to this activity, believing that God will meet us, we receive more fully into our lives the transforming power of the Spirit.

God's transformation of our lives is both painful and joyfully liberating. Exposure to the sufferings of others connects us with our own grief and fear. We are brought face-to-face with the immense forces of selfishness and prejudice that lurk inside us all. We discover the hardness of our own hearts and our capacity for evildoing and destruction. And yet it is precisely in these parched and barren places that, if our hands remain open, God quietly goes about transforming our hearts. The implanted seed of divine compassion begins to flower. Nonsentimental and caring deeds are birthed. Courage is given to speak truth to those "principalities and powers" intent on destroying the lives of people. Our hearts begin yearning for a society where there is justice and compassion for all. That this can begin to happen in our lives is the testimony of our pilgrims.

> IT IS PRECISELY IN THESE PARCHED AND BARREN PLACES THAT, IF OUR HANDS REMAIN OPEN, GOD QUIETLY GOES ABOUT TRANSFORMING OUR HEARTS.

THE LONGING TO BE DIFFERENT

Holiness arouses longing and sorrow. Encountering God-touched men and women who are different for the sake of Christ and his kingdom always disturbs. Their depth exposes our superficiality, their realness uncovers our falseness, their compassion reveals our self-centeredness. In their presence we long to be different. These holy longings cry out for fulfillment. The good news is that the Spirit of God, who dwells inside these longings, wants very much to give us experiences of transformation and change. They are given to those who genuinely seek the Holy One in solitude and in the suffering of their neighbor. What is essential is that we begin the seeking.

Following the Signpost Together

1. Write the word *holiness* on a sheet of paper. Brainstorm your immediate responses to this word.

2. Discuss the flesh-and-blood vision of holiness that we see in the life of Jesus of Naza-
    reth. In what ways does the holiness of Christ revise our traditional understanding of
    this word?

3. Share your experience of the Holy Spirit in your life.

4. In what ways do you avoid the experience of silence and solitude?

5. What have you learned from suffering people?

Consider making yourselves accountable to one another with regard to some of the practical suggestions outlined in the chapter.

7

LOVING THOSE
CLOSEST TO US

The Signpost

COMPASSIONATE CARING IS THE ACID TEST of the authentic Christ-following life. Practices of spiritual disciplines that do not result in others, especially those closest to us, feeling more valued and loved are hollow and empty. Genuine growth in relationship with the Holy One evidences itself for the most part in an ever-deepening capacity to care for others. When this does not happen we have failed the acid test. There is no higher priority for the Christ-follower than learning to love as Christ loved.

Holy Experiment

Confession

Listening

Conscious loving actions

Reading

I once visited the home of a man highly respected as a devout person. Vocal in expressing his faith, regular in his church commitments and enthusiastic about evangelism, he had become a key figure in his local congregation. During our visit the phone rang. It was his pastor requesting his immediate presence. An urgent matter had arisen requiring prompt attention. As he left the lounge I was left alone with his wife, a rather tired-looking woman in her early fifties. One exchange in our brief conversation remains fresh in my memory.

"Your husband is certainly a deeply committed man," I casually remarked as we heard her husband's car speeding down the street. For a few moments she was quiet. I thought I sensed a hidden and smoldering resentment. Her sharp response confirmed my intuition. "Yes, I guess you can say that. But then you don't have to live with him on a daily basis."

We do well not to judge the man. Have there not been numerous occasions in our own personal lives when those closest to us have felt neglected, unloved and taken for granted? I recall one painful moment in my own marriage. I had just assumed responsibility for my first congregation. Obviously keen to succeed, I worked long, hard hours. Externally things were going well. Attendance was increasing, finances had improved, and a new sanctuary was on the drawing boards. Within my marriage relationship, however, I was not doing well. Often away from home, I was denying the person closest to me the attention, time and energy necessary for real communication and caring. Coming home late one night I found a note at my bedside table. It read: "Trevor I love you and want to be married to you. Sometimes I worry though that one day I may not be worried if you don't come home. I miss you and want to reconnect."

I had failed the acid test.

CHALLENGED TO LOVE

Learning to love particular individuals is an indispensable component of the Christ-following vocation. God, as we have already noted, is extravagantly, sacrificially and unconditionally loving. Jesus, God come in the flesh, lived this love and taught what he lived. The language of the kingdom is the language of self-giving love. Participation in this kingdom demands one central commitment. It requires sharing with others the same kind of compassion, mercy and caring that we have received from God. This is the essential distinguishing characteristic, "the acid test" as I've called it, of being a follower of Jesus. Ponder again those startling words spoken by Jesus: "A new command I give you: Love one another. As I have loved you, so you must love one another. By this all men will know that you are my disciples, if you love one another" (John 13:34-35 NIV).

This great commandment is given us for our wholeness, the well-being of our relationships and the healing of our societies. Shaping our lives into instruments of God's love breaks the tyranny of ingrained self-centeredness and narcissism. We step out of our cramped and suffocating worlds into the spacious milieu of the kingdom. We begin blossoming into the mature people God wants us to be. Our lives come alive with renewed responsiveness and fresh meaning. We discover how loving others releases within them immense possibilities for growth and change. And we realize that only the power of God's love, manifest in the lives of ordinary people, can heal our broken world. Mmutlanyane Mogoba describes love as "the Great Transformer of the Global Village." There is no higher priority for the Christ-follower than learning to love.

Elton Trueblood is a widely read Quaker author whose writings have influenced the lives of countless women and men. In the ninth decade of his life he continued to encourage others through the writing of a quarterly newsletter. In his newsletter dated June 1994 he described a banquet dinner given in his honor where he told the story of his own life, calling it "A Life of Search." Profoundly moved by the spirit of loving commitment that joined together the three hundred people who had gathered for this occasion, Elton Trueblood was prompted to write about the crucial priority of becoming a loving person. After quoting the many New Testament texts that support this central emphasis on love, he wrote these moving words:

> At the age of 93 I am well aware that I do not have many years to live. Consequently, I try very hard to live my remaining years in such a manner that I make a real difference in as many lives as possible. How do I want to be remembered? Not primarily as a Christian scholar, but rather as a loving person. This can be the goal of every individual. If I can be remembered as a truly loving person I shall be satisfied. Now I hope that this Quarterly Letter may help others to realise what comes first in the life of a Christian. The great idea is that a life of love is really open to all. Every individual who reads this letter can try to be more loving.[1]

What does it mean, as the Ephesians author writes, to "live a life of love, just as Christ loved us"? (Ephesians 5:2 NIV). Wrestling with this question moves one from the abstract to the concrete, from the universal to the particular, from theory to practice. I have struggled with this question for almost twenty years. In this chapter I focus particularly on loving those closest to us—spouse, child, parent, brother, sister, partner, faithful friend. Something is radically wrong if we talk about caring within the wider community and neglect those in our intimate circle.

Conscious that my greatest failures have been those in loving, it is with a certain reserve that I offer the following three suggestions. Representing my own growing edges, they arise from an ongoing engagement with the gospel story, insights gleaned from mentors along the Way and reflection on personal experiences of being loved and learning to love.

BEGIN WITH CONFESSION

Inside us all there are powerful ingrained forces that block the flow of self-giving love, sabotage efforts at fostering intimacy and repeatedly alienate us from those with whom we live. We want to love, yet constantly fail. It would appear, as Paul confesses in the seventh chapter of his letter to the Romans, that there rages within the human heart a fierce "tug of war" to claim or to forfeit the loving destinies God intends for every one of us (see Romans 7:13-25).

There is the side that genuinely seeks to care and give itself away in self-forgetful compassion. This is our truest nature, the image of God imprinted on our souls, the person God wants us to be. There is also that side with its infinite capacity for self-centeredness that curves us inward upon ourselves, imprisons us in egotism and hobbles our attempts at loving: our sin condition. When estranged from the Source

WITHOUT HELP FROM BEYOND OURSELVES WE MISS THE MARK THAT GOD HAS SET FOR OUR LIVES.

of Love, it is the latter side that consistently triumphs. When it wins, evil finds a firmer foothold in our lives. Damage is inflicted on those around us and on ourselves. Without help from beyond ourselves we miss the mark that God has set for our lives.

Only those, I would dare suggest, who

acknowledge their impoverishment when it comes to loving and come repeatedly into the presence of the Holy One with open hands learn to care in the spirit of Jesus. This is not easy. Admitting failures and weaknesses in loving can be humiliating. Letting go of virtuous illusions about ourselves is tough. Relinquishing rationalizations and excuses leaves us vulnerable. Taking back blame heaped on others for not meeting our needs confronts us with the challenge of sacrificial caring. However, we are encouraged in these processes by the knowledge that God in Christ is utterly for us, accepts us in our lovelessness and offers us moment by moment his empowering companionship.

A childlike exercise enables me to appropriate the resourcing benefits of confession. I learned this exercise from Morton Kelsey, Episcopalian priest and prolific author, who has written helpfully about the challenges of caring.[2] Involving our imagination, it is based on a familiar passage of the New Testament, written by John in the last book of the Bible and sent to some

---

CONFESSION—WHETHER IT HAPPENS IN THE INNER SANCTUARY OF OUR SOUL OR IN THE PRESENCE OF ANOTHER—OPENS CLOGGED CHANNELS BETWEEN GOD AND OURSELVES, ALLOWS FOR THE INPOURING OF HIS LOVE AND PROVIDES US WITH NEW RESOURCES FOR THE WORK OF LOVE.

---

lukewarm disciples as a message from the risen Jesus himself: "Listen! I am standing at the door, knocking; if you hear my voice and open the door, I will come in to you and eat with you, and you with me" (Revelation 3:20).

I imagine myself to be sitting alone in my own soul-room. Its darkness and untidiness represent my failure in reaching out compassionately and lovingly to those around me. As I look around at the clothes lying on the floor, the unmade bed, the cluttered washbasin, there is a dark voice that accuses me, "Trevor, you really are no good at Christ-following. Look at the way you disappoint those closest to you, fail to love them and let them down. Forget about following Christ and trying to live his way of love. It will never work for you." I hear that voice often in my moments of failure and disobedience. Whenever I hear it I am learning to respond firmly: "Keep quiet. You are a lying, deceiving voice and I will not allow you to define my life." As this dark voice fades I hear another sound—a gentle, persistent knocking at the door of my soul-room. When I ask the guest to enter he answers that he cannot, for the door is locked and the latch is inside. I realize that this guest is not a burglar who wants to intrude. He awaits my invitation to enter my life. Opening the door I am greeted by the risen Lord. Still bearing the scars of crucifixion, his continuing love for me is clear. The light of his presence shines into the darkness of my room.

"Dear Lord," I say to him, "my soul-room is a mess, but please come in." He enters, puts his arm around my shoulders and leads me to a table amidst the mess where we sit down. With quiet authority my guest becomes the host. As at Emmaus, bread is broken, wine is poured and we commune together. An inner assurance that I am loved, forgiven and accepted rises in my heart. I start sharing specifically the many ways in which I withhold myself from those I love, the symptoms of my self-centeredness, my uncaring thoughts and attitudes. After listening attentively he tells me not to give up. He will give me his transforming Spirit and will empower me anew for the tasks of loving.

As I conclude the exercise with a prayer of thankfulness, I usually feel renewed in faith, hope and love. I am ready to begin again. There are times, though, when I feel "stuck" in my struggles to become a loving person. Sharing these struggles with a faithful friend who will listen and pray with me helps tremendously. James may have had this kind of sharing in mind when he taught those belonging to the early church to "confess your sins to each other" (James 5:16 NIV). Our failure to become open, vulnerable, caring people could well be related to our resistance toward doing this. Confession—whether it happens in the inner sanctuary of our soul or in the presence of another—opens clogged channels between God and ourselves, allows for the inpouring of his love and provides us with new resources for the work of love.

Holy Experiment

CONFESSION

After reading through the way I have adapted this exercise for my own use, you may want to take a few minutes and practice it yourself where you are. Begin by imagining yourself in your soul room. Look around. What do you see? Are there any messes? failures in loving? Do you hear any dark voices of accusation and harsh self-judgment? Now allow yourself to hear the sound of the risen Lord knocking on the door of your soul room. How do you respond?

LEARN TO LISTEN

The Scriptures are clear: the God who loves is the God who listens. The biblical God, whose face we have seen in Jesus, hears the cry of the oppressed, listens to the distress of the psalmist and is attentive even to those groans we cannot put into words. Jesus lived in the constant awareness of this listening presence. "Father," he once prayed, "I thank you that you have heard

> LISTENING IS ONE OF THE MOST PRECIOUS GIFTS THAT WE CAN GIVE TO SOMEONE WE LOVE.

me. I knew that you always hear me" (John 11:41-42 NIV). God joins love and listening inseparably together.

Listening is one of the most precious gifts that we can give to someone we love. Stop for a moment and recall your own feelings when you last felt truly listened to. When this experience is ours we feel valued for who we are, recognized as a unique human being and affirmed as a God-created person. Listening says to the other person: "I care for you. I respect your uniqueness. How you feel and what you say matters to me. And in order to make

> SEVENTY YEARS AGO DIETRICH BONHOEFFER, GERMAN PASTOR AND MARTYR, MADE THIS VERY RELEVANT OBSERVATION: "MANY PEOPLE ARE LOOKING FOR AN EAR THAT WILL LISTEN. THEY DO NOT FIND IT AMONG CHRISTIANS, BECAUSE CHRISTIANS ARE TALKING WHEN THEY SHOULD BE LISTENING."

this clear, I'm willing to set aside my own concerns, give you space to share yourself and offer you my focused attention. I want to try to understand the inexhaustible mystery of your inner world."

Consciously making the effort to listen well involves three basic ground rules: respectful silence, total attention and appropriate response. Without bridling our tongue, restraining ourselves from interrupting and becoming quiet inside, it is impossible even to begin listening. Without concentrating intently on what someone is saying, the feelings that accompany the words and the silences in between them, genuine listening seldom occurs. Without indicating some understanding of what is being said and felt in our verbal response, it is improbable that the person will feel listened to. This kind of real listening makes empathy possible.

Empathetic listening is difficult, requires persistent effort and takes time to learn. Few people are able to listen effectively without practical guidance and experiential training. Strangely enough, local congregations are often the last place where classes in listening are provided. We talk more about the "gift of tongues" and little about the "gift of ears"!

If I am to give this kind of quality listening to those closest to me, we will need uninterrupted time together. On my weekly day off, my wife and I have an appointment for breakfast. It gives us a leisurely opportunity to share and to listen. Few practices have enriched our relationship more than this simple arrangement.

CHRISTLIKE CARING ROOTS ITSELF IN ACTION

"My children," teaches John, beloved dis-

Holy Experiment

LISTENING

Make an appointment with a loved one with no agenda other than being together, and focus on listening to them.

ciple and wise spiritual guide, "our love should not be just words and talk; it must be true love, which shows itself in action" (1 John 3:18 Good News Bible). Jesus enfleshed these words. His love was a love-in-action. He touched lepers, shared meals with outsiders, hugged children, fed hungry people, washed dirty feet and ultimately laid down his life on a cross for us all. To Jesus, love meant far more than a fleeting feeling, a sentimental thought, a wistful emotion. Love implied a priority decision and commitment to act in a loving way that would leave others feeling valued and important.

Love in action is chiefly a matter of the will. Jesus invites decision and commitment when he commands us to love as he loved. This commandment does not address our feelings and emotions. Not that these are unimportant. There are times when we do feel warm and affectionate, and these feelings need to be expressed. However, loving actions are not dependent on good feelings. There are many moments when the Christ-follower inwardly decides: no matter how I may be feeling, with God's help, I commit myself to act in a loving way.

I recall a birthday card my wife made for me one year. After an exceptionally long day, I noticed her going to the lounge with scissors, card, glue and old magazines.

Early the next morning I was awakened with a hug and the gift of a homemade card. Debbie had extended herself and, in

LOVE IN ACTION IS CHIEFLY A MATTER OF THE WILL. JESUS INVITES DECISION AND COMMITMENT WHEN HE COMMANDS US TO LOVE AS HE LOVED.

spite of feeling weary and tired, acted in a loving way. I felt appreciated, valued and loved.

I deliberately choose a very ordinary episode from our family life together to illustrate my point: the ways in which we commit ourselves to be channels of God's love are usually down-to-earth. Characterized by thoughtfulness, creativity and kindness, they are within the reach of us all: cooking a favorite meal, buying a surprise gift, writing an overdue letter, re-

THE WAYS IN WHICH WE COMMIT OURSELVES TO BE CHANNELS OF GOD'S LOVE ARE USUALLY DOWN-TO-EARTH.

membering an anniversary, giving space for a loved one to be alone and, yes, creating a homemade birthday card! Simple ac-

Holy Experiment

CONSCIOUS LOVING ACTIONS

Take a few moments to engage in a holy experiment designed to unite your praying and loving. I find it helpful to repeat this experiment at regular intervals. Begin by asking God for the discernment that the Spirit gives. List the names of those with whom you share most closely your daily life. According to your best knowledge of each person, think about his or her individual hopes and needs. Write down next to each person's name what practical expression of caring would most contribute to that person's greater wholeness. Without fuss go about putting these written intentions into practice. Allow these actions to become channels of that extravagant love and gracious acceptance which we have been given by God. Reflect on the results of the experiment, asking God to guide you as you continue seeking to be an instrument of his love in your close relationships.

tions like these are sacramental. They connect us with God's loving presence and give us a taste of the heavenly banquet. Apostle John describes the experience in a single sentence: "those who abide in love abide in God, and God abides in them" (1 John 4:16).

Caring for those closest to us signposts us toward genuine growth in God. Through confession, empathetic listening and caring actions, we embark on the loving way. Stepping into this world of compassion, we step into the world of the self-giving God. Miracles of the Spirit begin to occur. Our lives and relationships are gifted with healing and newness. Hearts of stone become hearts of flesh. We pass the acid test.

Following the Signpost Together

1. What do you think about the statement "There is no higher priority for the Christ-follower than learning to love"?

2. What is a struggle you have in loving those closest to you?

3. What blocks you from listening actively to those with whom you relate most deeply?

4. "Loving actions are not dependent on good feelings." How do you respond?

End your time of group sharing by sharing together in the imaginative meditation outlined in the chapter. It may be helpful if someone in the group would prepare this meditation beforehand and then lead the rest of the group through it.

8

DISCOVERING GOD'S CALL
FOR OUR LIVES

The Signpost

AS FOLLOWERS OF CHRIST WE ARE CALLED to participate in God's kingdom dream for a renewed society. For every one of us, God has a unique kingdom assignment in mind. This good work that God has prepared to entrust to each individual is our personal calling. Discerning and growing in this dynamic calling nourishes us and others as we are equipped by the God who calls.

Holy Experiment

Discernment

Reading

Recently I watched a television documentary portraying the remarkable life and ministry of Mother Teresa among the suffering poor of Calcutta. At one stage there was a poignant exchange between her and the commentator. He asked whether she found her work futile and hopeless given the immensity of the task facing her and the sisters. In her typically humble fashion she replied: "I was not called to be successful, but faithful. Each one of us has something beautiful to do for God."

You are not alone if you struggle to believe this for yourself. Often we feel our smallness, are filled with self-doubt and

have little sense of ourselves as instruments of God's kingdom in his suffering world. So when someone like Mother Teresa suggests that God has something special for each of us to accomplish, we are only half convinced. Yet her words signpost the inescapable challenge facing every Christ-follower to discern the task God wants him or her to fulfill.

Call is the biblical word that describes this challenge. It is a central scriptural theme that threads its way through the actions of all the key figures on its pages. Abraham was called, as was Moses, as was Jeremiah, as was Mary, as were the early disciples. Neither are we excluded. Writing to the enthusiastic Corinthian congregation, Paul makes it clear that every Christ-follower is a called person: "let each of you lead the life that the Lord has assigned, to which God called you" (1 Corinthians 7:17).

Upon opening our lives to the crucified and risen Lord and his family, we are invited into a threefold vocation: to become the person God wants us to be, to care for those closest to us as Christ has loved us *and* to participate in God's kingdom dream for a healed and healing society. Earlier chapters sought to probe the first two components of this Christ-following adventure. Exploring the third involves clarifying the biblical features of personal calling, unraveling its relationship with our daily job, and finally, offering some practical suggestions for discerning and following this call in our individual lives.

PERSONAL CALLING IN THE BIBLE

God has a kingdom assignment in mind for you and me. This good work, which has our unique name written across it, is our personal calling. An ancient Christian tradition celebrates this truth when it states that God sends every person into the world with a special message to deliver, with a special song to sing for others, with a special act of love to bestow. No one else can speak my message or sing my song or offer my act of love.[1] Paul puts forward the biblical basis for the tradition in a single sentence: "For we are what he has made us, created in Christ Jesus for good works, which God prepared beforehand to be our way of life" (Ephesians 2:10). Do you not

intuitively sense this truth stirring in your own depths? Underneath persistent feelings of emptiness and unfulfillment there often lies hidden the unexplored treasure that is one's personal calling.

Before unpacking four biblical features that describe God's personal calling in our lives, one important exception must be noted: those in deep depression and those who are mentally ill are often unable to wrestle with the challenges of personal calling. Sometimes it is even difficult to experience any kind of significant relatedness with the Holy One. Often in our excitement about what God is calling us to do, we very easily neglect or overlook those around us who simply don't have the available resources to deal with these kinds of faith issues. Indeed there may well be those in the local congregation for whom caring for the depressed and mentally ill is their primary call.

Discovering our personal calling nourishes our lives and those of others. This biblical feature of personal calling finds its origins in our picture of God. The God who calls is the God who loves us and longs for us, together with the rest of all creation, to be made whole. His call will never diminish or restrict our lives. Engagement with the task to which God calls us brings us alive, releases locked-up potential and gives real fulfillment. We know we are doing what we were created for. We are speaking our message, singing our song, bestowing our act of love. We are becoming the person God wants us to be. Jesus, whose whole life was integrated with this theme of call, captures this nourishment in a memorable metaphor: "It is meat and drink for me to do the will of him who sent me until I have finished his work" (John 4:34 NEB).

But a personal call is not for our own sake alone. It continually points our hearts and minds toward our neighbor, connects us with some segment of the world's pain and meets real human need. Living out our call becomes a way in which we, like Jesus, lay down our lives on behalf of others. We become instruments of God's *shalom* and healing.

> Where there is hatred, we sow love;
> where there is injury, we bestow
>   pardon;
> where there is doubt, we bring faith;
> where there is despair, we bring
>   hope;
> where there is darkness, we shed
>   light;
> where there is weakness, we inspire
>   strength;
> and where there is sadness, we
>   bring joy.
> (St. Francis)

Awareness of a personal call usually evokes deep feelings of resistance. This biblical characteristic is vividly illustrated in the burning-bush encounter between the God who calls and Moses. Before Moses eventually responds he seeks to sidestep his personal call with a litany of excuses. Upon close examination these excuses echo familiar whispers of resistance inside us all. In my rather loosely paraphrased version of Moses' five excuses you may recognize one or another of them from personal experience:

• I'm nobody.

• I don't know enough about God.

• What happens if I fail?

• I don't have what it takes.

• Someone else can do it better.

I am well acquainted with these whispers of resistance. At present I am testing—one word at a time—what may be a calling to write. In my primary vocation as pastor I spend long hours placing words together that seek to proclaim the sacred story in a way that is fresh and faithful. I enjoy working with words and have observed their powerful effects on my life and those of others. Perhaps sensing this, one or two companions along the Way have suggested that I write. Their interest has given me the courage to risk trying. But it has not lessened the forces of resistance within myself. Feelings of self-doubt and inadequacy mock me constantly. I struggle to believe that I may have anything to say. The task ahead seems impossible, and with Moses I want to say: "No, Lord, please use someone else."

We are not left to face these resistances alone. The God who calls also empowers us in a multitude of ways. The joy we experience in pursuing our call strengthens us. Our souls are nourished by the meat and drink that doing his will provides. Helpers mysteriously cross our paths with gifts of affirmation and encouragement. For those with eyes to see and ears to hear, the word of promise given to Moses is made real for us.

The biblical God calls his people into an amazing variety of tasks. A random selection of scriptural stories makes this clear: Moses invests himself in the work of people-liberation and nation-building; Isaiah proclaims an unpopular message to a stubborn people; Mary bears the Christ-child into a hostile world; Joseph heeds his God-given dream and courageously protects wife and child from Herod's death squads; Simon and Andrew are invited to become fishers of men and women; Dorcas knits garments for the poor and needy; Paul builds Christ-centered faith communities that transcend race and class. Personal calls do not come in stereotyped and standardized categories. They portray the infinite creativity of the Creator-Redeemer, God.

While amazingly varied in content, these calls unite in common cause. All serve the purposes of God's kingdom in a torn-apart and fractured world. In some particular way the Spirit-breathed call will, in the language of the prophet, bring good news to the oppressed, bind up the broken-hearted, proclaim liberty to captives, bring release to prisoners and comfort to those who mourn.

I have frequently been asked by laypeople about the circumstances in which my own calling to be a pastor originated. When I respond I also inquire about their experience of call. The taken-aback responses I usually receive indicate a commonly held conviction that it's only the pastor who is the called person. Nothing, as we have seen, can be further from biblical truth. Every human being has something beautiful to do for God. I have become increasingly convinced that one of my essential tasks as a pastor is to evoke these personal callings in the lives of those in my pastoral care.

Personal calling is dynamic. This biblical feature can be traced in the life of Jesus as he went about his Father's work during the various stages of his own pilgrimage. For almost thirty years there is the Nazareth phase of hidden preparation, culminating in his baptism and wilderness choices. This is followed by the Galilean phase of public and popular ministry: leisurely wandering through the countryside villages and towns, sharing meals with outcasts, feeding the hungry, healing the sick, choosing and training a band of disciples, and an-

---

PERSONAL CALLS DO NOT COME IN STEREOTYPED AND STANDARDIZED CATEGORIES. THEY PORTRAY THE INFINITE CREATIVITY OF THE CREATOR-REDEEMER, GOD.

---

nouncing the availability of the kingdom for all people. The Jerusalem phase, with its conflict and opposition, turns the spotlight in word and deed on the themes of sacrifice and suffering servanthood. Finally, the resurrection phase bursts forth with its joyful work of consolation and commissioning.

My primary calling is to be a pastor. In its outworking there have been clearly discernible phases. There was a lengthy period of pregnancy when I carried my call around within me. For nine years there was a time of preparation and supervision. Then I invested my energies in a decade-long task of building a local congregation. During the past twenty years my calling has found expression in three different people contexts: regular teaching and preaching in the local congregation; participating in retreats, workshops and conferences that explore these signposts for the Christ-following journey; and befriending fellow pilgrims on the Christ-following road. I do not know what the next phase will look like. God requires only that I be open to his initiatives and responsive to his promptings.

PERSONAL CALLING AND DAILY WORK

It is also helpful to consider the relationship between personal calling and our daily jobs. The way in which the two relate varies tremendously from person to person. Francis Dewar, an Anglican clergy person who runs courses and retreats to enable people to link prayer and action, has helped me enormously in clarifying this relationship between personal calling and daily job. The latter, he suggests, is accompanied by a job description, has defined expectations and carries with it a clear role prescription. Think of the work you do each day. Whether you are a secretary or a senior manager, your job is directed and defined by others. In return for doing what is required, you receive a wage. Dewar discusses the consequences of this state of affairs: "Many of us can hardly conceive what our daily activity would be if it were not *demanded* of us, *expected* of us, or at least *asked* of us by someone else."[2]

Personal calling involves living from the inside out. It is freely responding to the inner promptings of the Spirit, expressing the unique essence of who we are and giving ourselves away in some particular way that enriches the lives of others. This may be something that we do as a large or small part of our daily job; it may be an activity we pursue outside of work hours. For the growing number of unemployed and retired people, personal call becomes an even more urgent issue since it often preserves a sense of personhood and dignity.

Three stories of friends come to mind. Through the painful death of a loved one, a self-employed middle-aged man who spends his working hours doing small building alterations felt a sense of call to care for the dying. After processing his own grief over an extended length of time, he applied to, and was accepted for, a hospice care-giving course. Now he shares in his congregation's intentional ministry to those who are dying. Amidst the turmoil leading up to our country's first fully democratic elections, a legal adviser in a construction company sensed a call for peacemaking. He made himself available to the local peace structures and invested his personal giftedness and skills in its work. An elderly lady retired to a small coastal resort and was moved by the loneliness of the town's many senior citizens. Each day around lunchtime she makes sandwiches for two, packs them in her bag, sits down on a bench overlooking the ocean and waits for someone to join her. When a stranger sits beside her, she offers him or her a sandwich and reaches out in listening friendship.

These examples describe people living out their call without financial remuneration. We can consider ourselves extremely fortunate when personal calling and daily job coincide and we are paid for doing what we believe God is calling us to do. I think of a long-term friend who works in the area of organizational development and training. His personal calling, in his own words, is "the development of people." While his job description outlines many routine tasks, a large percentage of his time is given to what he believes is his life's vocation.

His working hours offer him numerous opportunities to live out his inner calling. Going to work each day is an energizing and fulfilling adventure.

In whatever way calling and job may relate, I do not want to undervalue the importance of our daily work. Unemployment is a major soul-killing form of oppression. One night I sat for two hours with a devastated man on the brink of suicide after being retrenched for the third time within the year. Made in the image of the worker-God, it is good and right for us to work.

DISCERNING AND FOLLOWING YOUR PERSONAL CALLING

Hopefully you are willing to consider the possibility that God may have something unique for you to do. You may be wondering how you can practically explore this possibility. Not every inner prompting or nudge is necessarily the voice of the Spirit. It may be the voice of culture, parents, peer pressure or our egos. Cynical stories abound of those who have claimed a call from God but whose actions have either been self-promoting or painfully destructive. Clearly there is a need not for a neat and tidy formula but for a discerning process that enables you and me to understand the source of a call, its content and what response is appropriate.

Personal calling implies a relationship with the One who calls. Calls are discovered and discerned within an ever-deepening intimacy with God. Walking along the signposted road places our lives consciously in the way of the God who calls, enhances the ability to discern the burning bushes across our paths and strengthens us to act on what we have discovered. Another way of stating this is to affirm that we are called to *being* before we are called to *doing*. Jesus invites his disciples to *be* with him in community and then calls them into their ministry tasks. Communion precedes commissioning.

WE ARE CALLED TO *BEING* BEFORE WE ARE CALLED TO *DOING*.

The primary gift we bring to the world is always who we are, the compassionate and responsive person that the Spirit is gradually forming. And it is into the internal fabric of who we are becoming that God writes the special message which we are called to deliver in our lifetime. Deciphering this message is what discernment is all about. Facilitating this deciphering process would be questions like: "What do I really care about?" "How can I follow my heart more faithfully?" "What are my gifts and where can they enjoy fuller expression in the cause of the kingdom?"

Personal calling intersects with the experience of pain. Perhaps this is why Paul, in that magnificent eighth chapter of the letter to the Romans, invites his readers to listen to three groans: "We know that the whole creation has been groaning. . . . Not only so, but we ourselves, who have the firstfruits of the Spirit, groan inwardly. . . . But the Spirit himself intercedes for us with groans that words cannot express" (Romans 8:22-23, 26 NIV). Paying attention to these groans—in our lives and those of others—puts us in touch with the Spirit who shares our suffering, speaks to us through pain, and calls us to be channels of healing and wholeness in a broken and tormented world. Discerning our call is rooted in this kind of listening.

Attending to our inner groans happens best with a trusted friend of the soul who can be our "wailing wall" and will listen

> COMBINED WITH THIS INNER LISTENING TO OUR OWN PAIN, THERE NEEDS TO BE A GROWING AWARENESS OF THE HUMAN STRUGGLES TAKING PLACE IN OUR MIDST.

prayerfully with us to the pain we bear. Planted there may be the buried seeds of those good deeds that God has purposed us to do.

I am reminded of the parents of two mentally handicapped children who, in their own anguish and despair, heard the call of God to initiate a "faith and light" ministry for others in a similar position. Their pioneering efforts resulted in the forming of a small community comprising fellow parents, their handicapped children and friends. For almost eight years they have gathered together, once every month, to celebrate their faith, share stories and struggles, and play together. Their testi-

mony encourages us to listen to our own inner pain and to seek there the clues that enable us to discern our calling.

Combined with this inner listening to our own pain, there needs to be a growing awareness of the human struggles taking place in our midst. Here we recognize the critical necessity of the spiritual discipline of planned encounter with those who suffer. Through this kind of exposure there is sometimes a particular human cry that penetrates our heart more deeply than any other. In this cry we may hear God addressing us and calling us to colabor in the work of making whole what is broken. Pause for a moment and ask yourself: "What human cry in my community disturbs me the most?" Is it the cry of the dying or the bereaved? Is it the cry of the homeless poor, the drug addicted, the children of the street? Is it the cry of the depressed, the lonely, the shut-in elderly? You may discover in this cry intimations of your own calling.

Personal calling unfolds slowly. Like a person walking through a dark forest with a torch, we take one step at a time, following whatever light is given.

Following the Signpost Together

1. How do you respond to the statement made by Mother Teresa, "Each of us has something beautiful to do for God"?

2. Which one of the biblical features described in the chapter sheds the most light for you on the theme of personal calling?

3. How do you understand the relationship between your daily work and your calling from God?

4. What "human cry" in your community disturbs you the most?

5. What is your own next step in exploring and following your call?

Holy Experiment

DISCERNMENT

Your own next step in exploring and following your call could include any of the following: writing down your responses to the questions suggested in this chapter, sharing your present understanding of what God may be wanting you to do with a trusted friend or group, getting more information about the area of concern to which you are drawn, sounding your call within your local congregation, and gathering others around it for future prayer and action. Whatever step we take, we should always check our understanding of personal call against its biblical features mentioned earlier. Does this step nourish my own life, connect me with others, evoke some measure of resistance, serve the kingdom and reflect the dynamic nature of call? If the answer is yes, you and I may be on the edge of doing something beautiful for God.

_____

_____

_____

_____

_____

_____

_____

_____

9

PRACTICING THE PRESENCE OF GOD

The Signpost

THE LIVING, ACTIVELY LOVING presence of God pervades all things and every experience. We cannot separate the sacred from the secular, but must train ourselves to be aware of this glorious reality in every present moment. In the training process we learn to turn our mind regularly toward Christ, remain constantly thankful and do everything we do for God. Within the companionship of God's presence and God's family we shall be able to become all that we're intended to be.

Holy Experiment

Mindfulness

Thankfulness

Welcoming God into your next task

Reading

"Practicing the presence of God," a phrase often associated with Brother Lawrence's book *The Practice of the Presence of God*, has become increasingly instructive for my own pilgrimage. Constantly it enters my mind, reminding me that it is within everyday life—cooking meals, cleaning the house, going to work, enjoying friendships, playing with the children—that my union with the resurrected Christ must be lived out. Sacred and secular are not to be separated. The presence of God can be practiced wherever we are and in whatever we are doing.

I failed to grasp this truth in the early years of my walk with Christ. Everyday life seemed segregated into strict "spiritual" and "unspiritual" compartments. There was the sacred sphere of prayer, Bible reading, worship and other church-related activities where we might expect to encounter God. Then there was the secular segment—those routine, mundane junctures of daily life in our jobs, our families, our leisure times—which was somehow perceived to be devoid of God's active presence. Frequent exhortations by preachers to "take Christ into the world," where he was supposedly absent and non-active, deepened this division even further.

Gradually it dawned on me that the people in the Bible saw things differently. Repeatedly the Scriptures witness to the presence of God being encountered everywhere and in everything. In his temple vision of the Lord seated high on the throne, Isaiah speaks of the seraphim in the Divine Presence calling out to one another, "Holy, Holy, Holy is the LORD of hosts; the whole earth is full of his glory" (Isaiah 6:3). Preaching to the Athenians, Paul declares boldly that God is always near, for "in him we live and move and have our being" (Acts 17:28). Writing later to the Ephesians, he gives this truth even sharper focus: "There is . . . one God and Father of all, who is above all and through all and in all" (Ephesians 4:4, 6). In the closing moments of his earthly life Jesus assures his disciples that they shall continually be accompanied by his risen presence. "And remember," he says to them on the mountain in Galilee, "I am with you always, to the end of the age" (Matthew 28:20).

This way of understanding God's relationship with his world has profoundly altered my understanding of the Christ-following life. No longer is the Holy One to be encountered only within particular places, special times and certain states of mind. His living presence pervades all things and every experience, and waits only to be invoked. Wherever we may be standing—in the kitchen or at the work-place—is holy ground. We are continuously encircled and enfolded in the heart of God. Not for one second can we escape the presence of the Lord. For as the psalmist

THE PRESENCE OF GOD CAN BE PRACTICED WHEREVER WE ARE AND IN WHATEVER WE ARE DOING.

affirms: "If I went up to heaven, you would be there; if I lay down in the world of the dead, you would be there" (Psalm 139:8 Good News Bible).

Our picture of God develops this truth further. The God in whom we live and move and have our being is the Christlike God who loves every one of us sacrificially and extravagantly. Like the shining sun that continuously sends forth its rays of light and warmth, there is no time in our lives when God is not actively loving us. His transforming love radiates toward us in every single moment and experience of our lives. This never-failing, always-present love is the kingdom, the eternal realm of God, which Jesus has made accessible to us now, and into which we shall fully pass at the moment of our dying. Training ourselves to be aware of this glorious reality in the present moment signposts the challenge facing every Christ-follower.

LIKE THE SHINING SUN THAT CONTINUOUSLY SENDS FORTH ITS RAYS OF LIGHT AND WARMTH, THERE IS NO TIME IN OUR LIVES WHEN GOD IS NOT ACTIVELY LOVING US.

This is not easy, especially for those who

have suffered greatly. Not every moment is filled with sunlight. Not every experience at first glance appears to be a sacrament of God's loving presence. Not every event suggests a divine epiphany. There is an obvious conflict raging in our midst between the forces of Christ and those of darkness and evil. Oppression, poverty, torture and pain scar the life experience of more people than we will ever know. Often the darkness can be overwhelming, and we may feel that God has forgotten or forsaken us.

Writing after a lifetime characterized by both immense personal pain and an intense sharing in the sufferings of others, medical doctor and author Paul Tournier observes that while some people are transformed by suffering, far more are destroyed by it.[1] We do well, therefore, in our reflections about practicing the presence of God in all things not to speak too glibly or easily.

This is also why I have found it essential to take with utmost seriousness the teachings of Jesus about the afterlife. For countless people this earthly life has meant continual suffering, which has made belief in a loving God nearly impossible. The twentieth century witnessed human misery on a scale unparalleled in human history. If this life is all there is, then it is ultimately an absurd and cruel joke. Yet, as was made clear in our earlier chapter, at the heart of the message of Jesus is the promise of the kingdom of heaven. Partially available to us now as we open our hands to receive it, this realm of infinite love and goodness will be fully known beyond the space-time dimensions of our present world. Within the endless companionship of God's presence and God's family we shall be able to become all that we're intended to be. In-

deed without these eternal dimensions, the love of God is no love at all.

Numerous Christ-followers in both biblical and modern times have personally witnessed this reality of a fuller kingdom. Their testimonies encourage a vital belief in life beyond the grave. One powerful biblical example is that of Stephen, the first Christian martyr, as he was being stoned to death. In the book of Acts we read about his experience when he "gazed into heaven and saw the glory of God and Jesus standing at the right hand of God" (Acts 7:55). This vision reflects the passionate conviction of the early church that *nothing* would ever be able to separate them from the love of God revealed in Jesus Christ. Little wonder this vulnerable band of disciples outlived the ancient world. They were not counting on their lives coming to a meaningless end. They understood themselves to be eternal beings, living lives that would never cease to be. They took with absolute seriousness the assurance of Jesus that those who kept his Word would never see death (John 8:51).

Recently I came across a very moving written testimony in which the widely respected theologian and writer Henri Nouwen shares his glimpse into God's eternal realm. On a dark winter's morning in 1988 he experienced a near-lethal accident that brought him into that shadowland between life and death and also led him into a new experience of God. In his remarkable little book *Beyond the Mirror* he describes this experience within the portal of death. He writes:

> What I experienced then was something I had never experienced before: pure and unconditional love. Better

still, what I experienced was an intensely personal presence, a presence that pushed all my fears aside and said, "Come, don't be afraid. I love you." A very gentle, non-judgmental presence; a presence that simply asked me to trust, and trust completely. . . . I had spent countless hours studying the Scriptures, listening to lectures and sermons, and reading spiritual books. Jesus had been very close to me, but also very distant; a friend, but also a stranger; a source of hope, but also of fear, guilt and shame. But now, when I walked around the portal of death, all ambiguity and all uncertainty were gone. He was there, the Lord of my life, saying, "Come to Me, come."

A few paragraphs later he continues:

This experience was the realization of my oldest and deepest desires. Since the first moment of consciousness, I have had the desire to be with Jesus. Now I felt his presence in a most tangible way, as if my whole life had come together and I was being enfolded in love.[2]

Only those empowered by this kingdom hope will venture forth and experiment with a training program designed to practice the presence of God in all things. The kingdom of God is made accessible through the presence of the crucified and risen Christ, and this presence needs to be invoked in order for us to experience the kingdom. How we go about invoking the Divine Presence is what constitutes a training program. One possibility consists of simply

- turning the mind regularly in a Christward direction
- keeping constantly thankful
- doing everything we do for God

Finding their origins in the wisdom of Scripture, these practices have been explored in the great spiritual classics and are accessible to us all. For those who live busy, active and filled lives, an extra plus is that they demand no additional time commitments away from family or work. They do, however, demand the discipline of consistent effort.

Over recent years I have experimented with these practices within the nitty-gritty

THE KINGDOM OF GOD IS MADE ACCESSIBLE THROUGH THE PRESENCE OF THE CRUCIFIED AND RISEN CHRIST, AND THIS PRESENCE NEEDS TO BE INVOKED IN ORDER FOR US TO EXPERIENCE THE KINGDOM.

of my own daily routines and relationships. In spite of frequent lapses and having constantly to restart the program, they have become the channel for numerous blessings. These range from receiving strength and help in times of difficulty to a far broader awareness of God's active presence in commonplace occasions and duties. Without engagement in practices like these I am convinced that we shall not cultivate a sense of the holy amidst the ordinary.

TURNING IN A CHRISTWARD DIRECTION

The meaning of the Greek word for repen-

> Can you think of some external sign which, if strategically placed in your home or place of work, would encourage you to be more mindful of God's nearby presence?

tance, *metanoia,* once again helps us here. It means "thinking about our thinking." Whereas prior to conversion we lived our lives without reference to Christ, there is

SOMETIMES JUST REPEATING THE NAME OF JESUS CENTERS OUR LIVES IN THAT PORTABLE INNER SANCTUARY WHERE THE MOST HIGH DWELLS.

now the desire to let him be the center of our thinking and living. Regularly turning our minds toward him is one practical way of ensuring that this happens.

This does not mean thinking *only* about the Holy One all the time. This could have disastrous consequences concerning the tasks we have to accomplish. I like the story which David Sheppard, bishop of Liverpool, tells about himself. He was playing in a crucial cricket test match between Australia and England. He had recently been ordained as a priest. In the outfield he dropped a vital catch. An Australian spectator shouted at him from the stands: "Hey, parson, keep your eye on the ball and take your mind off God."

We direct the mind Christward by frequently affirming the closeness of the Divine Presence. Whether washing dishes, doing housework, sitting in the boardroom, working on the factory floor or typing reports, we acknowledge God with us wherever we are. These repeated affirmations may find their shape in a short prayer

inwardly whispered, the recall of a biblical phrase, a silent pausing. Sometimes just repeating the name of Jesus centers our lives in that portable inner sanctuary where the Most High dwells. This way of invoking the presence of Christ is made known through an easy-to-read little book called *The Way of the Pilgrim.* It tells the story of a Russian pilgrim peasant who repeated the name of Jesus wherever he went and describes the experiences that resulted from this practice.

With these "little affirmations" we are not trying to generate or manufacture the presence of God. The bottom line has already been clearly established: in God we live and move and have our being. Or as Paul elsewhere reflects, "in him all things hold together" (Colossians 1:17). Developing the practice of this mental habit means we are taking this truth seriously and acting boldly on it. There come times when dark circumstances, painful relationships and feelings of spiritual barrenness will mock our attempts at this practice. In such moments, continuing with our affirmations demonstrates a trusting faith that there is nothing "able to separate us from the love of God that is in Christ Jesus our Lord" (Romans 8:39 NIV).

This simple practice yields life-transforming benefits. In his personal journal, written while he labored as a missionary in the southern Philippines, Frank Laubach describes the results of his holy experiment with God. On January 3, 1930, he

Holy Experiment

MINDFULNESS

Decide upon the shape of your "little affirmation." Is it going to be a short prayer, a favorite scriptural verse, the loving repetition of the name of Jesus? Begin to use it right now. Refuse to be discouraged by what Quaker Thomas Kelly calls frequent "lapses and forgettings." Without self-accusation, gently remind yourself of your intentions and begin again just where you are. After a period of experimentation, reflect on the experience and see whether your relationship with God and awareness of the Divine Presence has been deepened.

resolved to direct his mind Godward for one second out of every minute. Twenty-nine days later he made the following journal entry:

> The sense of being led by an unseen hand which takes mine, while another hand reaches ahead and prepares the way, grows upon me daily. I do not need to strain at all to find opportunity. It piles in upon me as waves roll over the beach, and yet there is time to do something about each opportunity. . . . I feel, I *feel* like one who has had his violin out of tune with the orchestra and at last is in harmony with the music of the universe.[3]

Habits of holy mindfulness are not easily formed. In their awkward early stages they need all the help they can get. Tangible symbols of the Holy help us in this regard. Orthodox Russian believers place an icon in the corner of each room that communicates a sense of the sacred to anyone who enters. A business executive friend of mine writes out a biblical verse on his desktop pad. A stay-at-home mom I know plays a music tape of Taizé chants while she dusts and sweeps.

KEEPING CONSTANTLY THANKFUL

Choosing to remain constantly thankful nurtures the awareness of God's immediate presence. This could be one reason why thanksgiving is central to biblical prayer. Throughout Scripture we receive repeated invitations to grow in the way of gratitude. We stumble across one of these invitations tucked away in Paul's first letter to the Thessalonians. Crammed with wise insight it reads: "Be joyful always; pray continually; give thanks in all circumstances, for this is God's will for you in Christ Jesus" (1 Thessalonians 5:16-18 NIV).

By addressing his words to the wills of his readers, Paul assumes that gratitude is a choice. In whatever circumstance we find ourselves we are given the freedom to choose our response. Particularly in painful and difficult circumstances we can ask, as Baptist minister and author John Claypool has pointed out, the resentment question—"Why did this have to happen to me?"—and focus on the negative. Or we can ask the gratitude question—"What is there to be thankful for that we can use in constructing a new future?"—and focus on the positive. The first choice leads us into despair and paralysis while the latter increases our sense of God's presence and results in courageous and victorious living.

DELIGHT IN THOSE SMALL RITUALS OF EVERYDAY LIFE THAT ARE USUALLY TAKEN FOR GRANTED.

Pastor Claypool makes his point not from an academic ivory tower but from within the crucible of personal suffering and grief. At the tender age of ten his daughter, Laura Lue, died from acute leukemia. In the desolate days following her death he wrestled with bitter resentment and despair. "What kind of God are you?" he raged. "Why did you allow an innocent little girl to suffer as she did and then die? What right did you have to take away the one I cherished?"

Claypool chose, however, not to travel down the road of resentment. With what must have been immense courage he asked himself the gratitude question and answered:

> Who was Laura Lue, really? She had been a gift—not something I had created and therefore had the right to clutch as an owned possession, but a treasure who had always belonged to Another. She had been with me solely through the gracious generosity of that One. . . . At every given juncture, we humans are given the freedom to choose the attitudes we assume, and so it was with me. I could be angry that Laura Lue had died after only ten short years, or I could be grateful that she had lived at all and that I had been able to share in her wonder. I chose then, and I still do, the way of gratitude.[4]

John Claypool's words show us that gratitude is not a dutiful obligation—it is an appropriate response to the sheer giftedness of our lives. What do we have that has not ultimately been given? Awakening to this truth releases the flow of gratitude and thankfulness. Nothing is taken for granted anymore. Our posture toward life shifts from grabbing, demanding and complaining to one of receiving, celebrating and delighting. Everywhere and in everything the goodness of God is seen—in every warm embrace we receive, every drink of water we take, every mouthful of food we eat. When we are caught up in the immeasurable grace and generosity of the Giver, the sense of God's presence in all things is enhanced and deepened.

DOING EVERYTHING WE DO FOR GOD

An ancient story goes as follows: Three masons were building a cathedral. When asked about what they were doing, the first mason answered: "I am putting one stone upon another in order to build a wall." The second mason said: "I am working so that I can purchase food and clothing for myself and my family." But the third mason replied: "I am building a house of God so that people may know God's presence and be joyful."

Three attitudes toward everyday tasks and occupations are reflected in this simple story. We can live and work mechanically,

---

Holy Experiment

THANKFULNESS

We can decide to embark on this way of gratitude immediately. Delight in those small rituals of everyday life that are usually taken for granted. This could mean enjoying a walk around the block, eating slowly or just lingering over a cup of coffee. Fill the day with gestures of thankfulness—saying thank you, writing notes of appreciation, giving a hug. Pause at regular intervals to give thanks to God for every sign of his goodness. Thank the Holy One for gifts of sleep and rest, food and work, friends and family. In all these good gifts God is present, pouring himself out in self-giving love for us to receive and enjoy. Write about what you discover.

putting one stone upon the other, day after day, until the wall is built; or we can live and work solely for ourselves and our loved ones without thought for others and their needs; or we can offer up our daily work to God, whether it be washing dishes or selling insurance or being a doctor, and so build a world in which the Divine Presence is made manifest and where people can find joy.

Dare we adopt this last attitude toward those mundane and unspectacular tasks that fill our lives? Ninety percent of what we do every day bears little overt religious significance. Think for a moment through your own daily schedule. Make a mental list of those routine and regular tasks that occupy most of your waking time. If my guess is accurate, most of these activities are neither very pious nor churchy. We wake up, go about our jobs either at home or in the workplace, have our meals, enjoy some leisure moments with friends and family, and retire to bed. Yet it is my

THERE IS A HASIDIC STORY ABOUT A DEVOUT RABBI WHO WAS KNOWN TO HAVE LIVED AN UNUSUALLY FULFILLED AND ABUNDANT LIFE. AFTER HIS DEATH ONE OF HIS PUPILS WAS ASKED, "WHAT WAS MOST IMPORTANT TO YOUR TEACHER?" WITHOUT HESITATION THE PUPIL ANSWERED, "WHATEVER HE HAPPENED TO BE DOING AT THE MOMENT."

firm belief that Paul had tasks like them in mind when he offered the following nugget of spiritual direction to the Corin-

thian church: "So, whether you eat or drink, or whatever you do, do everything for the glory of God" (1 Corinthians 10:31).

The ordinary is made holy when we resolve to do everything we do for God. Brother Lawrence models what this may mean for us. For fifteen years amidst the hustle and bustle of a monastery's kitchen, this semi-literate Christ-follower endeavored to live and work with a constant sense of God's presence. One of the ways through which he sought to realize the presence of God was to direct all his actions to God's glory. Nothing was too trivial or ordinary. Whether it was baking pancakes or picking straws off the floor, he sought to do everything for the sake of his King. Abbe de Beaufort, who edited his conversations and letters, provides us with a glimpse of Brother Lawrence at work: "And it was observed, that in the greatest hurry of business in the kitchen, he still preserved his recollection and heavenly-mindedness. He was never hasty nor loitering, but did each thing in its season, with an even uninterrupted composure and tranquillity of spirit."[5]

To do everything for God is to put your whole heart into whatever you are doing at the present moment. Imagine the difference such wholehearted living would make to the quality and meaningfulness of our daily labor.

Wholehearted living eludes many of us. Preoccupied with external demands and internal pressures, we find it hard to concentrate on the task at hand. The more routine and menial the task, the harder it is to be fully present. Before we realize it our attention drifts someplace else and no longer are we attentive to what is before us. This happened for me in a counseling experience. While listening to a distraught man I suddenly caught myself anxiously wondering how I was going to meet the fast-approaching deadline for the completion of this manuscript! Doing one thing and thinking of another is a sure sign of a scattered and half-hearted way of living.

Help is needed from beyond ourselves if we are going to engage in the present task with the whole of our hearts. Consciously welcoming the Holy One into every new activity before we begin it opens our lives to this aid. Invoking God's presence into our work enables us to do it differently. We become present where we are and more focused on what we are about to do. There is given to us a deepened sensitivity to the sacredness of the now-moment and to the ethical challenges it may present. Certainly this was my experience in the above counseling encounter. Upon realizing that I had disengaged from the present moment, I immediately asked for help. "Lord," I inwardly prayed, "please help me to put my preoccupations to one side and to bear your listening love to this man." Within seconds I felt myself reestablished in God's presence and was genuinely able to do what I was doing for his sake.

CONSCIOUSLY WELCOMING THE HOLY ONE INTO EVERY NEW ACTIVITY BEFORE WE BEGIN IT OPENS OUR LIVES TO THIS AID.

Precisely here, amidst the ordinary and commonplace, the life of the kingdom is made available. Through practices like these, daily life is integrated into the kingdom, the Divine Presence is known in all things and everyday life becomes for you and me nothing less than "the house of God . . . the gate of heaven" (Genesis 28:17).

Holy Experiment

WELCOMING GOD INTO YOUR NEXT TASK

Since we are exploring the practice of the presence of God, let me suggest another holy experiment. In a few moments you will complete your reading of this chapter and move on to your next task. Before you begin that task, welcome the Holy One into whatever you are about to do. Say something like "With your help, Lord, I commit myself now to the task of playing with the children," or "With your help, Lord, I want to be present to my spouse," or "With your help I want to give myself to the task of writing this letter." After your brief prayer give yourself wholeheartedly to your planned task. Resolve inwardly not only to do it with God but also to do it for God.

Following the Signpost Together

1. How would you describe your experience of God amidst the routines of your everyday life?

2. Share your attempts to remain aware of God's presence during the day. What do you find most helpful?

3. When in difficult and painful circumstances, do you tend to ask "the resentment question" or "the gratitude question"? Discuss your responses.

4. How would daily life be different if you sought to offer everything you did to God?

5. Select one way of deepening your awareness of God's presence in your everyday life in the coming days, and share this resolve with your group.

IO

OPENING OUR
HEARTS TO GOD

The Signpost

The witness of Scripture is clear: The God who speaks is also the God who listens. We can be certain that everything we communicate to God is heard, even when we struggle to believe this is true. Growing in a prayer life of sincere conversation deepens our intimacy with God's transforming Spirit, allows us to discover our true selves and changes the way we relate to others.

Holy Experiment

Praying our feelings

Praying the Psalms

Praying the Lord's Prayer

Reading

My earliest memory of talking to God is not very pious. When I was six years old my mother and I selected four horses to win the jackpot at the local racecourses. We listened eagerly to the results as they were announced on radio. By five o'clock I was sitting on the edge of my chair. Three of our selected horses had won their respective races and the final race was due to be run. I can remember going into our backyard, looking up at the heavens and pleading with the Holy One: "Oh God," I begged, "please let our horse win." The horse finished third!

Mulling over that childhood memory, I am struck by my simple belief that, as a child, I could speak directly to God. No one had given me any formal instruction in the ways of prayer. To the best of my knowledge, I had not been to Sunday school, nor had I participated in any church service or in any form of family prayer. Yet somewhere, from a deep place within, there was this childlike intuition that God listened to those who prayed. Even as a six-year-old with a dangerous penchant for gambling, I was sensing something quite remarkable about our relationship with the Holy One. Many years later, my explorations into Scripture would convert my early intuition into firm conviction.

WRITTEN INTO THE PRAYING LIVES OF BIBLICAL WOMEN AND MEN IS THE PASSIONATE CERTAINTY THAT WHEN WE SPEAK TO THE HOLY ONE, WE ARE HEARD.

The biblical witness is clear: the God who speaks is also the God who listens. Written into the praying lives of biblical women and men is the passionate certainty that when we speak to the Holy One, we are heard. Everything we say, every desperate request, every sigh of unmet longing, every thankful cry—even those groans unable to find articulate expression—everything is heard by our listening God. While he may not answer each prayer as we would like, he hears us.

Jesus, who lived in daily awareness of this listening presence, expresses biblical faith when he prays: "Father, I thank you for having heard me. I knew that you always hear me" (John 11:41-42). Learning to pray as Jesus would if he were in our place ushers our lives into the grace-filled adventure of exploring how we can share our hearts with the God who listens.

Persistently sharing your struggle and asking for what you desire often begins an authentic prayer journey.

WHAT HAPPENS WHEN WE PRAY?

Talking with the God who listens has three life-changing consequences. First, maturing in the art of holy conversation *baptizes us into an intimate relationship with Abba Father.* Critics of prayer sometimes accuse those who talk with God of merely communing with their own thoughts, of projecting upon the giant screen of the universe their infantile wishes for an ideal father figure. Reflection on the actual experience of prayer challenges this accusation. As we share our hearts regularly with the listening God, not only do we experience greater closeness with the Holy One, but we undergo a gradual and profound character transformation. Conversation with God deepens intimacy with the Whol-

---

How confident are you that God listens when you pray? You may find it easy to answer affirmatively, or you may be more doubting and hesitant in your response. The question may touch a raw place in your soul; it could trigger the memory of a desperate prayer that went seemingly unanswered; it may surface painful intellectual questions about your sense of aloneness in the vast universe. How do you respond? If the question is a difficult and painful one, besides sharing your thoughts and feelings with a trusted fellow pilgrim, it may be helpful to voice them in a plain request to the Holy One: "Dear God, I struggle to believe that you listen to me. Please show me, in whatever way you choose, that you do listen."

ly Other, opens our lives to the impact of the living Christ and links them to the power of his Spirit.

A second benefit of speaking openly with the Holy One lies in *coming to know ourselves*. As we disclose who we are in prayer, take off our masks and acknowledge the dark emotions that lurk in our inner depths, our self-knowledge increases. While this growth in consciousness is seldom flattering and usually uncomfortable, it reminds us of our basic neediness. Knowing ourselves more fully teaches us what to ask, identifies our Achilles' heel where we are most vulnerable, and highlights the humbling fact that we need help from beyond ourselves to live well. Most importantly, we discover that sharing our broken selves with God does not diminish our belovedness, but draws us deeper into the Divine Love and submerges our lives afresh into the infinite ocean of his transforming grace.

The third byproduct of genuine dialogue with God *is a change in the way we relate toward others*. Talking with God has social consequences. After all, we are speaking with One from whom, in the direct language of Paul, "every family in heaven and on earth takes its name" (Ephesians 3:15). Not surprisingly, therefore, when we converse with this social God, people really begin to matter. Herein lies the litmus test for authentic prayer: it forges within our self-centered hearts a greater concern for others, beginning with family members and friends closest to us, and stretching out to include suffering neighbors, our enemies, and even strangers. A prayer life not finding practical outward expression in caring action can hardly be called Christian.

For many, prayers are mechanical and secondhand, seldom articulating who we really are before the Holy One. How do we begin to speak out from our inner depths

---

MOST IMPORTANTLY, WE DISCOVER THAT SHARING OUR BROKEN SELVES WITH GOD DOES NOT DIMINISH OUR BELOVEDNESS, BUT DRAWS US DEEPER INTO THE DIVINE LOVE AND SUBMERGES OUR LIVES AFRESH INTO THE INFINITE OCEAN OF HIS TRANSFORMING GRACE.

---

to God? I offer three suggestions. Experiment with them in your own dialogue with the God who listens.

PRAYING OUR LIFE EXPERIENCE

Honestly praying our life experience provides an excellent starting point. Martin Luther once suggested that the most important principle for anyone wanting to develop a conversational prayer life is: Don't lie to God. To say what we think God wants to hear, or to use religious-sounding clichés unrelated to our everyday realities, spells the end of any possibility of genuine prayer taking place. We must come to God truthfully, as we are, warts and all. In the helpful words of Ann and Barry Ulanov: "In prayer we say who in fact we are—not who we should be, nor who we could be, but who we are. All prayer begins with this confession."[1]

Practically, how do we begin praying our life experience?

Ask for what we need. Start by asking for what you need. Recall Jesus' response to his disciples' request about learning how to pray. He offers them what we call "the Lord's Prayer," shares a brief story illustrating the importance of persistence and concludes with a brief summary (Luke 11:1-13). Notice the centrality of asking in Jesus' answer: the Lord's Prayer contains six petitions; the main character in the parable asks for bread; the wrap-up comment commences, "So I say to you, Ask . . ." To pray the Jesus way is to ask. Asking for what we need puts us in touch with who we are, moves us beyond pretense and facilitates an honest relationship with the Holy One.

For some, this may prove difficult. As we grow up we tend to hide our real needs from each other and God, and sometimes from ourselves. We want to appear capa-

---

ASKING FOR WHAT WE NEED PUTS US IN TOUCH WITH WHO WE ARE, MOVES US BEYOND PRETENSE AND FACILITATES AN HONEST RELATIONSHIP WITH THE HOLY ONE.

---

ble, self-sufficient, in control. Asking for what we need becomes foreign to our everyday vocabulary. While writing this chapter, I spent time with a couple married for over twenty years and battling to hold their marriage together. After listening to them unburden their hurts and unmet needs, I enquired whether they had shared their pain and had ever asked one another for what they needed. "I don't ask anyone for anything!" answered the husband. "I'm too scared to ask!" responded the wife. It was deeply moving to observe the couple break through these self-imposed barriers,

risk becoming vulnerable and offer their requests to each other.

Real engagement with the Holy One begins in a similar manner. We get in touch with our immediate needs and, by articulating them aloud to God, allow them to become the "stuff" of our daily prayers. There is no need to use special language. We simply share our struggle and ask for what we need: "God, I'm at my wits' end with the kids. Please give me patience and wisdom." "Lord, I don't know how we are going to make it this month. Show me the way forward." "God, I'm battling with depression. Shine your light into my life and help me to keep going." Simple petitions like these express who we are, connect us with God, and open our lives to his grace and help. Begin talking now with God. Ask for what you need. You will discover that the Holy One frequently encounters us at the point of our deepest need.

Express our feelings. Another way into praying our life experience involves expressing our feelings to the Holy One. This suggestion may surprise you. We are not accustomed to acknowledging our real feelings as Christ-followers, especially those that are angry and full of rage. Much of the teaching we receive downplays the importance of feelings. They are better left alone, and certainly not to be trusted or openly owned. Not surprisingly, it isn't too long before a split appears in our praying and living; a split between our conscious relationship with God and what we are experiencing in our emotional world. This is a sure-fire recipe for our relationship with the Holy One to become unreal and unrelated to our daily concerns.

Our feelings are important. They are an integral aspect of our God-given humanity and are not to be neglected. When acknowledged and appropriately shared in our human and divine relationships, they deepen our experience of intimacy and provide a life-giving way for our growth in self-knowledge. They uncover what goes on in our depths, reveal the hidden condition of our hearts and highlight those attitudes requiring ongoing conversion. Owning and expressing our feelings to the God who came in the flesh helps us to live

WHEN ACKNOWLEDGED AND APPROPRIATELY SHARED IN OUR HUMAN AND DIVINE RELATIONSHIPS, OUR EMOTIONS DEEPEN OUR EXPERIENCE OF INTIMACY AND PROVIDE A LIFE-GIVING WAY FOR OUR GROWTH IN SELF-KNOWLEDGE.

fully and maturely. Usually this is easier done with gratitude and joy, than with anger and rage. After many years of seeking

Holy Experiment

PRAYING OUR FEELINGS

Begin by identifying and naming the feelings that are present in you. I cannot overestimate the importance of this step. Unspecified emotions tend to have a draining and depressing effect. Now own the feelings: "This is what I am feeling—my anger, my sadness, my envy, my joy." Finally, express them aloud to the Holy One and let them go in your prayer. Build this honest sharing of feelings into your dialogue with the Holy One. You will find that it renews closeness with God, imparts additional strength for everyday tasks and channels the energy within your feelings into creative action.

to relate my devotional life to my emotional world, I still find it difficult to own my angry and fearful feelings and bring them into the orbit of my daily conversations with the Holy One.

LEARNING TO PRAY FROM THE PSALMS

Regularly praying the Psalms trains us how to speak to God. Originally crafted as both the prayer book and the hymnbook of the Jewish people, the Psalms were prayed by Jesus and by his followers. They serve us today as God's gracious resource for the building of a faithful prayer life. When left to our own resources, real dialogue with the Holy One tends to break down. We find that the words we pray bear little relation to those which God has already addressed to us. Instead, our praying becomes narrowly determined by our own inner agenda. We hear ourselves repeating the same requests, the same feelings, the same concerns. By expanding our prayer vocabulary, and teaching us how to answer the words previously spoken by the Holy One, praying the Psalms safeguards us from this common danger.

Imagine disclosing your innermost thoughts and feelings to a friend. How would you feel if the response you received revealed no connection to what you had just shared? Most probably, you would find the experience hurtful. Something similar can easily occur between ourselves and God. In our praying, we may fail to respond to those words that the Holy One has directed toward us. It could be that we simply don't know how to answer. Here the Psalms prove to be a magnificent gift. Initially prayed by people who knew they had been addressed by God and who wanted to respond, they show how we can answer the Holy One.

The Psalms also enable us to bring our *whole* lives before God. In support of her conviction that the Psalms act as good psychologists, writer and poet Kathleen Norris points out that they are "unrelenting in their realism about the human psyche. They ask us to consider our true situation, and to pray over it."[3]

Certainly if you were to work through all 150 Psalms and summarize the emotions and experiences represented, you would be hard-pressed to make any significant additions. Praying them regularly makes us more aware of those feelings and memories we are inclined to hide. Through his own vulnerable transparency, the psalmist helps us to confess our secrets, own our hatreds, face our fears and acknowledge our doubts. If we cannot immediately identify with the human condition represented, we will most surely find ourselves being pulled into a prayerful solidarity with those fellow human beings who can.

Presbyterian author Eugene Peterson, who has helped many rediscover the importance of praying the Psalms, writes: "In the Psalms we do not primarily learn what God says to us, but how to honestly, devoutly and faithfully answer his words to us. . . . The Psalms train us in answering God."[2]

Holy Experiment

PRAYING THE PSALMS

Choose your favorite psalm. If you don't have a favorite, start with Psalm 103. Read it aloud, slowly, repeatedly. Allow the words of the psalmist to simmer silently within, to become part of your own praying heart. Without trying to make anything happen, be attentive to your own experience. You may discover the psalm directing your attention toward the Holy One in praise and thanksgiving; it may connect you more intimately with some aspect of your own life experience; it will certainly provide vocabulary with which to pray. Following this time of simmering silence, share aloud with God whatever lies in your heart and mind. Should you find the practice awkward in the early stages, don't give up. Be encouraged by the knowledge that you are participating in a centuries-old practice whereby millions of Christ-followers have learned how to dialogue honestly with God.

I once had the life-changing privilege of spending six weeks with the Church of the Saviour in Washington, D.C. Few people have challenged me more in this matter of psalm prayer than Gordon Cosby, founding pastor of this remarkable congregation. For one year, he buried himself in the book of Psalms. Each week he would select one psalm, and pray it regularly until it had become embedded in his memory. By the end of the year, over forty psalms were in his possession. Many of these were filled with praise and spoke of God being our security and strength. His reflection on the year-long experiment bears powerful testimony to the way praying the Psalms enlivens our experience of God: "You use these Psalms, and you begin to really feel that you are kept by God. You go over and over again 'The heavens are telling the glory of God, the firmament proclaims his handiwork,' and the first thing you know, you look at the heavens and they are telling the Glory

of God. Before, you looked at them and they were just heavens."[4]

PRAYING THE LORD'S PRAYER

The Lord's Prayer is perhaps the greatest gift given to those desiring to speak with God. Crafted by Jesus, it provides an all-inclusive framework for our communications with the Holy One. Its subject matter covers areas essential for living life at its best—yet it was not intended to be prayed by everyone. As Richard Foster has pointed out, the Lord's Prayer "is the prayer given by the Lord for disciples of the Lord."[5] The early church took this fact seriously. During the first three centuries, the prayer was hidden from the outside world and taught only to those intent upon following Jesus. Embodying concerns vital for passionate discipleship, these prayer words were not to be recited thoughtlessly, but prayed with a clear understanding of their meaning.

Clearly, then, when it comes to our use of the Lord's Prayer, there is a vast difference between saying it and praying it. Mechanically repeating the words, without grasping their meaning for our lives, robs us of reality in our walk with God. When we truly pray the Lord's Prayer, the conse-

WHEN WE TRULY PRAY THE LORD'S PRAYER, THE CONSEQUENCES CAN TRANSFORM OUR LIVES.

quences can transform our lives. Not only does this prayer draw us into greater intimacy with the Holy One, it reveals the nature of our real needs and draws us into greater solidarity with the rest of the human family. Paying attention to the content of this model prayer, as recorded in the Gospels of Matthew and Luke, makes this clear. Notice how this prayer addresses God, shapes our petitions and opens our hearts toward others.

It begins with the simple invitation to call God "Father." Except for one desolate occasion, namely the cry of dereliction from the cross, Jesus continually used this form of address in relation to the Holy One. Throughout his earthly life he spoke di-

PRAYING THE LORD'S PRAYER IN THIS WAY BRINGS OUR NEEDINESS BEFORE GOD, PROVIDES ACCESS TO DIVINE RESOURCES AND EMPOWERS US TO LIVE AT OUR BEST.

rectly to God in Aramaic as "Abba," meaning "my own dear father." Never before in the history of Judaism had anyone dared to pray like this. Imagine the astonishment of the disciples when invited to pray as Jesus did. They were being offered the privilege of sharing in Jesus' own unprecedented closeness with God. This is the gracious gift given to all Christ-followers: intimate access into the Abba-heart of the Holy One. Listen to the way Jesus describes this gift-experience: "No one knows who the Son is except the Father, or who the Father is except the Son and anyone to whom the Son chooses to reveal him" (Luke 10:22).

Calling out "Abba Father" bonds us to the person of God and opens our hearts to a new realm of intimacy in our praying. Often when I pray these words, I imagine myself as the prodigal returning home. Running down the road toward me is the Father, arms flung wide open to welcome me home. Here is Abba Father accepting me as I am, assuring me of my belovedness and receiving me home. Holding this picture helps me realize that I can be totally open and vulnerable in the Divine Presence. This is the intimacy promised by Jesus to his disciples—the same kind of intimate relationship that he enjoyed with God.

From each of the five petitions we learn something vital about the nature of our real needs:

- Hallowing the divine name enables us to affirm the wholly otherness of the Holy One, fills our lives with reverence and hushes our hearts into silent adoration.

- Praying for the coming of the kingdom indicates our willingness to be transformed into the image of Jesus Christ, that we ourselves may become agents of kingdom transformation wherever we live.

- Asking for daily bread makes us mindful of basic necessities—food, shelter, clothing, health, security—that we all need for a full human life.

- Opening ourselves to the ever-flowing stream of God's forgiveness challenges us to confess our sins and to forgive those who have sinned against us.

- And finally, the requests for protection and deliverance alert us to the evil one who seeks to destroy human life from within and beyond.

Using these petitions as a *pattern* for our praying enables them to accomplish their intended purpose. While there is nothing wrong with reciting them during a worship service, this was not their primary purpose. According to the Gospel writers, they emerged not within a liturgical discussion but in connection with how the disciples could learn to pray. When offering these petitions, Jesus was saying, in effect, "If you want to know how to pray—be it for a few minutes or the whole day—here are the essentials. Use each petition as a point from which to begin your conversation with Abba." Praying the Lord's Prayer in this way brings our neediness before God, provides access to divine resources

and empowers us to live at our best. Episcopalian author Everett Fulham describes these consequences well: "To pray the Lord's Prayer as Jesus intended is to pray for life as God intended. To live the Lord's Prayer is to live in the will of God."[6]

It is nearly impossible to pray the Lord's Prayer without our hearts being engulfed with concern for others. Throughout this prayer, the pronouns *our* and *us* predominate. They remind us that our lives are invisibly interwoven and bound together in Christ. "Alone with God" is a contradiction in terms. We come to Abba Father never as an only child, but with fellow sisters and brothers, whether they are physically present or not. Whatever we ask for ourselves—daily bread, forgiveness, guidance, deliverance—we ask also for others. To pray the Lord's Prayer without affirming this interconnection turns praying into an escapist activity, hinders the spread of the gospel and mocks our common belonging in the family of God.

This became clear while watching a television documentary featuring an interview with a respected national leader who had been imprisoned on Robben Island. He felt

Holy Experiment

PRAYING THE LORD'S PRAYER

I invite you to experiment with a more meditative approach to the Lord's Prayer. It will take a little longer than usual. Set aside about twenty minutes during which you can genuinely seek to enter the realities described by this prayer. Come into the presence of Abba Father and imagine the joy and warmth of your welcome. Allow each petition to become an entrance to the vastness of your need before God. Ask for those crucial resources without which human life cannot be fully lived. Remind yourself that you are a family member, praying also for the needs of your neighbor and wanting to know how best to be a bearer of the Divine Presence.

that he could not embrace fully the claims of the Christian faith. When pressed for a reason, he replied: "In prison we longed for bread, but it was constantly denied us. Yet twice every day we would hear the wardens pray, 'Our Father . . . give us today our daily bread. . . .' However to them we were not part of the 'us.'"[7] Prayer unaccompanied by practical concern for others is likely to be hollow and empty.

An effective way of developing this social awareness is to pray the Lord's Prayer specifically for someone in need. If Debbie is the person I am praying for, I say:

> Our Father in heaven,
> May Debbie live today with
>   reverence toward you.
> Please reign and rule in her life.
> Do your will in her as it is done in
>   heaven
> Give her the things she needs
>   for today.
> Forgive her sin as she forgives those
>   who sin against her.
> Bring her through her trials and

> temptations and deliver her from
>   every kind of evil.
> For the kingdom, the power, and the
>   glory are yours forever.
> Amen.

While I pray, I picture Debbie in the light and presence of the risen Lord Jesus.[8]

Communicating with the Holy One is an immense and awesome privilege. In prayer we are able to open ourselves to God and allow God's Spirit to come and dwell in us. We journey from isolation to intimacy, from illusion to reality, from self-interest to compassion. Speaking to the listening God leads us closer to the Father's heart, confronts us with who we are and awakens us to our suffering neighbor.

Neglecting this gift of prayer costs our lives more than we shall ever fully realize. If we are wise, giving time and attention to how we deepen our dialogue with God will become a priority. Little wonder that the only time the disciples ask Jesus to teach them anything, they ask: "Lord, teach us to pray" (Luke 11:1).

Following the Signpost Together

1. Recall and share your earliest memory of speaking with God.

2. How confident are you that God listens when you pray?

3. In what ways, if any, can you identify with the three consequences of talking with God?

4. What suggestion did you find most helpful for the deepening of your own prayer life?

5. Describe your experience of putting this suggestion into practice.

6. How would you like to develop your conversational relationship with the Holy One?

11

OVERCOMING EVIL
WITHIN AND AROUND US

The Signpost

As the beloved of God, we are thrust into an intense spiritual battle. We must recognize the dark forces opposing us while knowing that in Christ they are already defeated. As we learn to understand and overcome the evil within and around us, we have access to the victorious example and powerful presence of the resurrected Christ. We are invited to join him in overcoming evil and to become instruments of his liberating love.

Holy Experiment

Journaling your inner struggle

Overcoming evil with love

Intercessory prayer

Reading

The struggle we enter as Christ's followers engages us, to put it quite bluntly, with the powers of evil. Interpenetrating the entire fabric of human existence, these dark forces affect every aspect of the world that the Creator has made good: the visible and the invisible; the personal and the public; the individual and the institutional. The good news is that the destructive spiritual forces have already been defeated decisively. So no matter how costly or painful the present contest, connected with the conquering Christ we shall ultimately overcome.

Discerning the nature of this spiritual battle and our practical responsibilities is essential. C. S. Lewis observes that

> there are two equal and opposite errors into which our race can fall about the devils. One is to disbelieve in their existence. The other is to believe and to feel an excessive and unhealthy interest in them. They themselves are equally pleased by both

errors and hail a materialist or a magician with the same delight.[1]

Certainly this remains true today. Many reject the notion of a spiritual war, while others are dominated by a paranoid worldview that sees demons everywhere. Hence the pressing need for careful discernment.

Two newspaper articles lying on my desk verify this observation made by C. S.

> "THERE ARE TWO EQUAL AND OPPOSITE ERRORS INTO WHICH OUR RACE CAN FALL ABOUT THE DEVILS. ONE IS TO DISBELIEVE IN THEIR EXISTENCE. THE OTHER IS TO BELIEVE AND TO FEEL AN EXCESSIVE AND UNHEALTHY INTEREST IN THEM."

Lewis. In the one, a deeply committed activist reflects on the challenges facing present-day South Africa and remarks: "Forget Satan, I believe darkness is an economic system designed to make the majority of people poor." In the other article, the contrasting paranoid perspective is sharply criticized by a British psychiatrist who pleads for a responsible investigation into the clinical status of supposedly "possessed" persons before embarking on any form of deliverance ministry. In his letter to the British *Church Times*, he writes: "In making this point, I have in mind an attempt to exorcise a 'demon' held to be responsible for the depression, altered behavior and severe headaches of a woman who had an operable tumor within her skull."[2]

Clearly there are questions that must be asked. What exactly is meant by the "warfare" metaphor? How does spiritual battle actually take place inside and outside our lives? How do we learn to overcome dark forces? Questions like these deserve thoughtful and rigorous reflection; otherwise human lives and communities will continue to be disrupted and oppressed. Fortunately, as we try to understand and overcome the evil within and around us, we have access to the victorious example and powerful presence of the resurrected Christ. Let us stay close to him, learn from his encounters with evil, and allow his Spirit to teach and guide us.

JESUS THE WOUNDED OVERCOMER

Overcoming evil is an essential ingredient in the gospel life of Jesus. Not only does he conquer evil in the guise of personal temptation, but he constantly wrenches women and men free from malignant evil as it manifests itself in human suffering and pain. Jesus, according to the New Testament witness, is the divine agent sent by the Holy One to shatter the strengths of the evil one. John, his closest companion, summarizes his ministry thus: "The Son of God was revealed for this purpose, to destroy the works of the devil" (1 John 3:8). Notice how this is accomplished through his life, death and resurrection.

First, Jesus' life engages the powers of evil. Witness, as one example, his personal engagement with the evil one during his forty-day wilderness retreat. There his adversary bombards him with temptation. The assault is threefold: change stones into bread, throw yourself down from the pinnacle of the temple, pay homage to the devil. Jesus rejects each one. He will not provide material needs at the expense of the spiritual, compromise the way of sacrificial servanthood for the sake of becoming a religious superstar or exchange his God-allegiance for worldly power. The encounter ends when the devil leaves "until an opportune time" (Luke 4:13). Resisting temptation is not something Jesus does once—it is something he successfully does throughout his ministry.

Jesus also engages the destructive powers as they seek to spoil and destroy the lives of others. Much of his public ministry centers around pastoral encounters with hurting men and women held captive by the evil one. Little wonder that when he is in the presence of the Capernaum demoniac the hosts of darkness cringe and cry out, "What have you to do with us, Jesus of Nazareth? Have you come to destroy us?" (Mark 1:24). The very next verse demonstrates emphatically his answer. "Be silent!" says Jesus sternly. "Come out of him!" (1:25). Telescoped into this dramatic encounter we witness Jesus' firm resolve to deliver human beings from the clutches of the evil one.

Unquestionably, according to those who know him best, Jesus lives a human life that engages the powers of evil head-on. He looks squarely into the face of temptation, resists its glittering options and steadfastly refuses to compromise his listening, obedient relationship with Abba. Outwardly he exercises his authority over the evil one on several fronts: he delivers the inwardly bound, restores the mentally tormented to their right minds and forgives those paralyzed by their sin. Summarizing his earthly ministry, Peter, one of his closest colleagues, says that Jesus "went about doing good and healing all who were oppressed by the devil, for God was with him" (Acts 10:38).

Second, Jesus' death absorbs the powers of evil. Until the last week of his earthly life, his ministry is predominantly pastoral. For three action-filled years he preaches, teaches and heals. Each of these ministry activities exposes and defeats evil. Yet these victory moments only represent the prelude to the central act in the cosmic drama between the servant Messiah and the evil one. If there is to be a decisive victory, there needs to be a victorious encounter with evil's most deadly weapon—death. Jesus deliberately sets the stage for his final encounter when, seated unarmed on a donkey, he rides into the Holy City to face the full fury of the powers of evil.

Upon the cross the crucified Christ confronts the entire mystery of evil. New Testament writers believe firmly that behind the human perpetrators of this torturous act—Judas, the religious elite, the soldiers, the crowd, the carpenter who made the

> KNOWING THAT EVIL CANNOT BE ULTIMATELY DEFEATED WITH ITS OWN WEAPONS, JESUS RESPONDS BY ABSORBING ALL THE EVIL INTO HIMSELF WITH THE VULNERABILITY OF SELF-GIVING LOVE.

cross—there are destructive spiritual forces intent on wrecking the redemptive purposes of God. The apostle Paul expresses this view when he boldly insists that "the rulers of this age . . . crucified the Lord of glory" (1 Corinthians 2:8). Stretched out on the instrument of death, it was as though Jesus was saying to the evil one: "Throw at me every weapon you have in your arsenal. Once and for all I am going to unmask, disarm and defeat you."

On the cross, evil unleashes its worst to the very best that walked upon this earth. Its weapons are all too human—mocking laughter, taunting abuse, excruciating pain, gratuitous violence, senseless brutality. Jesus' response is strikingly different. Knowing that evil cannot be ultimately defeated with its own weapons, he responds by absorbing all the evil into himself with the vulnerability of self-giving love. Evil, even as it finds radical expression through those human agents involved in the crucifixion, cannot keep Jesus from loving. Calvary love—that is, the incomparable suffering, self-giving love of God in Christ—cannot be stopped by all the powers of evil put together.

Finally, Jesus' resurrection proclaims his victory over the powers of evil. Recall the shattered lives of his desolate followers the day after the crucifixion. The One who gave them a new vision of what their lives could be had been killed. Although he had faced death with immense courage, and demonstrated a remarkable depth of forgiveness, his life and message now appeared to be a ghastly failure. Jesus' upside-down way of sacrificial servanthood, voluntary vulnerability and self-giving love had led into a cul-de-sac. Evil, with its destructive weapons of deceit and violence, seemed to have spoken the final word. Imagine the disciples' despair and torment as they spoke about what had happened to their friend and master.

Then they are suddenly transformed! Something happens that restores their faith, causes their hearts to burn again and sends them outward with the startling news that evil and death have been overcome. They preach, teach and live this message. In the process, they meet opposition, endure hardship and are killed, yet their allegiance to Jesus and his Way does not waver. What has changed them? The only hypothesis that fits this historical data is the explanation outlined by Paul: "For I handed on to you as of first importance what I in turn had received: that Christ died for our sins in accordance with the scriptures, and that he was buried, and *that he was raised on the third day*" (1 Corinthians 15:3-4, italics mine).

The resurrection reveals what really happened in the crucifixion. For a terrifying moment it had seemed that selfishness was stronger than sacrifice, deceit stronger than truth, violence stronger than nonviolence, hatred stronger than love. With Jesus powerless on the cross, and later buried in the tomb, evil appeared to be the victor. But—and this is the most powerful *but* ever written—God acted and raised the crucified One from the grave. The Holy One was declaring that there is a more potent force than evil—the power of self-giving love. New Testament scholar Tom Wright describes it well: "The cross was not the defeat of Christ at the hands of the powers; it was the defeat of the powers at the hands—yes, the bleeding hands—of Christ."[3]

Admittedly, there are times when it becomes extremely difficult to keep believing in the victory of the cross. As I read about certain atrocities carried out against ordinary civilians during the apartheid era, a serial killer charged with the murders of thirty-eight women, the escalating incidence of abuse and violent crime toward children, I feel myself becoming over-whelmed by the power of radical evil.

Again, I sense myself confronted with a choice. Do I yield to the temptations of cynicism, despair and immobility—or do I recommit myself, in partnership with the wounded Overcomer, to engage the evil within my own life and surrounding society? Only by continually celebrating the resurrection message that evil will not ultimately triumph am I enabled to choose the latter.

How do we participate today in the victory of the cross? Without considering this practical question at some depth, it is doubtful whether we shall experience the resurrection power of our ever-present Christ. Thankfully, as we search for our response to this question, we can learn from the way Jesus engaged the powers of evil. From his Gospel example, there are three practices that I have found helpful in my own endeavors to become a resurrection person.

FACING EVIL WITHIN

It was an eye-opening moment when I realized for the first time that Jesus, during his temptation experience in the wilderness, actually listens to what the Tempter has to say. The Gospel record makes it clear that he hears the voice of the evil one. He does not cut off the evil one and say, "I want nothing to do with you." As Morton Kelsey observes, "He sat and listened to everything that the devil had to offer. . . . If he knew what the devil was like, he could make sure that his life was not like the devil's but according to God's will."[4] Jesus demonstrates that to defeat the evil that constantly harasses us we must first face and acknowledge it.

How differently we treat the spiritual evil that confronts us. From personal experience, I know how difficult it is to admit evil tendencies. Rather than acknowledge any temptation to harm others, or allow harm to come to others, we cling steadfastly to a virtuous view of ourselves. We insist on seeing ourselves as decent, respectable and well-meaning individuals. Sometimes our ability to remain deliberately unconscious of our readiness to do and promote evil can reach remarkable extremes.

Consider this operating principle for our ongoing engagement with the powers of evil: the more we acknowledge our capacity for evil, and our complicity in societal evils, the more we are able to share in Jesus' victory over the evil one. Undoubtedly, this self-examination will be a disturbing and difficult process. Confessing personal selfishness and self-centeredness can be painful. Admitting our cooperation with oppressive structures, whether it be active or passive, shatters virtuous illusions about how decent we are. Not surprisingly, many shy away from looking inside themselves and, as a tragic consequence, repeatedly fall prey to the snares of the evil one. Facing the depths of our inner evil positions us to receive help from the invincible Christ.

Experiencing this divine assistance is seldom automatic. The always-present

FACING THE DEPTHS OF OUR INNER EVIL POSITIONS US TO RECEIVE HELP FROM THE INVINCIBLE CHRIST.

Christ comes to those who call out for him. As we recognize the tentacles of evil inside and around our lives, we must consciously turn toward Christ and ask for his empowering presence. Jesus, in the Lord's Prayer, taught his followers to pray "but deliver us from evil." He knew that on our own we cannot overcome the clutches of evil. Asking for aid from beyond ourselves is essential. As we acknowledge our readiness to do evil, let us also invite the risen Lord to strengthen us. "Come, risen Christ," we can pray aloud, "and empower me to share in your victory over the evil one."

Let me illustrate how this process takes place through my own experience. One area where I experience myself as an attacked human being is marriage. There is a part of me which yearns to give itself away in sacrificial loving, and a part which wars against this yearning and seeks to remain firmly self-centered. At one time when I found myself yielding to the latter and choosing to withdraw into a sullen detachment, I decided to spend time in quietness, face the temptation head-on and hear out the destructive voice. With my journal on my lap, I penned these words:

> Debbie and I are struggling to connect at the moment. The temptation to withdraw and escape into compulsive busyness is exceptionally strong. To some degree I confess that I have already yielded to its powerful urgings. I hear the Evil One's mocking voice reminding me that I'm hopeless at loving those closest to me, and it would be far better to give up even trying to love as Christ did. Just look after yourself, it seems to be saying, and don't pay any attention to the needs of your spouse.
>
> Dear Lord, I turn again to you with empty hands. Thank you that you understand temptation from the inside. Today I need your strength and wisdom. I cannot handle these destructive forces within my life on my own. Without you, I'm defeated. Please come to my aid. Empower my will to choose life, strengthen my capacity to love and show me how best I can reach out and bridge the distance between Debbie and myself.

I find it helpful, when calling on Christ like this, to place my imagination at the service of my faith. As I wrote out the above prayer, I took time to imagine the risen Lord coming directly to my aid. I heard his voice affirming me as his beloved, forgiving me for my failures in loving, and inviting me to reach out afresh to Debbie. A thought, bearing the distinctive characteristics that I've come to associate with the divine whisper, burst into my consciousness. Immediately I wrote it down: "Take the initiative and reach out to Debbie." Later that day, with a renewed awareness of Christ's overcoming presence, I reconnected with Debbie, shared honestly my feelings and chose life in our marriage.

Sometimes the struggle with inner evil becomes too much for one person to handle alone. Then we need a wise soul-friend, or a close-knit fellowship of recovering sinners, where we can share the battles that rage beneath the surface of our visible lives. Sharing temptations, as Jesus did, strengthens the spirit against the onslaughts of the evil one. This could be one reason why group members of Renovaré, a renewal movement founded by author Richard Foster, ask each other on a weekly basis: "What temptations did you face this week?"[5] Al-

Holy Experiment

JOURNALING YOUR INNER STRUGGLE

Experiment with this prayer exercise in your own struggle against inner evil. Here are the guidelines implicit in the process:

- *Find a quiet place where you will not be disturbed.*

- *Ask the Holy Spirit for courage and insight to read honestly the condition of your heart.*

- *Reflect on a temptation intent on sabotaging your personal integrity or harming a close relationship or enticing you into darkness. Hear out this temptation as coming from the evil one, and write it down.*

- *Now turn to Christ and, using your imagination if you find it helpful, invoke his risen presence. See his blazing light pierce into your darkness, open your inner being to receive his power, and listen for the divine whisper.*

- *Afterward, you may find it helpful to write about your prayer experience.*

lowing faithful friends to know how we are tempted not only decreases our spiritual aloneness, it also opens our lives to vital life-giving resources of the Spirit.

DEMONSTRATING CALVARY LOVE

Jesus' entire life-and-death resurrection drama reveals that there is one power stronger than evil—the power of self-giving love. Dare we build our lives on this conviction? I believe that we must. To be a Christ-follower is to live life as he would if he were in our place. As Andrew Walker points out, "The pattern of victory is the same for us, the followers of Jesus, as it was for our Lord."[6]

Let us explore, to the limit of our vision, what it may mean to shape our lives into instruments of Calvary love.

Forgiving others. Demonstrating Calvary love means forgiving those who have done evil against us. Hear again the petition of the crucified One as nails are hammered into his unprotected body: "Father, forgive them; for they do not know what they are doing" (Luke 23:34). Jesus knows that evil cannot be defeated with evil, violence with violence, hurt with hurt—and so he dies freely offering forgiveness to his killers. Following him today involves reaching out with a similar love to those who hurt us. When Peter asked Jesus how many times he should forgive, he was told, "Not seven times, but, I tell you, seventy-seven times" (Matthew 18:22). In other words, stop counting. There can be no limit for forgiveness, for there is no limit in God's forgiveness for us.

Few Gospel commands are more difficult. Speak with parents whose children

---

EXTENDING FORGIVENESS IS ONE OF THE HARDEST THINGS ANYONE CAN BE CALLED ON TO DO. YET THERE IS NO QUESTION WHATSOEVER THAT BEING A CHRIST-FOLLOWER INVOLVES FORGIVENESS.

---

have been killed by senseless violence, civilians traumatized by armed robberies, women victimized by abusive mates, spouses betrayed by unfaithful partners, business persons deceived by unscrupulous colleagues, detainees tortured by callous interrogators, and they will tell you that forgiveness can seem an impossible

task. You may already know this from your own experience. Extending forgiveness is one of the hardest things anyone can be called on to do. Yet there is no question whatsoever that being a Christ-follower involves forgiveness. How do we go about forgiving the hard-to-forgive?

Usually the process begins when, with a listening friend or counselor, we express our anger and pain about the hurt done to us. A second step occurs when we see ourselves as capable of hurting others. We, too, violate trust, act thoughtlessly and do evil. Accepting ourselves as fallible, sinful human beings lessens the temptation to be judgmental and morally superior. Like the person who has harmed us, we similarly need the mercy of God and our fellows. The crucial step, however, occurs when we inwardly release the offending person from the evil they have done. As psychologist David Benner writes: "Forgiveness . . . is letting go—letting go of the anger, letting go of the right to retaliate, and letting go of the right to savour any of the emotional consequences of the hurt."[7]

Working through these stages—and this process can take months or even years—does not remove automatically all angry and painful feelings. Hurts have a stubborn way of returning to our minds. We should not be surprised. Christlike habits are slowly formed. We may need to revisit the hurt we received, express again our negative feelings, see ourselves anew as no different in kind from our offender and resolve once more to let go of our victim role. It may be important to remind ourselves that the Holy One shares our struggle, and that we must be patient and gentle with ourselves. As we remain firmly resolved to become forgiving people, and rely constantly on the victorious Christ, the day will come when we are finally released from our old hurt feelings.

Forgiveness overcomes evil. It brings liberation from resentment, release from the bondage of past hurts, deliverance from bitterness, and the freedom to live fully in the present moment. The wrong done to us, inexcusable as it was, loses its power to determine the way we live. No longer are we imprisoned within the role of victim. Instead, our lives reflect the family likeness of the crucified Forgiver and the power of his resurrection. This could account for the radiant dignity and victorious spirit present in a sixteen-year-old South African who testified during the Truth and Reconciliation hearings, "I want to know the name of the person responsible for killing my father," she said quietly, "so that I can learn to forgive him."[8]

Being with others. Demonstrating Calvary love means being with those crushed by evil. As the crucified One, Jesus identifies with every sinned-against human being. In his cry, "My God, my God, why have you forsaken me?" (Mark 15:34), he becomes one with all who feel cut off from God in their suffering. On the cross he joins himself in holy love with every victim of torture, rape and abuse; with every Alzheimer's patient and child born with AIDS; with every homeless and displaced person; with every parent grieving the loss of a dearly loved child; with every elderly person forgotten by an uncaring society. So totally present is Christ with those who suffer that he says,

> FORGIVENESS OVERCOMES EVIL. IT BRINGS LIBERATION FROM RESENTMENT, RELEASE FROM THE BONDAGE OF PAST HURTS, DELIVERANCE FROM BITTERNESS, AND THE FREEDOM TO LIVE FULLY IN THE PRESENT MOMENT.

"Truly I tell you, just as you did it to one of the least of these who are members of my family, you did it to me" (Matthew 25:40).

Christ's special closeness with suffering men and women models the gospel way of caring for the hurting. Calvary love, in a nutshell, entails being present. This necessitates getting close to the broken and devastated, listening respectfully to their human cries and seeking greater understanding of their turmoil. It means paying attention to the person before thinking of what we can do for them. This takes patience, time and disciplined effort. Being with our suffering neighbor in this way can be our greatest gift.

Being with those who suffer forms an essential component of our vocation as Christ-followers. Evil is not merely an academic and abstract issue—it finds tangible expression wherever there is human suffering. "The thief," Jesus reminds us, "comes

When the Russian spiritual writer Catherine de Heuck Doherty was asked by a priest about the kind of contribution he could make in a world torn apart by evil, she answered simply, "Your presence, Father."[9]

only to steal and kill and destroy" (John 10:10). The dark mystery of evil manifests itself in our inhumanity to one another through violence, crime and gossip; it is witnessed where people live in abject poverty and want, as well as in physical sickness, mental torment and marital strife. In these situations, and others like them, we are called to be present in the spirit of Calvary love. Should we respond faithfully, we discover that the Holy One uses our presence to overcome darkness with light, despair with hope, conflict with peace, and evil with good.

Each December I spend time with congregation members who have suffered tragedy during the year. Before each visit, I remind myself that ministry with the suffering primarily involves being present. I visited a young widow and mother of two small children whose husband's life had tragically ended through illness. I listened silently as she poured out her grief. I tried to enter her pain as deeply as I could, in-

Holy Experiment

OVERCOMING EVIL WITH LOVE

Discover in your own experience how evil can be overcome by Calvary love. Set up a practical experiment in self-giving. If you are carrying resentment, this may mean embarking on the forgiveness road. Perhaps it will involve taking time to be actively present, in face-to-face compassion, with someone devastated by pain and tragedy. Or it could necessitate committing yourself, either financially or with your own practical efforts, to certain compassionate deeds aimed at relieving human suffering. Ask the Spirit of the risen Christ to empower and guide you as you prepare to give of yourself on behalf of the gospel. Later, reflect on your experience, and observe what occurs within and around you as you follow in the way of Jesus.

wardly praying for the light of Christ to penetrate her darkness. After a time of shared prayer affirming the victory of the Resurrected One over every form of evil and death, she quietly said, "Thank you for being here with me. It helps me to face tomorrow."

Taking action against evil. Demonstrating Calvary love means taking action against evil. All through his earthly ministry, Jesus, out of his infinite compassion and care, liberates men and women from evil. Wherever people are hindered from experiencing abundant life, he takes loving action. He feeds hungry people, confronts callous exploiters, heals the ill, welcomes the marginalized and frees the bound. Always he acts against evil. Interpreted from this perspective, his dying on the cross becomes his greatest act of self-giving love. On our behalf he walks willingly into an excruciating death to defeat evil in its most radical manifestation. For our sake and salvation, to use the words of Paul, the crucified One "disarmed the rulers and authorities and made a public example of them, triumphing over them in it" (Colossians 2:15).

Calvary love goes beyond words in response to evil. This means for you and me, as it did for Jesus, confronting oppressive structures, doing good whenever we can, including outsiders scorned by society, and sharing what we have with the neglected and forgotten. We dare not delegate this gospel responsibility to governmental programs and welfare bodies, critical as their task is in building a God-pleasing society. Christ calls all of his followers to discern some specific way whereby they can connect practically and personally with the poor, the despairing and depressed, the traumatized and shattered, or those who are sick. Every loving action wins strategic ground against the powers of evil.

One woman who pushes back the darkness with gospel actions of Calvary love is Judy Bassingthwaite. She ministers on the

EVERY LOVING ACTION WINS STRATEGIC GROUND AGAINST THE POWERS OF EVIL.

streets of Johannesburg amid the homeless. She coordinates a weekly feeding scheme, arranges funerals for the unidentified dead, counsels the despairing, speaks on behalf of the voiceless, and commits herself to learn the names of those she serves—all in the name of Jesus. She lives the Calvary love I'm trying to describe. Not everyone is called to Judy's particular vocation. Nor can we take upon ourselves all the injustice and human misery around us. But we can and must ask: "Lord Jesus, where do you want me to counteract evil with the deeds of Calvary love?"

INTERCESSORY PRAYER

I am constantly challenged by the Gospel passage where Jesus, the night before his crucifixion, interceded for his disciples. One particular sentence of that high priestly prayer bears special significance for our present exploration. Jesus pleads on behalf of his followers: "[Father,] I am not asking you to take them out of the world, but I ask you to protect them from the evil one" (John 17:15). Intercessory prayer, it seems for Jesus, is one indispensable means through which we engage in spiritual warfare.

Certainly the writers of the New Testa-

Holy Experiment

INTERCESSORY PRAYER

How then, practically, do we practice intercessory prayer as a form of spiritual warfare? We practice by holding particular people, especially those in physical pain and mental anguish, in the healing presence of the risen Christ. We practice by speaking against the demonic forces of self-interest and greed and racism, wherever they are operative, and commanding them to leave. We practice by persistently asking God to bring the kingdom near in places of injustice, oppression and darkness. We practice by silently listening to the human groans in our midst, and to the groaning of the Spirit within our lives, and articulating them before the Holy One.

ment, as they wrestle with the realities of evil in their time, take seriously the prayerful example set by Jesus. Paul is well aware, for example, that the struggle of the early Christ-followers is "not against enemies of

SAINT AUGUSTINE WRITES: "WITHOUT GOD, WE CANNOT; WITHOUT US, GOD WILL NOT."

blood and flesh, but against the rulers, against the authorities, against the cosmic powers of this present darkness, against the spiritual forces of evil in the heavenly places" (Ephesians 6:12). He knows that the spiritual battle cannot be won by human efforts and programs alone. Only prayer can engage these destructive forces at their roots and release the power of God necessary to overcome evil. Before ending his letter, Paul instructs his readers to intercede earnestly: "Pray in the Spirit at all times in every prayer and supplication" (Ephesians 6:18).

I do not fully understand how intercession works. What I am learning is that the Holy One desires to labor *with* us in healing human lives and communities. Intercessory prayer is one vital way in which we interact with God in this kingdom work. In other words, we work together by speaking together. Our intercessions, when prayed with integrity and commitment, boomerang with the challenge and power to become answers to our prayers. But intercessory prayer is more than a spur toward action. In itself, it forges a milieu in which God can act decisively without overriding our freedom.

As human experience makes painfully obvious, God does not always answer our intercessions immediately. It seems that the powers of evil, operative in oppressive structures and human disobedience, can temporarily block the Holy One's response. Daniel, interceding for the nation of Israel, provides a biblical case in point. While God hears Daniel's prayer the moment he prays, it takes twenty-one days before God answers. Unseen powers, at work in the nation of Persia, thwart God's purposes (see Daniel 10:1-14). According to Walter Wink, intercessory prayer involves God and people and the Powers. He concludes: "It takes considerable spiritual maturity to live in the tension between these two facts: God has heard our prayer, and the Powers are blocking God's response."[10]

This tension could be one reason why Jesus encourages persistent intercession. Look again at his parables about the persistent widow and the friend who comes at midnight (Luke 18:1-8; 11:5-13). Both stories teach us to persevere in prayer, to keep interceding until the breakthrough comes. There is a cosmic struggle taking place, and every time we intercede we increase the openings through which God's power can freely flow. Resurrection faith believes that, while destructive spiritual forces can impede God's purposes, our intercessions for the coming of the kingdom will ultimately prevail. The empty tomb reminds us that no matter how entrenched and pervasive these powers, the victory shall be with God.

We are invited, as followers of the Wounded Overcomer, to implement the victory of the cross. Together we have explored three ways in which this can be accomplished: facing inner evil, demonstrating Calvary love and practicing intercessory prayer. Since actions indicate our beliefs better than words, let us venture forth immediately to overcome the powers of evil. Giving constant expression to these three gospel behaviors enables us, and the communities to which we belong, to recover life at its best. We should celebrate the victory that our risen Lord has won by following him into the spiritual battle and putting into practice those actions that characterize his own defeat of the evil one.

Following the Signpost Together

1. Write the phrase "spiritual warfare" on a sheet of paper. Brainstorm your immediate responses, as a group, to this metaphor.

2. What strikes you most about the way Jesus faces evil?

3. What is one way in which you experience yourself as a tempted human being?

4. How is God calling you, in some specific way, to set up an experiment in Calvary love?

5. "Intercessory prayer is one vital way in which we interact with God in kingdom work." How do you respond to this comment?

6. How do you feel about the invitation to implement the victory of the cross in your own life and community?

12

WITNESSING TO
THE GOOD NEWS

The Signpost

ONE OF THE PRACTICES that contributes most powerfully to a vibrant life of faith is witnessing. This is not an optional extra in the life of faith, but should be a natural and normal part of our everyday discipleship as followers of Jesus. Sharing Christ with others makes him more real to us, conforms our lives to the example and command of Jesus, and addresses the deepest needs of our society.

Holy Experiment

Witnessing without words

Divine openings

Testimony

Reading

The first nugget of spiritual counsel that I ever received remains firmly etched in my memory. The evangelical rally where I had made my first public commitment to Jesus Christ had ended, and I was sitting with one of the prayer counselors. We were discussing how I could nourish my newly born faith and grow in the never-ceasing life of the kingdom. After showing me some biblical passages that underlined the importance of making a conscious choice to be a disciple, and explaining the necessity

for regular habits of Bible reading and prayer, my counselor extended a parting challenge. "Make sure that you tell someone soon about the step you've taken tonight," he said.

"But why must I do that?" I asked, already feeling nervous about the possibility of speaking about Jesus.

"If you don't share your faith," he responded matter-of-factly, "it will die."

I took my counselor's challenge seriously. Almost immediately I began, with a close friend, to engage zealously in witnessing activities. Unfortunately, our manner of witness was not always congruent with the spirit of the gospel we sought to share. One favorite strategy involved hitch-hiking down the main road of our hometown. We had no intention of reaching any particular destination; we simply wanted to get into a passing car and, once inside, present the claims of Christ to a captive audience. "We want to tell you about Jesus," one of us would say to the unsuspecting driver after we had traveled for a few minutes, "and ask whether you have accepted him in your life." Mission accomplished, we then asked to be dropped off and prepare ourselves for the return trip, when we would repeat the exercise!

Over thirty years have passed since those first, somewhat naive attempts at faith-sharing. While I now have a broader understanding of witnessing than I did during those hitch-hiking ventures, I still yearn to share my faith on a person-to-person basis.

Few other practices, I believe, have contributed more significantly to the ongoing aliveness and growth of my faith experience as that of giving personal testimony. Learning how to share the good news with those around me constantly serves to stretch my thinking, challenge my lifestyle and deepen my dependence on the Spirit. Affirmatively stated, my counselor's prediction has proven itself accurate in my own experience. Sharing Christ with others has made him more real to me.

Members of Alcoholics Anonymous (AA) affirm the value of witnessing from a similar perspective. Their twelve-step program, although not consciously Christian, underlines public witness as a vital ingredient in the recovery journey. The twelfth step reads: "Having had a spiritual awakening as a result of these steps, we try to carry this message to others and to practice these principles in our affairs."

IF YOU DON'T SHARE YOUR FAITH, IT WILL DIE.

Implied in this step is the clear belief that, for the recovering alcoholic to stay alive spiritually, he or she must share what has been received. Not surprisingly, most AA gatherings resemble old-style testimony meetings.

But we don't only witness because it keeps us spiritually alive. More significantly, we become witnesses because the witness-motif that pervades the life of Jesus, and the growth of the early church, invites us to do so. Exploring relevant biblical data highlights the urgency of an immediate response to this invitation. Witnessing is not an optional extra in the life of faith, or an activity for those especially drawn to it—it

WE DON'T ONLY WITNESS BECAUSE IT KEEPS US SPIRITUALLY ALIVE. . . . WE BECOME WITNESSES BECAUSE THE WITNESS-MOTIF THAT PERVADES THE LIFE OF JESUS, AND THE GROWTH OF THE EARLY CHURCH, INVITES US TO DO SO.

is intended to be a natural and normal part of our everyday discipleship as followers of Jesus.

WHY WITNESS?

Numerous voices rise up today against the practice of witnessing. The arguments range from the assertion that "religion is a private matter" to the argument that, in South Africa and elsewhere, the Christian faith has been used to legitimize political structures that have brought untold suffering to millions of human lives. "What right," contend these objectors, "do you have to share your faith with others?" Objections like these, some more serious and valid than others, raise real tension in many thoughtful hearts and undermine the confidence of many aspiring witnesses. They also give reason for us to engage with the question "Why witness?"

Jesus did. We witness to the good news because Jesus did. Throughout his earthly ministry, he makes known the priceless gospel offer that, as dearly beloved children of God, we can choose to live with direct access to our infinitely loving Abba Father. In this interactive communion with the Holy One, an extra-human spiritual power is at our disposal to help us live more creatively and fully. These realities of God's love and power enter our lives as we apprentice ourselves to the One appointed as the gateway to abundant life. This was the message to which Jesus constantly witnessed: "I am the gate. Whoever enters by me will be saved. . . . I came that they may have life, and have it abundantly" (John 10:9-10).

The Gospels make very clear that the witness by Jesus to this good news goes far beyond verbal announcement. Wherever he goes, and in whatever he does, he makes known God's love and power. In the well-known phrase of Marshall McLuhan: "The medium is the message." When he feeds the hungry and heals the sick, he witnesses to the love and power of God. When he befriends the marginalized and shares meals with the rejected, he witnesses to the love and power of God. When he welcomes little children and washes his disciples' feet, he witnesses to the love and power of God. When he dies and rises again, he witnesses to the love and power of God. His entire life, in word and deed, models the vocation of witness. For this reason, one of his closest friends describes him as "the faithful witness" (Revelation 1:5).

Jesus insists that we do. We witness to the good news because Jesus insists that we do. Consider, as one example of this insistence, how the command to witness brackets his teaching ministry. At the beginning of his disciples' formation, in the well-known Sermon on the Mount, Jesus urges: "let your light shine before others" (Matthew 5:16).

But this is not his final word on the subject. Further reinforcement of the witness imperative comes with his last recorded words. Speaking to the gathered group of disciples just prior to his ascension, he charges them to be "witnesses in Jerusalem, in all Judea and Samaria, and to the ends of the earth" (Acts 1:8). Those left behind had one central assignment—they were to communicate their lived experience of the Lord to the world, beginning with their closest friends and family.

Those early Christ-followers rose to the challenge and became an incendiary community of witnesses. With the enablement of the Holy Spirit, they witnessed to the love and power of God as Jesus had done. They shared their possessions, responded to human suffering, overcame cultural and racial barriers, stood for the truth, and constantly revealed through their contagious aliveness the transformation that the risen Lord brings in yielded lives. People listened when they boldly named the source of their different kind of life. They had earned the right to be heard. Their remarkable witness challenges you and me to reevaluate our commitment to be faith-sharers wherever we live and work.

Society needs it. We witness to the good news because our society needs it. Writing for a national Sunday newspaper, Peter Storey, a seasoned leader in the South African church, incisively diagnoses the condition of post-apartheid society:

> The new South Africa is thrashing around in search of its soul. There is a growing consensus that our society is in need of moral renewal. We lack strong values to govern our behaviour toward one another. We must recover an ethical framework for our attitudes to work, money, sexuality and power. We need large doses of selflessness if the economic gap between the haves and have-nots is to be bridged. We need the standards to recognise corruption and the strength to resist it. In short, we need to learn the difference between right and wrong.[1]

The problem facing us is primarily a spiritual one, and so, therefore, the cure must be a spiritual one as well.

How does the good news which we celebrate as Christ-followers fit into this cure? We believe that Jesus discloses supremely God's way in which human life can be lived at its best. When we become his apprentices and learn from him how to live our lives, we are enabled to know and to do what is best—both for ourselves and for

THOSE LEFT BEHIND HAD ONE CENTRAL ASSIGNMENT—THEY WERE TO COMMUNICATE THEIR LIVED EXPERIENCE OF THE LORD TO THE WORLD, BEGINNING WITH THEIR CLOSEST FRIENDS AND FAMILY.

the common good. This is the good news that will, when backed up with God's action and our matching lives, remedy the soul-sickness of our nation. To believe this message leaves us with only one option. We must, as an act of neighbor-love, share the good news.

It is one thing to underline the importance of witnessing from a biblical perspective; it is quite another to know how to go about doing it in a practical way. Not all methods of gospel witness are valid. As James Houston observes: "It is perfectly possible to bear witness to a religious faith in a manner that is neurotic, ideological and even toxic, one that wholly betrays the reality of the 'truth that is Christ Jesus.'"[2]

In my search for a way forward, I constantly return, as my main touchstone for faithful witness, to the overall lifestyle chosen by Jesus. Reflection of his life suggests that authentic witness consists of three interactive components: fasting from many words, discerning the right time, and sharing our faith with others.

FASTING FROM MANY WORDS

Have you ever been struck by the intriguing gospel fact that Jesus, before he goes public with the good news, spends almost thirty years in hidden silence? We know little about these incognito years spent among family and friends in Nazareth, sharing their working conditions and daily struggles. Nonetheless, they have come to represent, in the reflections of many spiritual writers, the silent witness of a hidden and faithful life.[3] Frequently I have mulled over the significance of these obscure Nazareth years for public witness. Their message sounds surprising for contemporary ears: that witnessing the Jesus way begins when we fast from many words.

This challenge overturns prevailing assumptions about what it means to witness. There is a common tendency among Christ-followers, especially in our discussions about witnessing, to emphasize strongly the role of talking. Yet verbal witness can go wrong when it neglects the silent dimension. Talkative Christianity collapses into an empty chattering that fails to penetrate people's

THERE IS A COMMON TENDENCY AMONG CHRIST-FOLLOWERS . . . TO EMPHASIZE STRONGLY THE ROLE OF TALKING. YET VERBAL WITNESS CAN GO WRONG WHEN IT NEGLECTS THE SILENT DIMENSION.

hearts, reveals a lovelessness in our own and cheapens the gospel's unsearchable riches. There are countless moments when our silence, accompanied by a positive interest in those we are with, serves the good news of Jesus far more than our speech. This may be the reason why James, brother of Jesus, encourages us in our conversations to "bridle [our] tongue" (James 1:26).

In the early 1980s, as I searched for ways to express a credible gospel witness in the apartheid era, I stumbled across a small Catholic order whose rule of life emphasizes this Nazareth quality of silent witness. Called the Little Sisters of Jesus, they live unobtrusively in small communities of two and three among the poor and marginalized. Their passion for evangelism is movingly articulated in the words of their founder, Charles de Foucauld, a twentieth-century martyr who once exclaimed: "I wish to cry the gospel with my whole life." These followers of Jesus have pledged themselves not to preach, or to give formal instruction, or to employ any intentional evangelism strategy. Their call is that of being silent witnesses to the divine friendship, offering to their neighbors and colleagues the rare gifts of sustained attention, true listening and genuine concern.

I recall one Christmas Day visiting a Little Sisters community in Mayfair, a predominantly Muslim suburb west of Johannesburg. The nuns had become good friends, and I wanted to drop off a small gift. Walking into their lounge I was surprised to find the room filled with people who, like myself, had been touched by their silent witness. Among the guests were banned political activists, homeless men and women, children from the neighborhood, and their Muslim neighbors. Listening to the sounds of relaxed conversation and joyful laughter, I gave quiet thanks for the lived-out witness of our hosts. Later that evening, before going to sleep, I made the following journal entry:

> Spent an enjoyable hour this afternoon with the Little Sisters, together with some of their friends. I find the

traditional way we understand witness deeply challenged by the way they communicate their faith. They connect with the kind of person whom the organized church seldom reaches. Their secret seems to have something to do with the manner in which they reach out. While they don't conceal their faith, they certainly listen much more than they

FEW FACTORS UNDERMINE THE COMMUNICATION OF THE GOOD NEWS MORE THAN INCONSISTENCIES BETWEEN WORDS AND DEEDS.

speak. People feel respected and valued in their presence. Even though I realize that their way of life cannot

Holy Experiment

WITNESSING WITHOUT WORDS

Join me in the adventure of learning how, in a prayerful and sensible way, we bear witness to the good news through fasting from words. Next time you find yourself sharing with a friend or colleague who stands outside the Christian faith, rather than rushing into speech, offer the gifts of your quiet presence. Be attentive to what is being shared. Listen discerningly to what lies unexpressed beneath the spoken words. Show interest in the well-being and life situation of the speaker. Above all, know that as you engage yourself in the discipline of bridling your tongue, the Holy Spirit is working ceaselessly to generate in the heart of your companion a fresh awareness of the living Christ. Maybe, as we learn from Jesus how to be silent witnesses, we shall discover how others can "be won over without a word" (1 Peter 3:1). Make some notes about what you experience.

be considered normative for all Christ-followers, I must learn from them. Lord Jesus, please teach me how to be silent with others in a way that bears witness to your personal concern for every human being.

Fasting from many words forges the necessary time and space for us to embody what we want to say. Too often we gallop into speech with unbridled tongues before

---

PUSHING MATTERS OF GOD ONTO OTHERS WITHOUT A KEEN SENSITIVITY TO THEIR STATE OF READINESS SEVERELY DAMAGES THE CAUSE OF THE GOSPEL.

---

we have internalized the good news. And when our lives fail to back up our verbal witness, we end up communicating opinions rather than convictions, gossip instead of gospel. Few factors undermine the communication of the good news more than inconsistencies between words and deeds. The old saying "What you are speaks so loudly that I can't hear what you are saying" remains painfully true. Elton Trueblood's insight deserves our most careful thought: "If I speak to a neighbour or to a colleague at work, and speak too soon, I may kill the thing I love. . . . We must let our lives speak, before our words can be heard!"[4]

DISCERNING THE RIGHT TIME

Jesus witnesses to the good news with an amazing sense of timing. Ponder again the beginnings of his vocal ministry after thirty years of living as a hidden witness. According to Mark's Gospel, he only goes

public with the gospel when "the time is fulfilled" (Mark 1:15). Yet, on another occasion, he says to his disciples, "I still have many things to say to you, but you cannot bear them now" (John 16:12).

Right timing is of the utmost importance to Jesus. To use the words of an ancient biblical writer, he possesses the wisdom of heart that knows when it is "a time to keep silence, and a time to speak" (Ecclesiastes 3:7).

Witnessing as Jesus would if he were in our place takes seriously the matter of right timing. Words inappropriately spoken about God, even with the sincerest intentions, trivialize the truth that they seek to communicate. Moreover, these words are frequently resented by those to whom they are addressed. Pushing matters of God onto others without a keen sensitivity to their state of readiness severely damages the cause of the gospel. There is a critical importance in the work of witness of discerning the right time to speak. Thankfully, we are not left alone with this challenge—our constant Mentor and Friend is forever providing us with openings to give meaningful expression to our faith. For these opportunities we must watch and wait.

Responding to questions. One opening that the Spirit of God creates occurs when others ask us about the nature of our lives. If we make a concerted effort to embody the gospel values of confident reliance on God, nonpossessive caring and willing helpfulness, there is a high probability that someone will say to us something like: "I have known you for a while. There is something different about you that I don't seem to have. What is the secret to your life?" Questions like these open up precious opportunities for us to speak about the life that we are discovering in the company of Christ. They are not to be wasted.

I remember, at the age of sixteen, asking that question of a new friend. I had just switched high schools and begun to develop a friendship with a young Christ-follower. He made no attempt to convert me, but what I observed in his life, through our times together, connected deeply with the question of my own soul. When I inquired about the secret of his life, his witness in response pointed me toward the good news. He said, "I've opened my life to Jesus Christ and he has given me the gift of a new life." These words, spoken simply and plainly, found their way into my searching heart and prompted my first conscious steps toward the abundant life that God gives.

Divinely arranged circumstances. Another opening arises when we find ourselves in the midst of what is best described as a set of divinely arranged circumstances. Consider the biblical illustration of Philip who, upon receiving an inner nudging, immediately heads toward the Gaza highway. On this very road, riding home after a visit to the Holy City, is a highly placed Ethiopian official reading about the suffering servant in the Old Testament. At the desert road Philip receives a further prompting—this time to go across and join the chariot. Again he obeys. Overhearing the traveler reading from the book of Isaiah, Philip asks him whether he understands what he is reading. The Acts record describes the ensuing conversation:

> He replied, "How can I, unless someone guides me?" And he invited Philip to get in and sit beside him. . . .

> The eunuch asked Philip, "About whom, may I ask you, does the prophet say this, about himself or about someone else?" Then Philip began to speak, and starting with this scripture, he proclaimed to him the good news about Jesus. (Acts 8:31, 34-35)

The Spirit continues to organize these moments of divine synchronicity. The day before I was due to fly from Los Angeles to San Francisco, I purchased *The Cloister Walk* written by Kathleen Norris, a record of the author's relationship with a Benedictine monastery. Immediately upon taking off from the airport, I reached for my book and began to read. Next to me sat an elderly middle-aged lady who, as the plane became airborne, also pulled out a book. I couldn't help noticing the title—the same one that I was reading. Sensing that I was in the midst of a set of divinely arranged circumstances,. I began a conversation.

I turned to my fellow passenger and pointed to our two books: "It seems like we are both interested in monasteries."

"Yes, it does seem like it," she answered, obviously taken aback by the remarkable coincidence. "I am a Buddhist and deeply interested in spiritual practice. What is your interest?"

"I'm a Christ-follower," I responded, "and I'm also seeking a deeper life with God."

My answer appeared to surprise her. For a few moments she remained quiet, almost as if she was trying to fathom what my response meant. I stayed quiet, inwardly praying for the Spirit of God to be present in our sharing. Eventually she broke the silence between us and gave expression to her thoughts with a direct question: "What's a Christ-follower? I've never come across that term before."

Her question opened up a conversation that lasted the entire trip. I shared, as openly as I could, my relationship experience with the risen Christ and how I was seeking to be his student in daily life. She spoke about her disillusionment with her religious upbringing within her childhood church—"materialistic" and "superficial" were the ways she described it—and her adult search for meaningful spirituality. She seemed genuinely intrigued by the good news that the life offered by Christ included the possibility of a transforming meditative encounter with the Holy One. As the aircraft wheels touched the tarmac she asked whether I would write down the names of some books that would expose her more fully to the gospel of Jesus Christ. This I gladly did, giving inward thanks for the opening to share my faith.

Voluntary suffering. A third opening presents itself when our allegiance to Christ results in voluntary suffering. According to the Gospel records, Jesus clearly expected his followers to undergo opposition. "If they persecuted me," he tells them the night before his own death, "they will persecute you" (John 15:20). Yet these painful experiences would open up important opportunities for bold witness. In another setting, when Jesus forewarns the disciples that they will be flogged in the synagogues, handed over to the ruling authorities and dragged before kings, he also assures them that the Holy Spirit will testify through them. "When they hand you over, do not worry about how you are to speak or what you are to say; for what you are to say will be given to you at that time" (Matthew 10:19).

An accountant acquaintance can vouch for the truth of Jesus' words. For eight years he has managed the finances of a medium-sized engineering concern. One day he was ordered by his directors to submit false figures to the firm's bank. He refused, knowing that his refusal would

---

Holy Experiment

DIVINE OPENINGS

Experimenting with a simple prayer request alerts our hearts to these divine openings. We can pray:

> *Lord, thank you that you are already active in the lives of all whom I shall meet today. You desire that every human being hear and respond to your good news. Help me to discern the right time to speak about you. Grow within me your gifts of insight and wisdom that I may possess your sense of timing in all that I do and say.*

A prayer like this reminds us that the Holy One always goes before us, preparing the hearts of others to receive the words we may share.

place his job on the line. Asked for his reasons, he shared with his superiors his commitment to live as a disciple of Jesus. In spite of ongoing pressure, including manipulative threats, he stuck to his initial decision. Aware that his convictions may have sidelined possible advancement, he continues working in his managerial position. Outwardly, his words and actions appear to have had minimal positive effect. But who of us will ever know the eternal consequences of his brave witness?

SHARING OUR FAITH WITH OTHERS

Faithful witness involves, according to the gospel method of Jesus, "the daily conversational use of the words in the service of the gospel."[5]

His manner of faith-sharing moved from the nonverbal to the verbal, and so must ours if we desire to follow closely in his footsteps. The claim that our lives alone will communicate the good news borders on the arrogant. Few human lives radiate the love and power of God in such a way that it renders words unnecessary. Naming the Name from whom we receive our new life is essential, or others will not be led to live in the company of Christ. As the apostle Paul writes about those outside the Christian faith, "How are they to believe in one of whom they have never heard?" (Romans 10:14).

Many sincere followers of Jesus resist the verbal dimension of witness. Associating the practice of giving testimony with boastful claims, superior attitudes, heavy-handed selling tactics and empty clichés, they want to distance themselves from those who talk publicly about their faith. Understandable

as this reaction may be, if we desire to live as Jesus did, we cannot dodge his invitation to tell others about the good news. How do we use words wisely in the service of the gospel? Here are some thoughts that guide my own attempts to share my faith in conversations with others.

Respecting the listener's personhood. Peter underlines the importance of this attitude when, in his first pastoral letter, he counsels Christ-followers to share the hope that is in them "with gentleness and reverence" (1 Peter 3:16). At the very least this means, when we speak about our faith, that we leave others in their freedom to choose. We make no attempt to manipulate, coerce or pressure them into a relationship with the Holy One. We simply testify to the different kind of life that we are receiving from God, and trust that the magnetism of the Holy Spirit will attract their hearts to the living Christ. By refusing to violate the freedom of others, we reflect the manner of Jesus, who never once forces his message upon those around him.

Using the first-person singular. Authentic faith-sharing models itself on the per-

---

THE CLAIM THAT OUR LIVES ALONE WILL COMMUNICATE THE GOOD NEWS BORDERS ON THE ARROGANT. . . . NAMING THE NAME FROM WHOM WE RECEIVE OUR NEW LIFE IS ESSENTIAL.

---

sonal testimony of the man born blind who, upon experiencing the healing touch of Jesus, cries out: "One thing I do know, that though I was blind, now I see" (John 9:25). Likewise, we become faith-sharers

Holy Experiment

TESTIMONY

Aimed at helping us become more aware of our experience of the Holy One, the completed sentences in the following questionnaire place at our fingertips a few experiences that, if appropriately shared, may benefit someone else.[6] The exercise directions are twofold: write out your answers as frankly and spontaneously as you can; then share some of these responses with a trusted fellow pilgrim.

- I have come to experience God as . . .

- I seldom, if ever, experience God as . . .

- I feel more "in touch" with God when . . .

- One moment in my life when I was most aware of God's power working in me beyond my limits was . . .

- For me, Jesus is . . .

- The most significant difference that Christ has made in my life is . . .

- I have experienced the Holy Spirit active in my life when . . .

- What I want most to share with someone about my experience of God is . . .

- When I am faced with my own personal sinfulness I sense God as . . .

- What delights me most about God is . . .

- When I reflect on God's love for me I am . . .

- For me, the surest sign of God's presence in my life is . . .

When you have completed these sentences, you will have the beginnings of your own personal testimony.

in the gospel tradition when we dare to say, with gratitude and thankfulness, "This is the story of my faith pilgrimage. Here is how I have experienced the love and power of God within my everyday life." One cannot underestimate the impact of such first-hand testimony, especially when our words are undergirded by a Christ-formed life. Describing how we have experienced God often engenders in others the faith and the courage to discern and discover the Divine Presence in their own lives.

Be relevant. If we are conversing with someone who confesses to living an empty and boring life, it may be helpful to verbalize how we have found purpose in our life with God. Overwhelming the other person with our entire testimony will most likely only foster antagonism and resentment toward the good news. An honest and vulnerable testimony of how the Holy One has led us into a meaningful life could be deeply appreciated. As the missionary D. T. Niles

> OVERWHELMING THE OTHER PERSON WITH OUR ENTIRE TESTIMONY WILL MOST LIKELY ONLY FOSTER ANTAGONISM AND RESENTMENT TOWARD THE GOOD NEWS.

states, faith-sharing is all about "one beggar helping another beggar to find food."

Every Christ-follower has a unique story of faith. There are no dittos in the creative life of the kingdom. We are surrounded by people who desperately need the Word of Life. However undramatic and ordinary your story may appear, know that the Spirit can use it for the glory of God.

Following the Signpost Together

1. Describe briefly one person who you consider to be an effective witness for the gospel.

2. What are your feelings about "witnessing"?

3. Where do you find it hardest to be a witness for Jesus Christ?

4. Name one area in which you need to grow to become a more credible gospel witness.

5. What do you think of the following concept: "Jesus' . . . manner of faith-sharing moved from the nonverbal to the verbal, and so must ours if we desire to follow closely in his footsteps"?

6. Discuss your testimony questionnaire responses (see pp. 134-35) as you are comfortable doing so.

13

STEWARDING FAITHFULLY
WHAT WE POSSESS

The Signpost

IN THE GOSPELS, JESUS TALKS openly about money and possessions. He challenges listeners with imperatives that invite them into freedom from fear and bondage. Jesus commands us to put God and his kingdom first, to give generously and to manage our resources responsibly. It is not easy to be faithful stewards in a world stricken with need and poverty, but as we grow in obedience in the service of all, we participate in kingdom work that is so deeply needed.

Holy Experiment

Pledging to tithe

Divine ownership

Reading

As I sit down to begin this chapter I feel a little apprehensive. A large part of me would prefer to avoid writing about the economic invitation of the gospel. Indeed, I experience myself as a beginner in these matters, hardly competent to guide and instruct others. Yet, in spite of the anxiety and tentativeness within, the still small voice insists that I proceed. My hope is that, as we open our hearts to the teachings of Jesus about money and possessions, we shall enter more fully into the wholeness of life offered by the Holy One.

My apprehensiveness stems from several sources. First, I'm deeply aware that I am not as free as Jesus was when it comes to material things. My attitudes and feelings toward money and possessions have been significantly shaped by my childhood experiences as well as the society in which I grew up. Looking back, I'm aware that my parents never owned property, purchased their first secondhand car in the fifties and often battled to make ends meet. Society bombards us each day with tempting messages to buy more, spend more, acquire more. Today, I recognize that my fear of scarcity and need for security, which sometimes prevent me from living in a spirit of joyful trust and gracious generosity, have deep childhood and social roots.

Second, my family and I struggle frequently with decisions about money and possessions. For example, there is a proposal by our church's leadership to build a family room onto our parsonage. Questions abound: Is such expenditure appropriate given the immense needs that surround us? Could this money be better employed in the service of the kingdom? How legitimate are our family's needs for greater living and hospitality space? What

> ALTHOUGH WE LIVE IN AN AGE OF
> INCREASING EMOTIONAL HONESTY AND
> OPENNESS, MANY REMAIN STUCK IN
> SECRET AND HIDDEN FINANCIAL
> OBSESSIONS.

does it mean to embody a simple lifestyle in a complicated technological world? Questions like these, and my uncertain responses, mock my intention to explore these issues in writing.

My third reason for hesitancy lies in the fact that I consider myself an amateur when it comes to economics. I cannot claim to bring any specialized financial expertise into what many consider to be a highly technical and complex field. Those professionally versed in the complexities of macroeconomics and modern finance may well disregard my reflections as naive and simplistic. Only the firm conviction that the Gospels possess the best information on

how to live encourages me to keep going. I dare to believe that, while interaction with contemporary perspectives on money management remains essential, Jesus, our ever-present Friend, is always our best Teacher.

By sharing some of my personal feelings toward money, I hope that I can encourage you to verbalize your own. Even though financial factors play a critical role in determining the quality of our personal and social lives, we find it difficult to express our feelings on the subject. Casual observation suggests that we are enmeshed in a culture of deafening silence on the issue of money. Although we live in an age of increasing emotional honesty and openness, many remain stuck in secret and hidden financial obsessions. Acknowledging honestly our feelings makes us far more receptive to engage the teachings of Jesus and gradually find the freedom they promise.

Recently the members of our church's executive body began the process of identifying their feelings toward money with a fairly low-key and non-threatening exercise. Before we engaged the business agenda for the evening's meeting, each of us shared our response to the question "What has been your happiest and saddest experience with money?" We discovered that this simple question arouses deep feelings, and helps to identify where present attitudes about money may originate. Before reading any further, you may want to pause and reflect on your own responses. Writing out these memories about money in a journal usually proves beneficial.

In contrast to our reticence and reserve, Jesus talks openly about money and possessions. Numerous biblical scholars have pointed out that he speaks more about this subject than any other topic, except for the kingdom of God.[1] Jesus strongly warns against the spiritual danger of wealth and greed, yet makes it clear that wise use of our financial resources can enhance our relationship with the Holy One and contribute to the common good. Careful reflection on this paradoxical perspective gives rise to three gospel imperatives which, when understood as a whole, represent the divine invitation to move from fear and bondage into greater joy and freedom. May this be true for each and every one of us.

PUTTING GOD FIRST

The first gospel imperative involves a fundamental choice between God and money. Aware that we cannot have two ultimate points of reference, Jesus confronts us with a clear either-or decision. Either we put God first, or we allow money to capture the devotion of our hearts and become our god. We cannot serve at both altars or divide ourselves between two allegiances. Jesus firmly impresses this lesson upon our hearts when he declares: "No one can serve two masters; for a slave will either hate the one and love the other, or be devoted to the one and despise the other. You cannot serve God and wealth" (Matthew 6:24). Allegiance must be given to the one or the other.

By giving wealth the status of a rival god, Jesus personifies money and gives it a spiritual character. We underplay this parallel between God and *mammon* (an Aramaic word that usually means "money" or "wealth") at our peril. Jesus clearly regards money not as a neutral moral object but as "a power which tries to be like God, which makes itself our master and which has spe-

cific goals."[2] Money, in other words, actively seeks to capture our hearts, secure our trust, make us servants and control our lives. Unless we consciously reject these godlike claims of money and put God first, we place our souls in extreme spiritual danger.

It is precisely this decision that the rich young man chooses not to make (Mark

> UNLESS WE CONSCIOUSLY REJECT THESE GODLIKE CLAIMS OF MONEY AND PUT GOD FIRST, WE PLACE OUR SOULS IN EXTREME SPIRITUAL DANGER.

10:17-22). As the Gospel record describes, he approaches Jesus eager to discover life at its best. "Good Teacher," he enquires, "what must I do to inherit eternal life?" (v. 17). In the conversation that follows, Jesus discerns one serious problem in the youthful seeker's life. Money has become his god. Instead of controlling his possessions, his possessions possess him. Knowing that it is impossible to serve two masters simultaneously, Jesus tells him to sell everything he has, to give the proceeds to the poor and to become a disciple. The young man refuses: "When he heard this, he was shocked and went away grieving, for he had many possessions" (Mark 10:22).

It must be emphasized that Jesus, in this particular encounter, does not lay down a general commandment. This is a specific word to a specific person within a specific circumstance. Possessions are the single major focus of this young man's life. The god of money has gained his ultimate allegiance. He is addicted to his wealth and, to

If we truly desire to enter the kingdom of God and discover a gospel-sharing relationship with our material goods, we must honestly assess the place that money has in our lives. Several yes/no questions may prove helpful in this regard:

- Are our personal decisions primarily determined by economic considerations?

- Do we struggle to give sacrificially?

- Are we more respectful toward the affluent than we are toward the poor?

- Do we associate more easily with the rich than the needy?

- Do we find comfort by going shopping?

- Does our sense of inner well-being depend entirely on the clothes we wear, the car we drive, the salary we earn?

These questions deserve careful thought, prayerful reflection and an honest response. Should our answer be yes to any of these questions, it could be that we have succumbed to the godlike claims of money. Mammon, rather than God, occupies the central place in our lives.

put it in biblical language, has become a servant of mammon. Hence the strong challenge by Jesus for him to make a radical break with his possessions if he really wants to experience the abundant life that God alone can give. As Richard Foster writes: "The rejection of the god mammon is a necessary precondition to becoming a disciple of Jesus."[3]

After the rich young man goes on his way, Jesus continues the discussion about wealth with his disciples. His teaching assumes a more general character and, as a result, becomes extremely challenging for each one of us. He explains to his followers: "How hard it will be for those who have wealth to enter the kingdom of God! . . . It is easier for a camel to go through the eye of a needle than for someone who is rich to enter the kingdom of God" (Mark 10:23, 25). As could be expected, the disciples are startled by these words. Mark observes: "They were greatly astounded and said to one another, 'Then who can be saved?'" (Mark 10:26).

We must not sidestep the sharp warning implicit in these words spoken by Jesus. It *isn't* easy for the wealthy to enter the kingdom of God. Affluence is dangerous from the perspective of the gospel. Those who are rich in material goods—and I include myself in this category—know this from personal experience. Prone to believe the deadly lie that our well-being lies in what we possess, we worry endlessly about how we can secure ourselves by accumulating more. Instead of putting God first and learning how to embody gospel values, we focus our hearts on further acquisition. The consequences, as Jesus predicts, are tragic. By our own deliberate choice we exclude ourselves from the true security and carefree delight that comes to those who make the kingdom of God their focus.

If money rules, let us choose now to put God first in our lives. It is a decision that we will constantly renew if we want to find our true fulfillment in the kingdom. Money as an object of devotion does not satisfy the eternal hungers of the human heart. Worshiping material goods in the end leaves us feeling disillusioned, cheated and spiritually bankrupt. Centering our lives in the Holy One, and making this relationship foundational to all our other choices, ushers us through the doorway of the kingdom. Within this realm, amid the manifest presence of God, we begin to experience human life at its best.

It is not only the wealthy who must choose between God and mammon. The golden calf of materialism attracts to its shrine rich and poor devotees alike. Poor people become consumed by the love of money, just as the wealthy do, and can find themselves in spiritual bondage. Paul makes this point when, in his pastoral epistle to Timothy, he warns his young protégé in the ministry that "those who *want to be rich* fall into temptation and are trapped by many senseless and harmful desires that plunge people into ruin and destruction" (1 Timothy 6:9, italics mine).

"Haves" and "have-nots" both need to orient their lives Godward if they want to experience the fuller life of the kingdom.

GIVING GENEROUSLY

While Jesus stresses the spiritual hazards posed by having material goods, he also emphasizes how they can be used for good. Some familiar Gospel examples stand out: Jesus pointing out to his disciples how a poor widow's sacrificial offering expresses genuine devotion; telling the story of the good Samaritan who employs his personal financial resources as an instrument of neighbor-love; using an encounter with a rich tax collector who gives away half his possessions to show that the rich can enter the kingdom (Mark 12:41-44; Luke 10:25-37; 19:1-10). In each case, the practice of generous giving strengthens the relationship with God, redeems the spiritual power of mammon and brings to others a greater wholeness of life. Generous giving describes the second vital gospel imperative regarding the faithful use of what we possess. "Give," teaches Jesus, "and it will be given to you" (Luke 6:38).

In spite of these moving examples, many still find it difficult to give with generous hearts. I recall my own feelings, during the first church service I attended as a freshly

THE PRACTICE OF GENEROUS GIVING STRENGTHENS THE RELATIONSHIP WITH GOD, REDEEMS THE SPIRITUAL POWER OF MAMMON AND BRINGS TO OTHERS A GREATER WHOLENESS OF LIFE.

converted teenager, when the offertory was taken. I was amazed as the people around me voluntarily gave money away. When the steward arrived at my pew and the collection bag moved toward me, I began a furious argument with myself about the amount I should give. The prospect of freely giving away hard-earned cash terrified me. With extreme reluctance I slid my hand into my pocket, fingered around for the smallest coin and then gave my offering. I remember my regret as I watched the bulging red collection bag, with my money inside, move away from me forever!

How do we begin to overcome powerfully ingrained resistance to generous giving? This question has followed me ever since that illuminating confrontation with my own greed and stinginess. In my search for a greater freedom from material things, five biblically flavored insights gleaned from my studies of the money arena have proved liberating. Prompting regular experiments in generous giving, they have also opened my life to numerous providential and grace-filled visitations from the Holy One. I outline briefly these ideas in the prayerful hope that they will encourage you to embrace the second gospel imperative with an expectant and carefree spirit.

Our love for God. Generous giving symbolizes the depths of our responsive love for God. Because money occupies an important place in our daily lives, it is almost impossible to give sacrificially without si-

---

THROUGH EXTRAVAGANT ACTS OF GIVING
WE LITERALLY IMPART TO OTHERS
SOMETHING OF WHO WE ARE.

---

multaneously giving ourselves. Our material resources represent personal time, talent and toil. Large tracts of our lives are stored in what we possess. Through extravagant acts of giving we literally impart to others something of who we are. For this reason, when we give in response to all that the Divine Giver has given us, our financial giving expresses tangibly the extent of our devotion. Certainly this is how Jesus interprets the lavish gesture of the woman who breaks open her alabaster jar and anoints

his feet with expensive perfume (see Luke 7:36-50).

When sharing this insight with a home group, one person insisted adamantly that he could genuinely give himself to the Holy One without any need to involve his finances. "It's a spiritual relationship," he argued, "and money has little to do with it." Such an attitude, which is quite prevalent judging by much contemporary practice, sadly betrays the sacramental dimension of generous giving. Morton Kelsey puts it in even stronger terms when he writes that it is nonsense to maintain that

we are giving ourselves with utter sincerity to God and then to spend all but a tiny fraction of our financial resources on ourselves, on our own desires and interests, or the quest for more money. To say that we are truly committed and still to remain in such a selfish frame of mind is worse than nonsense, it is hypocrisy.[4]

God's sovereign activity. Generous giving plunges us into the divine milieu of God's sovereign activity. Consider, as one example, the story of Cornelius (Acts 10:1-48). Even though this upright and God-fearing Roman centurion was not a formal member of the Jewish religious community, we read that "he gave alms generously to the people and prayed constantly to God" (Acts 10:2).

One unforgettable afternoon, during a vision, an angel tells him that his prayerful giving has brought him to God's attention. Now he must send men to Joppa to fetch Simon Peter so that they can get together. Immediately he follows the instructions. The consequences stretch throughout history and into the present, for when Peter arrives at Cornelius's house and shares the message of the crucified and risen Christ, the Holy Spirit comes in Pentecostal power, his host's life is tangibly changed, and the Gentile church is born.

Should we decide to embark on an adventure in generous giving, we too can expect to live before a more open heaven.

Our lives will also become filled with surprising serendipities, unforeseen blessings and transforming encounters. A professor-friend tells the faith-building story of how he once, as a struggling student at university, decided to give away all surplus monies after paying his monthly bills. He and his young wife told no one about their action of abandoned giving. Imagine their astonishment when, just a week or so later, they found a substantial banknote pinned to the steering wheel of their parked car! Through their giving they had stepped into that divine sphere where miracles of the Spirit constantly occur.

Put money in its place. Generous giving debunks the godlike claims of money and returns it to its rightful place in our everyday lives. The point has been made that behind money and the material things it purchases, there lurk powerful spiritual forces determined to evoke our allegiance. When we greedily clutch what we possess, we yield ourselves to these dark powers. Like the rich young man, we become possessed by our possessions. We turn money into an object of devotion and are eventually enslaved in its service. This literal worship of wealth exacts a terrible cost. Paul makes clear that "the love of money is a root of all kinds of evil, and in their eagerness to be rich some have wandered away

from the faith and pierced themselves with many pains" (1 Timothy 6:10).

We dethrone money when, in a spirit of loving abandonment and confident trust, we give it away. French sociologist Jacques

---

SHOULD WE DECIDE TO EMBARK ON AN ADVENTURE IN GENEROUS GIVING, WE TOO CAN EXPECT TO LIVE BEFORE A MORE OPEN HEAVEN.

Ellul believes that giving "is one act *par excellence* which profanes money by going directly against the law of money, an act for which money is not made."[5]

Generous giving strips away money's sacred character, overcomes its oppressive powers and restores it within our lives as a mere means of exchange. Like any other created thing, money can be used to extend the compassionate purposes of God. However, we shall always need to be vigilant since the dark spiritual powers behind money never leave us alone.

Bless others. Generous giving blesses the lives of others. Opportunities abound for

---

WE DETHRONE MONEY WHEN, IN A SPIRIT OF LOVING ABANDONMENT AND CONFIDENT TRUST, WE GIVE IT AWAY.

---

us to show concern and compassion via the sharing of our material resources. We are surrounded by people in desperate need, and by numerous worthy charitable and religious agencies that require our support. Perhaps you know someone who has been retrenched, or a young person needing study sponsorship, or an elderly person unable to afford the basic necessities, or a single mother struggling to provide for her children. It may be an institution that needs our assistance, a hospice caring for the dying, a relief agency bringing famine aid, a mission project reaching out to the bruised and broken. In situations like these, our thoughtful and generous giving brings joy, restores hope and transmits blessing.

Blessing others with our giving builds up an eternal investment. Jesus alludes to this good news when, in his teaching about money, he urges his followers to store up for themselves "treasures in heaven" (Matthew 6:20). One way of transferring our investments from earth to heaven involves contributing to the good of those around us. We can be absolutely sure that, whatever else may be in heaven, people will surely be there. Money invested in people

Holy Experiment

PLEDGING TO TITHE

Kneel before a cross. Consider for a few moments all that the self-giving God has done for you in the crucified Jesus. Ask the Holy Spirit to help you to discern what it means, in loving gratitude for the incomparable gift of Christ, to give proportionately of your income to the work of the kingdom. As Elizabeth O'Connor writes: "None of us has to be an accountant to know what 10 per cent of a gross income is, but each of us has to be a person on his (her) knees before God if we are to understand our commitment to proportionate giving."[6]

Write down the figure that emerges. Imagine yourself giving this amount away. Pay attention to the thoughts and feelings that arise within you, and speak with God about them.

_____

_____

_____

_____

_____

_____

_____

_____

_____

_____

_____

earns interest forever. Timothy is encouraged to make the same connection when, in the letter from his mentor Paul, he is advised to command the wealthy "to be rich in good works, generous, and ready to share, thus storing up for themselves the treasure of a good foundation for the future" (1 Timothy 6:18-19).

Our giving, if it is to be faithful to God, must not deprive those closest to us. Income earners have a biblical responsibility to ensure that their dependents feel adequately secure. Tremendous resentment builds up toward us, and the God whom we represent, when loved ones perceive that our giving undermines our financial commitment to their own well-being. The apostle Paul makes this exact point when he emphasizes that "whoever does not provide for relatives, and especially for family members, has denied the faith and is worse than an unbeliever" (1 Timothy 5:8). Money invested in the lives of our loved ones, especially in the growth and development of our children, also constitutes an important eternal investment.

Tithe. Generous giving patterns itself around the tithe as a general bottom line. I borrow this insight from the faithful witness of my friends at the Church of the Saviour. When this community came into existence in 1947, its founders decided that, in order to nurture integrity with regard to membership, each member would voluntarily adopt a specific and definite set of spiritual disciplines. Over the years, this uncompromising commitment to a disciplined walk with God has released immense vitality and astonishing abundance into the church's life. One of these disciplines deals concretely with the issue of finance. Each year, members commit themselves to the pledge: "We covenant

OUR GIVING, IF IT IS TO BE FAITHFUL TO GOD, MUST NOT DEPRIVE THOSE CLOSEST TO US.

with Christ and one another to give proportionately, beginning with a tithe of our incomes."

Weaving a regular giving pattern into our lives provides a practical starting point for the faithful stewardship of our income. Otherwise, as so often happens, our financial giving becomes erratic, mood-dependant and undisciplined. I particularly like the above spiritual discipline because it holds together the Old Testament principle of the tithe and the emphasis in the New

WEAVING A REGULAR GIVING PATTERN INTO OUR LIVES PROVIDES A PRACTICAL STARTING POINT FOR THE FAITHFUL STEWARDSHIP OF OUR INCOME.

Testament on sacrificial generosity (see Deuteronomy 14:22-29; 26:1-15; 2 Corinthians 8:1-6; 9:6-8). In maintaining this creative tension, the pledge guides us toward discovering what it means to become a generous giver. You may want, as an expression of your love for Christ, to consider making the pledge your own.

MANAGING RESPONSIBLY

For many years I believed that, when it comes to the faithful stewardship of our material resources, generous giving was our primary responsibility as disciples of Jesus. This conviction developed mainly from my spiritual formation within the Wesleyan tradition. Very early in my faith pilgrimage, I was required to memorize one of John Wesley's well-known maxims, "Earn all you can; save all you can; give all you can." I assumed, consequently, that the only good thing that could be done with money and possessions was to give them away. I also developed a prejudice against the wealthy, and inwardly wondered whether they could really be genuine Christ-followers. After all, they had not given all they possessed away.

I was challenged to review my thinking when I attended a pastors' conference on the subject of the spiritual disciplines. We were invited to take a simple test concerning our attitudes toward the place of material possessions within the Christ-follower's life. I outline this test here, and hope that you find it as helpful as I did.

Compare two sincere and devout people who are seeking to be faithful in their discipleship. One, in a reckless act of giving, has totally divested himself of all his wealth. He has hardly enough to live on, depends largely on the generosity of others

---

BEING WEALTHY DOES NOT AUTOMATICALLY EXEMPT PARTICIPATION WITHIN THE KINGDOM OF GOD.

---

and shares generally the life of the poor around him. The other is a successful and prosperous businessperson who exercises her astute business skills in an honest and compassionate way, maintains significant financial resources and manages them re-

sponsibly for the sake of the common good and the glory of God. Is the poor person a more faithful and holier servant of Christ *merely* for having given away everything and keeping only enough money to get by?

This test triggered an internal revolution in my thinking about the nature of faithful stewardship. I answered immediately that the person who had given all away was the more committed. In my view, he had demonstrated greater faith, hope and love. The speaker gently challenged me to reconsider my quick answer. His argument was persuasive, logical and provocative. Surely, he said to me, it could take just as much faith, hope and love for the businessperson to manage her possessions creatively for the purposes of the kingdom—especially if she were able to bring greater benefit over a longer period of time than would have been possible by giving everything away. By the time the session ended, I knew that, besides needing to confront my prejudice against wealthy Christ-followers, I also had to rethink an understanding of stewardship that would include the responsible management of material goods.

This rethinking process continues. For guidance, I frequently consult the biblical record. I am struck by the many times God uses affluent people in significant ministry. The Old Testament describes numerous personalities—Abraham, David, Solomon and Job, to name just four—who are rich and rightly related to the Holy One. This trend continues in the New Testament. There several well-off Christ-followers involve themselves in the work of the gospel. Examples include wealthy women supporting the disciples, Nicodemus and Joseph of Arimathea using some of their consider-

Holy Experiment

DIVINE OWNERSHIP

To facilitate a freer use and control of money and possessions, I invite you to experiment with a journal exercise that I find particularly helpful. Begin by affirming that all you possess belongs to God. Whether it be your dwelling place, your car, your furniture or your savings, express to the Holy One your desire to place all personal possessions under divine ownership. List all these financial and physical assets and sign them over to the Lord. Then spend some time silently reflecting on your personal management of what you own. Is your underlying attitude, "What is mine is mine and I have the right to use it as I please," or do you consciously see yourself managing your material goods as a steward of God? Write out these reflections as honestly as possible. Ask the Holy Spirit to liberate you from all forms of greed and stinginess. Imagine Jesus placing his hands on your head, enfolding you within his love and bringing under his authority the dark spiritual power of your money. Describe this experience, paying special attention to your thoughts and feelings.

able substance to care for the body of Jesus, and the apostle Paul learning how to live contentedly with little and with plenty (Luke 8:2-3; John 19:38-39; Philippians 4:12). If the scriptural witness is a trustworthy guideline, being wealthy does not automatically exempt participation within the kingdom of God.

Further reflection on the lives of these wealthy believers reveals an important stewardship principle. In each instance, the person concerned manages their material resources for the greater purposes of God. They were not seduced by their wealth. In the light of these examples, I have come to realize that Wesley's formula requires revision. Generous giving, while remaining absolutely essential in the life of discipleship, cannot describe our entire responsibility as stewards under God. In the words of Dallas Willard, my mentor in these matters, I now believe that Wesley's maxim should read: "*Get* all you can; *save* all you can; freely *use* all you can within a properly disciplined spiritual life; and *control* all you can for the good of humankind and God's glory. *Giving* all you can would then naturally be a part of an overall wise stewardship."[7]

I have observed the stewardship principle concerning the proper management of material resources at work among quite a few wealthy believers. A family who owns an expanding engineering firm intentionally creates as many job opportunities as they can for the unemployed. One corporate executive makes available, at no charge, a seaside flat for those hard-pressed to afford a holiday away from home. Another successful businessperson enables budding entrepreneurs from marginalized communities to initiate small businesses with the assistance of interest-free loans. In each of these instances, Christ-followers have immersed themselves in the marketplace, earned lots of money and gone on to manage these financial gains for God's glory and for the good of their neighbor. They have been faithful and responsible stewards to whom, I'm sure, Jesus will one day say: "Well done good and faithful servant! You have been faithful with a few things; I will put you in charge

of many things. Come and share your master's happiness" (Matthew 25:21).

Managing responsibly our material goods for kingdom purposes requires rigorous self-honesty, prayerful planning and the mighty power of God's Spirit. It is no easy task to steward faithfully what we possess in a needy and poverty-stricken land. Moreover, our wealth constantly seeks to undermine our allegiance to the Holy One. We find it exceptionally difficult to keep things without clinging to them, to own things without treasuring them, to possess things without being possessed by them. Before we know it, we end up serving and trusting mammon rather than God.

People everywhere yearn for economic well-being. In South Africa, deeply rooted injustices keep millions in life-denying captivity. Social restructuring will certainly make a difference—good or bad—to the material conditions in which we live together. Our responsibility to forge a God-pleasing economic system is without question. However, what our world waits for is a mature company of sufficiently trained and empowered Christ-followers, distributed throughout society, who will faithfully steward the material goods of the world in the service of all, especially the poor, the marginalized and the little ones. This begins when ordinary people such as you and me learn how to put God first, give generously and manage responsibly what we possess. Perhaps then the shalom-vision of the kingdom will be experienced in our midst.

Following the Signpost Together

1. Describe your most precious possession.

2. What has been your happiest and saddest experience with money?

3. Why do you think it is so difficult to put God first in our lives?

4. What kind of feelings do you experience when you think about generous giving?

5. How do you respond to the test concerning attitudes toward the place of material possessions within the Christ-follower's life? (See page 146.)

6. Describe one practical step that would enable you to become a more faithful steward.

14

SPEAKING WORDS OF
LIFE AND POWER

The Signpost

ONE ESSENTIAL TRUTH WE LEARN in our relationship with God is the power of words. Our words enable us to reveal or hide ourselves, to build or break community, and to help or hurt our neighbor. We are called to halt all harmful speech and to employ our tongues in kingdom ministry by blessing and exhorting others.

Holy Experiment

Halting harmful speech

A blessing day

Offering encouraging words

Reading

I was sitting with six fellow pilgrims with whom I had been meeting on a weekly basis for several months. Each week the group leader, in order to facilitate personal sharing, would introduce an icebreaker similar to those outlined at the end of each chapter of this book. On this particular evening, we were asked to describe one significant change that our relationship with Christ had brought about in our lives. "He is changing the way I speak," I responded, "and has given me a new appreciation for the place of words in everyday life." My answer aroused a certain curiosity in the group.

"What do you mean by that?" asked the elderly man sitting next to me, obviously intrigued by my response.

Briefly I tried to explain how, since entrusting my life to Christ, my attitude toward words had undergone a radical conversion. Before my decision to become a Christ-follower, words were unimportant. Often I would use them flippantly, without caring about their effect on others. However, as I opened myself to the gospel message, God gradually seemed to impress on my mind that words are more than mere syllables. I began to see them as potential carriers of life and death. I began to honor them and to view them as one crucial way in which we participate in the abundance of life that God gives.

Words do matter. Among all of God's living creatures, human beings are the only ones who communicate with words. Our words, whether spoken or written, enable us to reveal or hide ourselves, to build or break community, to help or hurt our neighbor. When used carefully, words facilitate self-disclosure, foster communion and release healing. When used carelessly, they create confusion, generate conflict and cultivate chaos. Well aware of this immense potential that inhabits our words, the writer of the Proverbs exclaims without exaggeration: "Death and life are in the power of the tongue" (Proverbs 18:21)

History confirms this ancient observation. As Catholic theologian Walter Burghardt remarks: "Two words, 'Sieg Heil,' bloodied the face of Europe; three words, 'Here I stand,' divided the body of Christendom."[1]

In South Africa, vicious slogans have incited numerous actions of mindless violence, causing immeasurable grief and pain. From all sides of the political spectrum, perpetrators of these senseless acts have defended their evil deeds on the basis of these slogans. While I was writing this chapter, three young men were seeking amnesty for their killing of an exchange student, arguing in their defense that they had come from a political gathering where the slogan "One settler, one bullet" was repeatedly chanted.

There are also several instances when words have exercised a wonderfully positive effect on societal events. One example happened at a funeral during a time of tremendous civil unrest in the mid-1980s.

OUR WORDS, WHETHER SPOKEN OR WRITTEN, ENABLE US TO REVEAL OR HIDE OURSELVES, TO BUILD OR BREAK COMMUNITY, TO HELP OR HURT OUR NEIGHBOR.

Thousands had turned out for the burial of a young activist, and the atmosphere was thick with tension. During the service, mourning comrades spotted an informer and, in their pent-up rage, made preparations to burn him alive. Among the mourners was Nico Smith, a well-known Dutch Reformed pastor, who ministered in the township where the funeral was being held. In the midst of the uproar, a stranger urged him to do something. His testimony illustrates the life-giving power of the tongue:

> I was in a dilemma. I knew that the [tire] and petrol could as easily be turned on me as on the informer. Then my conscience said, "Let go and let God." I moved into the circle where the group had the informer and said, "In God's name, I plead with you not to kill this man." The words came from somewhere. I looked into the eyes of men who were about to kill the man they had condemned. I did not know how they would react. Then someone started clapping. The tension was broken. They took the man away to be judged

by the people's court. I felt sad that this could have happened.[2]

WHAT WORDS REALLY ARE

Given their powerful effects in human experience, it comes as little surprise to discover that Jesus places eternal value on the words we speak. On one occasion he says to the religious professionals: "I tell you, on the day of judgment you will have to give an account for every careless word you utter; for by your words you will be justified, and by your words you will be condemned" (Matthew 12:36-37). Words, according to Jesus, possess meanings that reach into eternity. Exploring these meanings, and building them into our own lives, motivates us to use words with much greater care and sensitivity. Thankfully, as we consider what words really are, Jesus mentors us with his insights into their nature.

First, words reveal the true condition of our hearts. Jesus assumes this connection when he declares: "out of the abundance of the heart the mouth speaks" (Matthew 12:34). He points specifically to the way in which what we say expresses the inward and spiritual nature of our lives. Our words manifest those attitudes, memories, thoughts, feelings, longings, inner wounds and choices that make up the substance of our souls. We learn the character of a person by his or her speech. No wonder our words form one part of the basis upon which our relationship with the Holy One is evaluated. They represent the sounds of our hearts which, as the Scriptures constantly remind us, constitute our essential point of contact with the Spirit of God (for examples, see Luke 24:32; Romans 5:5; Galatians 4:6).

Our words do not only refer to those heart sounds that come out of our mouths. They also concern the inner conversations we have with ourselves throughout the day. These hidden thoughts and internal monologues also express our character. Jesus deepens our understanding of this when, immediately after extending forgiveness to the paralyzed man, he turns to the critical religious professionals and uncovers their thought-words. Matthew perceptively records the encounter: "Then some of the scribes said to themselves, 'This man is blaspheming.' But Jesus, perceiving their thoughts, said, 'Why do you think evil in your hearts?'" (Matthew 9:3-4). Both our spoken and unspoken words reflect the real state of our hearts.

Second, words impart spiritual power for either good or evil, depending on their source. Jesus implies this word-view when he says to his disciples, "The words that I have spoken to you are spirit and life" (John 6:63). Simply interpreted, this text suggests that Jesus' words bear the invisible realities of love, joy and peace that enable us to live life at its best. His words accomplish the life-making purpose since the speaker himself fully embodies life. On another occasion, Jesus teaches his followers that their words will also be able to carry good into the lives of others. In giving them their ministry description, he instructs them: "Whatever house you enter, first *say,* 'Peace to this house!' And if anyone is there who shares in peace, your peace will rest on that person; but if not, it will return to you" (Luke 10:5-6, italics mine).

Personal experience testifies to the spiritual power of words. Thinking about their effect on our lives makes this clear. For some of us, our worst soul damage has been caused by words carelessly and unfairly spoken. Yet we can all recall moments when words spoken at just the right time have brought life and light and laughter into our lives. On these occasions, words have proved themselves to be an immeasurable force for good.

Third, words represent one way in which we work together with God to extend the divine will. Think for a moment how Jesus uses words during his earthly ministry. With words, he calls Lazarus out from the tomb, rebukes the unclean spirit in the synagogue worshiper, orders the paralytic to get up and commands the raging waves to become still (John 11:43; Luke 4:35; Mark 2:11; Matthew 8:26). Each of these episodes shows how words, spoken with faith and understanding, send forth the power of God to accomplish great things for the kingdom. Moreover, Jesus urges his disciples to work similarly with words. In one instructive passage, he says to them: "Truly I tell you, if you *say* to this mountain, 'Be taken up and thrown into the sea,' and if you do not doubt in your heart, but believe that what you say will come to pass, it will be done for you" (Mark 11:23, italics mine).

In the record of the early church in Acts, we witness Peter speaking "to the mountain" with startling consequences. However, the healing of the lame man with words should not really surprise us. Peter had come through an intensive three-year apprenticeship as a pupil of Jesus, undergone a profound inner transformation, experienced firsthand the agonizing heartache and volcanic joy of the first Easter event, spent ten days praying with the other disciples in the Upper Room, and been filled with God's gift of the Holy Spirit. One can hardly imagine his depth of faith, his understanding of the power and authority that was his as a kingdom citizen, his vivid awareness of the Divine Presence enfolding and filling him. So it is with the unforced confidence that characterizes those who walk in the company of Christ, that he says to the sufferer: "I have no silver or gold, but what I have I give you; in the name of Jesus Christ of Nazareth, stand up and walk" (Acts 3:6).

It is possible to become immobilized by the biblical examples that I have just described. Few among us are able to stroll

WORDS ARE PART OF OUR EVERYDAY INTERACTIONS, AND THEY CAN BE MARVELOUSLY EMPLOYED BY ORDINARY PEOPLE IN THE SERVICE OF THE KINGDOM.

into intensive-care units and raise people from their beds with words. Furthermore, some who try often come across as presumptuous, uncaring and downright offensive. I remember the heartbreaking anguish of a grieving family as they stood by watching well-meaning but misdirected university students attempt to raise their son from his coffin with loud shouts and incantations in the name of Jesus. Given these tragic abuses, together with our sense of immobilization, it's not unusual for many Christ-followers to bypass the gospel's invitation to speak words of life and power.

I want to encourage you to begin speaking on behalf of God and in the Name of

Jesus Christ. Words are part of our everyday interactions, and they can be marvelously employed by ordinary people in the service of the kingdom.

WE CANNOT UNDERESTIMATE THE DAMAGE THAT A LOOSE TONGUE CAUSES. IT CAN DESTROY CONFIDENCE, TARNISH REPUTATIONS, SPREAD RUMORS, SPLIT FAMILIES AND DIVIDE COMMUNITIES.

In my own efforts to put my tongue at God's disposal, I have been helped by three practical guidelines: (1) Be gentle with yourself and compassionate with others as you seek to experiment in appropriate and suitable ways. (2) Take a long-term view and refuse to give up learning, even if you feel that you are not making progress. (3) Remind yourself that you are God's beloved and that, with confidence in and reliance on Christ, you can make a significant difference in the lives of those around you with your words.

HALTING HARMFUL SPEECH

Recently I read a Jewish tale that strikingly illustrates how difficult it is to reverse the power of harmful speech. The setting is a small Eastern European town where a local inhabitant continually slandered the rabbi. One day, realizing the wrongfulness of his behavior, he asked the rabbi for forgiveness and offered to perform any penance required to make amends. The rabbi told him to fetch a feather pillow from his home, cut it open, scatter the feathers to the wind and then return. The man followed the rabbi's instructions to the letter, then came

back and asked, "Am I now forgiven?"

"You just have to do one more thing," answered the rabbi, "Go and gather all the feathers."

"But that's impossible," the man protested, "the wind has already scattered them."

"Exactly," explained the rabbi. "And although you truly wish to correct the evil you have spoken, it is as impossible to repair the damage done by your words as it is to recover the feathers."[3]

Like the feathers scattered to the wind, we cannot regather the harmful words we speak. Once they go forth, they echo repeatedly in the lives of those to whom they are spoken and determine how they themselves will think and speak. We cannot underestimate the damage that a loose tongue causes. It can destroy confidence, tarnish reputations, spread rumors, split families and divide communities. James, brother of Jesus, offers us a graphic word-picture of the power of the uncontrolled tongue to wreak havoc and devastation. He describes the tongue as "a small member, yet it boasts of great exploits. How great a forest is set ablaze by a small fire! And the tongue is a fire" (James 3:5-6).

If we want to use words helpfully, we must halt all forms of harmful speech. But what does this mean for our daily conversations? Joseph Telushkin provides important insight when he suggests that we hurt people with words in two ways. We can make negative comments about people in their absence, and we can speak cruelly to those in our presence.[4] If this observation is correct, we begin to understand what it means to put an end to harmful speech.

Speak kindly. We halt harmful speech

when we stop talking unkindly or negatively about someone behind their back. Usually stemming from a desire to improve our personal status or to gain revenge, the gossip virus infects many of us. Its devastating consequences spoil relationships, damage communities and breed a climate in which love cannot grow. Significantly, just two verses before the great commandment to love our neighbor as we love ourselves, appear the words "You shall not go around as a slanderer among your people" (Leviticus 19:16).

Should we genuinely yearn to be loving in our speech, as Christ would, we must confront our tendencies to gossip and eliminate them from our lives.

Does this imply that we can never talk about those who have hurt us or who may harm others? Obviously not. For us to find healing from our hurts, there are times when it is entirely appropriate to share them, even if this means naming particular people. Such conversation may happen with a confidential friend, a family member, a counselor or in a relevant professional setting. Some situations, particularly where the actions of people may bring harm to others and themselves, demand that we implement carefully the detailed instructions given by Jesus:

> If a fellow believer hurts you, go and tell him—work it out between the two of you. If he listens, you've made a friend. If he won't listen, take one or two others along so that the presence of witnesses will keep things honest, and try again. If he still won't listen, tell the church. If he won't listen to the church, you'll have to start over from scratch, confront him with

the need for repentance, and offer again God's forgiving love. (Matthew 18:15-17 *The Message*)

Stop lying. We halt harmful speech when we stop lying. Lies lurk behind nearly all the evil we do to one another. Most kinds of wrongdoing rampant in contemporary society—marital unfaithfulness, financial corruption, crooked business transactions, human rights abuse, racial stereotyping, to name only a few—rely on deceptive speech as their starting point. Jesus describes the evil one as "a liar and the father of lies" (John 8:44). Given this diagnosis of human evil, imagine the transforming impact on society by thousands of Christ-followers sensibly committed to honesty, noncooperation with falsehood, and truth-speaking? Life as we know it would look entirely different.

Great minds throughout history have wrestled with the complex ethical question of whether we must always speak the full

WHILE WE COMMIT OURSELVES TO TRUTHFUL SPEECH, WE MUST ALWAYS TRY TO UNDERSTAND WHAT IT MEANS TO SPEAK THE TRUTH IN LOVE.

truth. Are there times when, for the greater good of the other person, we need to withhold a portion of the truth? One example drawn from my pastoral experience raises precisely this concern: I have been meeting with a young mother of two children, greatly troubled by her stronger feelings of affection for the eldest. Sharing her lack of love with the youngest child, in total honesty, could cause irreparable harm. Telling

Holy Experiment

HALTING HARMFUL SPEECH

Halting our harmful speech begins with an honest acknowledgment of how we speak. As an experiment, you may want to monitor your conversations for the next few days. Note on a piece of paper every time you catch yourself saying something unkind or negative about someone behind their back. Record the lies you tell, especially those designed to create a more favorable picture of who you are. Keep track of the ways you express your angry feelings, and describe them below or in a journal. Allow this exercise to lead you into a time of confession before God. End the exercise with the request of the well-known chorus, "Change my heart, O God. Make it ever new."

the truth would amount to verbal sadism. Surely it is far more reflective of the Spirit of Christ for this mother to keep the truth of her feelings from her child, acknowledge them to a counselor and attempt to work through them. This simple case study suggests that, while we commit ourselves to truthful speech, we must always try to understand what it means to speak the truth in love (see Ephesians 4:15).

Control anger and rage. We halt harmful speech when we control expressions of anger and rage. We all get angry. Understood simply, anger can be described as a spontaneous and natural feeling-response that usually occurs when we are hurt, threatened or frustrated. As such, there is little inherently wrong. Indeed, should we deny ever having angry feelings, we are most probably deceiving ourselves. What cannot be justified is when our anger explodes into abusive and contemptuous speech. Such speaking causes incalculable harm, especially when directed to those closest to us, and goes against the way of Jesus. It cannot be justified and needs to be checked.

As Paul rather sternly admonishes us: "Be angry but do not sin" (Ephesians 4:26).

How do we express our anger without harming others? In my own attempts to deal constructively with hostility, I have found several practical suggestions helpful. First, we need to "catch" our anger before it rushes into speech. Pausing between the feeling and speaking increases our control over angry emotions. Second, we can ask ourselves whether our anger is proportionate to the situation that has caused it. Disproportionate feelings usually indicate that we are carrying around unresolved issues which need attention. Finally, should we choose to express our anger, we can use what some counselors call an "I message" rather than a "you message." It is one thing for my wife to say, "I am angry about you getting home so late," but it is entirely another for her to say, "You are an inconsiderate person who never thinks of others!"

EXTENDING BLESSING

There exists in the English vocabulary a very familiar and often-used phrase that gives us important insight into the character of God. These three simple words—"God bless you"—remind us that the One whom we have come to know in Jesus Christ constantly seeks to bless us. This means that, should we truly desire to live Christlike lives, we will endeavor to extend the divine blessing wherever and whenever possible. One practical way in which we bless this world, and all the people in it, is through words. As James teaches us in his down-to-earth manner, blessing is something that essentially comes from the mouth (James 3:10).

What does it mean to bless someone with our words? Considering the linguistic roots of the word "blessing" provides crucial clues. To bless in Latin is *benedicere*, which literally translates as "speaking good." This occurs when, with our words, we communicate gratitude for a person's life, verbally will his or her good, and invoke God's presence on his or her behalf. Certainly these meanings are implied in the great priestly benediction which Aaron is commanded to speak over the people of Israel:

> The LORD bless you and keep you;
> the LORD make his face to shine
>   upon you, and be gracious to you;
> the LORD lift up his countenance
>   upon you, and give you peace.
> (Numbers 6:24-26)

In a wonderful book *Life of the Beloved*, Henri Nouwen, perhaps one of the most spiritual writers of his century, recounts a deeply moving experience of blessing. He tells of how Janet, one of the handicapped members of the Daybreak community, asked him for a blessing. Almost ritualistically Henri traced with his thumb the sign of the cross on her forehead. Instead of being grateful, however, she protested vehemently, "No, that doesn't work. I want a real blessing!" So Henri promised her that he would try again and, when they gathered together for their daily prayer service, gave her a real blessing.

After the service, when all the community's members were sitting together, Henri shared Janet's request for a blessing. As soon as he said this, she stood up, walked toward him and buried her head in his chest. As they held each other, he said to her, "Janet, I want you to know that you are God's Beloved Daughter. You are precious in God's eyes. Your beautiful smile, your kindness to the people in your house, and all the good things you do, show us what a beautiful human being you are. I know you feel a little low these days and that there is some sadness in your heart, but I want you to remember who you are: a very special person, deeply loved by God and all the people who are here with you."

As Henri shared these words, Janet raised her head and looked at him with a smile that

> **THERE ARE NO MAGICAL FORMULAS OR RIGHT WORDS TO SAY. . . . WE SIMPLY USE WHATEVER WORDS WE CAN TO SPEAK GOOD INTO ANOTHER'S LIFE.**

showed she had heard and received the blessing. Afterward, nearly all the other handicapped people came forward, expressing the same desire to be blessed. Finally, one of the helpers, a young university student, raised his hands and requested a blessing. Henri put his arms around him and said, "John, it is so good that you are here. You are God's Beloved Son. Your presence is a joy for all of us. When things are hard and life is burdensome, always remember that

> **IMAGINE THE DIFFERENCE IN OUR WORLD IF, LIKE OUR FATHER IN HEAVEN . . . WE COULD LEARN TO EXTEND BLESSING TO EVERYONE AROUND US.**

you are loved with an everlasting love." As John received his blessing, he looked at Henri and responded, "Thank you, thank you very much."[5]

As we reflect on this encounter between the priest and his little "congregation," we see more clearly what it means to extend blessing with our words. There are no magical formulas or right words to say, for if there were, we would be entering the sphere of empty repetition and vain superstition. We simply use whatever words we can to speak good into another's life. It may be a traditional "God bless you" or "Peace be with you"—or it could assume a more spontaneous affirmation like, "I'm grateful for you," "You are a special person," "May your life be filled with the light of Christ." Words like these, spoken with accompanying faith and understanding, transmit immeasurable blessing and goodness to those around us.

Words of blessing need to be spoken to almost everyone. Unfortunately, as Father Andrew Miles writes in a helpful pamphlet on the subject, we can easily slip into a pattern of excluding certain people.[6] Often we take those closest to us for granted and forget to express our appreciation and gratitude for their lives. Sometimes we feel justified in withholding blessing from people who have hurt us, forgetting that Jesus specifically asks that we reach out to them in love. Nearly always we curse those involved in murders, hijacking incidents, drug dealing and other criminal activities. Instead, we could make it an occasion to bless: "Lord, bless that person with the grace of genuine repentance and true remorse. You died on the cross for all. Let him/her turn to you for salvation." Imagine the difference in our world if, like our Father in heaven who "makes his sun rise on the evil and on the good, and sends rain on the righteous and on the unrighteous," we

Holy Experiment

A BLESSING DAY

Make tomorrow a "blessing day." Ask early in the day that your heart and mind may be filled with God's overflowing love for people. Resolve to extend an appropriate blessing to each person you encounter—beginning with your own family. Remember that this exercise does not entail having to say "God bless you" throughout the day! Your blessing may be an expression of appreciation, a word of encouragement or an inwardly whispered prayer that invokes the manifest presence of God. Speak your blessings in the faith that God uses words to touch the lives of others. Review your experience at the end of the day, paying particular attention to the effects of the experiment on your own walk with Christ.

could learn to extend blessing to everyone around us (Matthew 5:45).

SHARING WORDS FROM GOD

Perhaps the most effective way of employing our tongues in the kingdom ministry is by sharing with others words from God. We have noted how, during his ministry in our midst, Jesus uses words to extend the purposes of God. With words, he brings life to the dead, freedom to the enslaved, wholeness to the broken and peace to our natural world. Yet he doesn't make up these words on his own; they originate from beyond himself. He clarifies this when, in dialogue with his disciples, he says: "he whom God has sent speaks the words of God, for he gives the Spirit without measure" (John 3:34). Jesus has given to us, as his pupils, the power and authority to speak God's words—though not "without measure."

Words and images from Scripture. We learn how to share words from God by pointing others to appropriate words and images drawn from the Scriptures. Bearing in mind the common tendency to quote the Bible as a weapon against those who see things differently, or as infallible proof of one's own righteousness, we must discover how to do this with care and sensitivity. If we don't, we will alienate those we are seeking to help and foster unnecessary resistance. A biblical sentence or picture, shared at the particular moment when the listener is able to receive it, releases powerful forces for healing and re-creation. When this happens, we experience the gracious

IN WHATEVER SITUATION YOU FIND YOURSELF, KEEP YOUR ANTENNAE OPEN TO PEOPLE AND TO THE SPIRIT.

power of God acting though our words to touch others with the life of the kingdom.

I experienced something of this joy when I visited a young woman battling against the horrendous effects of severe chemotherapy treatment. Her lips were blistered, her tongue swollen, and pain racked her body, making any kind of human touch unbearable. Sitting next to her bed, I didn't know what to say. I asked whether I could share some of my favorite memory verses from the Scriptures. She nodded and I began quietly to repeat, with lengthy pauses between, biblical sentences like, "I am with you always," "When you pass through the waters, I will be with you," "I am the Good Shepherd." As she listened, her eyes closed, a slight smile appeared and, within a few minutes, she drifted off into a restful sleep. I felt the strong nearness of the Divine Presence and

knew that I was on holy ground.

Divine insight. Offering what we believe the Holy One may be saying in a particular set of circumstances describes another way of sharing words from God. Whether it be a stressful management meeting, an informal conversation with a struggling friend or a conflict-ridden family matter, daily living regularly presents us with difficult situations that cry for divine insight. The good news is that Jesus' Abba Father frequently has something to say about these practical issues. Discerning these Spirit-prompted insights and intuitions, and articulating them appropriately, sometimes provides perspective and understanding that otherwise would not have been considered. This could be why one of my early mentors in pastoral training would repeatedly emphasize, "Trevor, in whatever situation you find yourself, keep your antennae open to people and to the Spirit."

When sharing possible words of wisdom and knowledge, as they are biblically described, it is important to refrain from making dogmatic statements. Claiming divine sanction for our utterances usually hinders open discussion, fosters argument and creates divisiveness. There also exists the very real possibility that we may have misheard the divine whisper! Therefore, when we attempt to share what the Spirit could be saying in our conversational encounters, let us start our sentences with phrases like "I believe that . . . ," "Have you considered . . . ," "The thought comes to me that . . . ," "I have the feeling that . . ." Beginnings like these ensure that our words build others up, invite response and "give grace to those who hear" (Ephesians 4:29).

Speaking the will of God. A third way of

sharing words from God revolves around the prayer practice of speaking the specific will of God. In his helpful description of this kind of bold prayer, Richard Foster writes: "We are not asking God to do something; rather, we are using the authority of God to command something to be done."[7] Jesus prayed like this and, as he did with his first disciples, invites us to go through a course of experience in which we can learn how to minister similarly. We enter this learning curve by specifically asking the living Christ to be our leader and teacher. "Lord Jesus," we can pray, "thank you for the authority and power you have delegated to me. Teach me how to speak and act on your behalf and in your name. Enable me to discern the divine whisper, and grow within me the confidence prayerfully to declare in your name how things are to be."

As we experiment with this form of sharing words from God in prayer, we must remind ourselves that we don't have to make things happen. We do not have to try to manufacture faith with loud shouting or repeated exclamations of "in the name of Jesus." Christlike faith, whenever encountered in the Scriptures, is characterized by a distinct ease. All that the Holy One requires of us when seeking to pray with oth-

WE DON'T HAVE TO MAKE THINGS HAPPEN.

ers in this way is that we listen for that faith-creating divine whisper about the situation at hand and speak (or act) in harmony with this word. Should no word come, we simply continue praying in a relaxed and compassionate manner that allows us to alternate times of silence with times of thankfulness and petition. We can also rest in the confidence that, if we seriously want to grow in this prayer-form, God will gradually increase our capacity to

Holy Experiment

OFFERING ENCOURAGING WORDS

If God has spoken to you through this chapter, join me in learning how to speak on God's behalf. Start by expressing your willingness to partner with the Holy One in the work of the kingdom with your words. Then picture a person in need for whom you already feel compassion. Ask the Holy Spirit to prepare your heart to receive whatever words may be given you about this person. Be especially attentive when you are with him or her to the movements of God on or in your heart and mind. Share any words or pictures that surface in your awareness and which bear those characteristics that you associate with the divine whisper. If you pray with this person, be prepared to speak forth any word that God may give regarding the situation for which you are praying. If nothing distinct arises in your thoughts and feelings, continue praying as you would normally.

discern what to command.

The time has come for Christ-followers to consider carefully how we speak. Too often our words reflect the incivility that plagues our society, breaks people down, negatively affects situations and conveys only our limited human perspectives. This does not have to be so. Authentic conversion transforms our hearts, converts our words and gives us a new vocabulary. Instead of speaking harmful words, we speak words that help; instead of cursing those around us, we bless them; instead of sharing earthly wisdom, we learn how to share words from God. We begin to speak words of life and power.

Following the Signpost Together

1. When have you experienced the positive value of words?

2. What is the most important thing that Jesus teaches you about words?

3. In what specific way do you need to halt harmful speech?

4. Share your experience with the "blessing day" experiment.

5. How do you feel about learning to share words from God?

6. Try the following exercise: Sit together in a circle. Quietly reflect on one another's lives, recalling especially what you have learned about each other's struggles and needs. Write out a one-sentence blessing for each person. Take time to share aloud these blessings by saying them directly to the person concerned.

15

LOOKING TO
THE LIFE BEYOND

The Signpost

OUR IDEAS ABOUT DEATH affect the quality of our present lives. If we are able to develop a well-founded and understandable view of life beyond the grave, we are empowered to live meaningfully and abundantly in the present. Central to Jesus' message is the promise that we can begin to live an eternal life today; we can partially experience the fullness of the kingdom of heaven in the here and now.

Holy Experiment

Centering prayer

The present moment

Relinquishment

Reading

Almost halfway through the writing of this manuscript, my father died. I was not by his side when he breathed his last. At that moment, I was counseling someone struggling to uncover meaning in the emotional pain of her own life. When the church secretary interrupted the interview, saying that there was an urgent call for me, I intuitively knew that this was the news I had been expecting for over two years. Picking up the receiver, I heard my sister's voice, heavy with numbness. "I'm phoning from the frail-care center," she said quietly, "Daddy has just died."

In an instant everything seemed different. While conducting funerals and caring for the bereaved had become a regular part of my working life as a pastor, this was the first time someone of my own flesh-and-blood family had died. As the phone call ended, I felt an aching sadness well up from deep inside, and I knew I would not be able to continue counseling. I shared my news with the young person sitting in the office and asked if we could postpone our time together. She agreed and, after offering a spontaneous prayer for my family and myself, left me alone to come to terms with the enormous changes that accompany the death of a father.

The days and months that followed were filled with contrasting emotions. Even though I could only be thankful that my father's struggle with Alzheimer's disease had finally ended, there came moments when I felt deeply the overwhelming weariness of grief and loss. As with all human interactions, my relationship with my father had been inextricably linked to my experience of his physical existence. For forty-five years I had heard his voice, felt the touch of his hand, looked into his eyes, conversed with him. But now that body, through which I had known and loved my father, was totally without life. Sitting beside his lifeless body at the funeral parlor, I thought to myself, *If this is where our lives end, then life is really a sick joke.*

> **I LEARNED . . . JUST HOW POWERFULLY OUR IDEAS ABOUT DEATH AFFECT THE QUALITY OF OUR PRESENT LIVES.**

One simple belief, nurtured by frequent study and repeated meditation, brought light into the darkness. It was the gospel conviction, embedded in Jesus' teachings and underlined by his own death-resurrection, that our lives continue beyond the grave. Acting on this belief, I began to give thanks for Dad's continued existence in the fuller presence of God. A quiet joy bubbled inside me whenever I reminded

myself that my father was at that moment more gloriously alive and fulfilled than ever before. While this belief did not take away the pain of my grief or fill the emptiness, it enabled me to grieve with hope and joy.

During the period following my father's death, I learned again—in this case from personal experience—just how powerfully our ideas about death affect the quality of our present lives. If we believe human life terminates when our physical body dies, then life indeed becomes a sick joke. This could be one reason why many people avoid the subject of dying. They cannot face the utter futility that accompanies the materialistic viewpoint that we cease to exist at death. If we are able to develop a believable, well-founded and understandable view of life beyond the grave, it becomes possible to live meaningfully and abundantly in the present.

Before seeking to understand death and the afterlife in the light of Jesus' life and gospel, you may find it helpful to consider your own thoughts and feelings on the subject. Questions that facilitate this particular reflection include:

- How do you feel about your own dying?

- What are your dominant thoughts at a funeral?

- What do you believe happens to your life at the point of death?

- What images come to mind when you think of the afterlife?

- How do you understand the relationship between this life and life beyond the grave?

Honestly working through questions

like these brings our ideas about death to the surface where we can critically evaluate them in the light of the gospel.

THE GOOD NEWS ABOUT HEAVEN

At the heart of the central message of Jesus lies the promise of the kingdom of heaven (Matthew 4:17). Partially available to us in the present as we open ourselves to the crucified and risen Christ, we step fully into this heaven-life when we die. Within the eternal community and infinite love and goodness that we experience when we live in the full presence of God, we develop into all that we are meant to be. Largely because of this hope, and supported by their experiences of the divine kingdom in the here and now, the first disciples witnessed to their faith even at the cost of personal death. Likewise, as we build this gospel of eternal life into our own belief systems, we begin to face death with expectant hopefulness and confident anticipation.

Death has been defeated. Underlying the good news about heaven are three closely connected New Testament convictions which, when held together, answer some of our deepest concerns about dying and the afterlife. The first of these affirms that death has been defeated by the resurrection of Jesus Christ. Easter Sunday demonstrates the reality of life beyond the grave. Because God raised Jesus from the dead, we can confidently assert that death does not speak the final word about our lives. Humankind's most feared enemy has been decisively conquered. Upon this historical reality rests our confidence for eternal life. As Paul joyfully celebrates:

"But the truth is that Christ has been raised from death, as the guarantee that those who sleep in death will also be raised" (1 Corinthians 15:20 Good News Bible).

At funeral services, it is my privilege to share this gospel conviction. Well aware that the shock of loss greatly limits our capacity to assimilate too many words, I usually describe death's defeat with a simple word-picture. Inviting the grieving worshipers to take a long look at the empty wooden cross suspended over our sanctuary, I talk about Jesus' death at the age of thirty-three, the grief of his mother and the disciples, the unbearable darkness of Holy Saturday, and the bursting forth of his resurrection life on the third day. I close by reminding my listeners that the vacant cross represents the mighty and conclusive victory that God has won over death. After sharing this meditation at a recent memorial service, a bereaved husband said to me, "I will always keep a picture of the empty cross before me. Because Christ lives, I know that my wife lives also."

We shall never die. The second gospel conviction stresses that, as God's dearly beloved, we shall never die. Arising from Jesus' staggering assurance that his disciples would not see death (see John 8:51; 11:25), this insight reminds us that we are essentially embodied spirits whose lives last forever. We are not merely a complex combination of cells and salt water, as some would define us, but never-ceasing spiritual beings created for eternal purposes. John Wesley underlines this perspective when, in one of his published sermons, he states:

Man is not only a house of clay, but an immortal spirit; a spirit made in

Revisit your own thoughts and feelings about death and the afterlife. This time around, allow the New Testament convictions to interact with your own. To facilitate this interaction, ask yourself the following questions:

- What is my gut-level response to these convictions?

- In what ways do they confirm or challenge my own beliefs about life beyond the grave?

- Is there any specific personal belief that needs reshaping in the light of New Testament teaching?

- What difference would it make to my daily living were I to make these biblical beliefs my own?

Giving time to questions like these, and writing out our personal responses, signifies our commitment to develop the mind of Christ regarding our future in God's kingdom.

the image of God. . . . Consider that the spirit of man is not only of a higher order, of a more excellent nature, than any part of the visible world, but also more durable; not liable either to dissolution or decay.[1]

What happens when we are declared medically dead? The Ecclesiastes writer answers with disarming simplicity: "the dust returns to the ground it came from, and the spirit returns to God who gave it" (Ecclesiastes 12:7 NIV).

These words indicate that, when we pass through the stage we normally call "death," our bodies decompose and enable nature to complete within us its cyclic process. However, the spiritual dimensions of our lives continue their existence in the Divine Presence. We do not, at the point of death, divest ourselves of who we have become. We lose only those limitations and powers that specifically relate to our earthbound bodies. I believe that when I die my body disintegrates, but the person I have become lives on.

We will receive new bodies. Building on these two gospel convictions, the third assures us that we will receive new, spiritual bodies in the afterlife. The early church based their confidence in this regard on the way in which the disciples experienced the resurrected Christ. These postresurrection encounters were characterized by two significant features. It was undeniably Jesus whom they encountered, the same person whom they had loved and related to before the crucifixion. But, as he was now clothed in an entirely new kind of body, his followers took time to recognize him. His transformed body, while sharing some distinctive characteristics with his previous one, was infinitely more glorious, and this, according to the New Testament, is going to be true for us as well. In the words of Paul, in the life beyond, "this perishable body must put on imperishability, and this mortal body must put on immortality" (1 Corinthians 15:53).

An analogy that I recently came across illustrates the biblical concept of our continuing lives beyond death, albeit within new spiritual bodies. Think of your personality, the "real" you, as a message, and think of your body as its present means of transmission. Like a message that remains the same whether spoken in words or flashed in Morse code, so, according to the New Testament teaching, you continue to be the same person no matter what transmitter is used to express your personality. At death, your earthly transmitter disintegrates and returns to dust. However, the message that is your unique personality continues existing—only now it finds expression through a new God-given transmitter better suited to the afterlife environment.[2] This is what we mean when, in the Apostles' Creed, we affirm, "I believe in the resurrection of the body."

Few immigrants set off for a new country without finding out about the place they intend on going to. Similarly, so must we if we are planning to spend eternity in heaven. If, as the gospel proclaims, we can experience heaven partially in this life, it behooves us to open ourselves to these experiences. Such intimations of heaven can only whet our appetite and increase our longing for the life beyond.

WHAT IS HEAVEN LIKE?

Is it possible to describe what heaven is like? Some scholars strongly believe that, since we are trying to describe an entirely nonphysical reality, we are in no position to speculate about the nature of heaven-

life. Encouraged by Christian thinkers like C. S. Lewis, Henri Nouwen, Morton Kelsey and Dallas Willard, I have come to believe differently. On the grounds that we have access to the Gospel words of Jesus and can partially experience the kingdom of heaven in the here and now, I believe that we are able to offer some insights into what life in God's fuller presence may be like. Thoughtfully exploring these insights, and regularly reflecting on them, builds faith for our future and enables us to live more abundantly in the present. Allow me to share four insights that mean a great deal to me.

God's eternal dwelling. Heaven refers to that eternal realm where the Holy One dwells. Throughout the Gospel record Jesus repeatedly makes this point. He challenges his disciples to live as children whose Father lives in heaven; instructs them to pray that the divine will be done on earth as it is done in heaven, and describes heaven matter-of-factly as his Father's house (see Matthew 5:45; 6:10; John 14:2). From these Gospel sentences, and many others, there emerges an image of heaven as God's home, where the overwhelming reality is the Divine Presence. These glimpses of God, which have come through faith in this life, give way to clear vision. Of this the New Testament authors were confident—in this world we see in a mirror dimly, but then we will see face-to-face (1 Corinthians 13:12).

Some dismiss talk about seeing God in heaven as nonsense, preferring not to discuss the subject. They believe adamantly that the present life represents all that we can be sure about; hence all discussion and speculation about the future is a waste of time. A delightful story-analogy describing the conversation between twins in their mother's womb challenges this particular viewpoint and invites us to think about our dying in a way more congruent with gospel faith—as a sacred transition bringing us face-to-face with God. This story begins with the twins lying snuggled up against each other. The sister suddenly turns to the brother and says, "I believe there is life after birth."

"Nonsense," answers her brother, "this dark and familiar place is all there is."

"There must be something more than this confined place," insists the baby girl, "There must be somewhere where there is light and vision and freedom to move."

Still she could not convince her twin brother. After a few moments of silence, she goes on hesitantly, "I have something else to say, and I'm afraid you won't believe that either, but I think there is a mother!"

"A mother, a mother!" shouts her furious brother, "What are you talking about? I have never seen a mother and neither have you. Who put that crazy idea in your head? This place is all we have. Why do you want more? It's not a bad place. We have all we need, so let's be content."

The sister is quite taken aback by her brother's fury and doesn't say anything more. However, she cannot ignore her thoughts and, since there is no one to speak to except her twin brother, she finally summons up her courage to ask him, "Do you feel those unpleasant and painful squeezes that come every once in a while?"

"Yes," he answers. "What is so special about that?"

"Well," his sister explains, "I think these squeezes are preparing us for another place, much more beautiful and spacious than this, where we will see our mother face-to-face."[3]

The family of God. Heaven includes all others who belong to the family of God. At this moment, the eternally creative Christ, according to his promise given to the disciples hours before his crucifixion, is preparing places in his Father's house for all his brothers and sisters (John 14:2-4). Jesus sees our final state as a shared life where we live together within the divine household. By coming home to God and to ourselves, we come home to each other. This is one reason why new spiritual bodies are critically important, for they imply that we shall be recognizable personalities, expressing our unique individuality and able to communicate. Morton Kelsey summarizes this second insight succinctly when he writes: "Heaven is the state of being in which we develop and grow in relationship with other human beings around us."[4]

In response to that often-asked question, "Will I recognize my loved one in heaven?" we can now give a positive answer. Jesus, in his transfiguring encounter with the eternal realm, clearly recognizes the individual personalities of Moses and Elijah (Matthew 17:3). However—and this requires constant remembering—life beyond will be far more than a mere nuclear family reunion! In our Communion liturgy there is a wonder-filled moment when, immediately after we have eaten and drunk the elements, the whole congregation prays, "We thank you, Lord, that you have fed us in this sacrament, united us with Christ, and given us a foretaste of the heavenly banquet prepared for all humankind." No doubt well aware of this future banquet, the famous theologian Karl Barth, when asked at a conference of pastors' wives, "Will we meet our loved ones in the afterlife?" answered, "Yes, but with others too."

No more suffering. Heaven promises an end to everything that oppresses and diminishes present human life. Countless numbers of people around the globe suffer indescribably in this life. Millions experience the devastation and turmoil caused by political oppression, unending famine and natural disaster. Other people's lives are reduced to an endless daily struggle as a result of their physical or psychological deformities. Some die prematurely because of accident or illness or crime, leaving behind heartbroken relatives and friends. Shining through the darkness of this immeasurable suffering comes the light of God's promise that, in the future kingdom, all the broken pieces of this life shall be mended. As John describes it in his Patmos vision, in the new Jerusalem

> [God] will wipe every tear from their
> eyes.
> Death will be no more;
> mourning and crying and pain will
> be no more,
> for the first things have passed away.
> (Revelation 21:4)

This vision of heaven touches deeply the hearts of those who suffer. This was reinforced for me while reading about the ministry initiatives of a small Anglican congregation from Hilton in KwaZulu-Natal. Ian Cowley, author of *A People of Hope* and the church's pastor for nine years, describes a visit with his ladies' group to nearby Sweetwaters, where over

100,000 people live amidst abject poverty and pain. After spending the morning working alongside the local inhabitants in self-help projects, the visitors gathered together with their hosts to worship. Ian spoke about heaven where, he said, there would be no more crying and pain, no more knives and guns. As the service ended, the congregation thronged to the front of the small church for personal ministry. Three days later, Ian received a message that the son of one of the worshipers had been shot dead outside their home. Reflecting on this series of events, he concludes: "We must not try to minimize the realities of evil in this world, and the need for us to resist it. But a sermon about heaven is very relevant in a community where people are being mercilessly killed, and where human life has become very cheap indeed."[5]

Serving God in heaven. Heaven continues our partnership with Christ in the ministry of God's kingdom. Biblical imagery of God's new world communicates rich possibilities of energetic action, participative worship, challenging responsibility and unimaginable creativity. Most obvious is the vision of heaven as a heavenly city where God exercises dominion with tender mercy and healing love (see Revelation 21 and 22). We can be sure that, among the functions of this city, there will be plenty for God's people to do. Those who have become gospel ministers will certainly be entrusted with greater occupations in the life beyond. We will not be idle, relaxing in some celestial retirement home! As the master says to the faithful servant in the parable of the talents: "Well done, good and faithful servant! You have been faithful with a few things; I will put you in charge of many things. Come and share your master's happiness" (Matthew 25:21).

THE KIND OF PERSON WE BECOME, AND THE CHARACTER WE FORM, BEARS DIRECT RELATION TO THE JOB DESCRIPTION WE WILL BE GIVEN IN GOD'S FULLER PRESENCE.

This particular insight stresses the crucial continuity between our earthly and heavenly lives. The kind of person we become, and the character we form, bears direct relation to the job description we will be given in God's fuller presence. What we develop in terms of self-giving love, creative goodness, life knowledge, sacrificial servanthood, people awareness and God-faithfulness will not be lost in our afterlife existence. The Holy One will take these spiritual qualities and employ them in the kingdom ministries that await us. Of course, the opposite holds true too. If we have given little attention to God's kingdom in this life, we will not likely find ourselves attracted by the possibilities of heaven-life. We can choose, now and for eternity, to distance ourselves from experiencing the blessedness of heaven. Present choices, as Jesus explains in his teaching, have ultimate consequences (for example, see Matthew 7:13-14).

You may find it worthwhile to experiment with the following long-term planning exercise. Find a quiet place where you can be alone and uninterrupted. Pray that God may meet with you and speak specifically to you. Fix firmly in your mind

these four biblical insights of heaven-life. Imagine what your future in the company of Christ is going to be like—seeing the invisible for the first time, delighting in community with loved ones and fellow pilgrims, experiencing complete wholeness, and creatively working in God's vast universe. Ask yourself how you can better integrate your present life with this glorious future hope. Carefully thinking through our responses enables us to draw direction and strength for our present lives from the perspective of the everlasting kingdom.

INTIMATIONS OF HEAVEN

Jesus announces the present availability of heaven to all who turn to him. The announcement—that we can begin to live an eternal life today—constitutes the central thrust of his gospel message. We do not have to wait for heaven until we die. Life eternal begins in this world. Jesus' life, death and resurrected presence throughout the universe opens the door to the undying life of the kingdom. Following Jesus, and building our lives on his words and example, leads us through this doorway. As the beloved disciple expresses it in his letter to the young church: "God gave us eternal life, and this life is in his Son. Whoever has the Son has life" (1 John 5:11-12).

Without some experiences of the kingdom's availability, our faith becomes deadly dull and coldly intellectual. As some have pointed out, abstract ideas without experience seldom transform. Through devotional exercises, exploration into church history and careful biblical study, I have learned three helpful ways of opening myself to the Divine Presence. While remain-

Holy Experiment

CENTERING PRAYER

One way to be still in the Divine Presence is the practice of centering prayer. Begin by choosing a simple word or phrase, expressive of your love-longing for God that you can repeat to yourself. Examples range from single words like Abba, Jesus *and* Maranatha *to the celebrated Jesus prayer from the Eastern Orthodox tradition: "Lord Jesus Christ, Son of God, have mercy upon me, a sinner" (a prayer based on Luke 18:13). Repeating our love word or phrase for fifteen minutes or so, and gently returning to it when our attention wanders, anchors us in that quiet place where we can attach ourselves more deeply to God. Others prefer to gaze at a picture or a symbol—a lighted candle, a crucifix, a single flower, an ancient icon—while they focus their minds and hearts on God.*

ing very much a beginner in these practices, I outline them with the hope that you find them accessible and meaningful. May your holy experiments with them confirm the reality of the spiritual, strengthen your connectedness with the Holy One, and empower you to live your life more fully and abundantly.

Be still. We open ourselves to heaven through the regular practice of becoming still. "Be still," we are encouraged, "and know that I am God!" (Psalm 46:10). Underneath this admonition lies the psalmist's firm faith-conviction that, within the experience of stillness, we can know the life and Spirit of God. This quiet place— referred to by spiritual writers as "the still point," "the inward temple," "the interior castle," "the deep center"—is accessible to everyone. As the Quaker Thomas Kelly confirms so beautifully: "Deep within us all there is an amazing inner sanctuary of the soul, a holy place, a Divine Center, a speaking Voice, to which we may continu-

ously return. Eternity is at our hearts, pressing upon our time-torn lives, warming us with intimations of an astounding destiny, calling us home unto Itself."[6]

Entering into this place of stillness in the faith that we are the temple of God's Spirit enables good things to occur. These positive consequences range from a growing intimacy with Abba Father, a stronger awareness of our heavenly citizenship, a keener sensitivity to the divine whisper, and a less frenetic, more centered and compassionate way of living. Furthermore, we discover that, as we build this inward pilgrimage into our everyday lives,

WE LIVE IN THE FAITH THAT THE DIVINE PRESENCE PENETRATES ALL THAT WE DO AND EXPERIENCE.

a portable pool of silence forms inside our hearts. This means that wherever we go during the day we carry within our hearts a quiet pool into which we can dip for renewal and refreshment. The busier our lives become, the more filled they are with activities and tasks, the greater our need for this still center.

Live fully in the present. We open ourselves to heaven by living fully in the present. Biblical faith affirms that each day we live and move and have our being in God (Acts 17:24). In other words, we live in the faith that the Divine Presence penetrates all that we do and experience—whether it be cooking, working on the computer, playing with the kids, driving through early morning traffic or reading the Bible. Eternity intersects our lives. The Invisible touches our lives in the visible. It follows that when we devote ourselves wholeheartedly to the moment at hand and enter into its unrepeatable "nowness," we begin to live sacramentally. According to one spiritual writer: "The present moment becomes the Communion bread that's broken to reveal the Presence of Christ."[7]

This expresses better my longing than it does my practice. Present-minded living often eludes me. Frequently my family complains that, although physically present, I am not "with" them. During a suppertime round-table discussion, my daughter suddenly remarked, "Earth calling Dad! When are you going to come down from Mars?" Obviously sensing that my mind was elsewhere, her honest feedback jolted me into a fresh awareness of how easily I estrange myself from the moment that matters most: the eternal now. Immediately I apologized and once again resolved to be more genuinely present in the here and now. *Lord,* I inwardly called, *please help me to live wholly in the present moment.*

Letting go and letting God. We open ourselves to heaven by letting go and letting

Holy Experiment

THE PRESENT MOMENT

Those practiced in the contemplative art of living fully in the eternal now tell us that, if we intend to give ourselves totally to the present moment, three basic habits are required. First, we have to train ourselves, amid the constant onslaught of life's pressures and demands, to take one thing at a time. Second, we must develop the skill of focusing on our immediate task, however trivial or mundane it may seem. This does not mean that we never plan for the future or reflect on the past; rather, it means entering with complete abandonment into the present, investing the full use of our abilities and attention. Third, we encourage ourselves to persevere with the first two steps if we constantly root our minds and hearts in the conviction that God's grace and power are always available to us in the present moment. As Paul affirms, there is "one God and Father of all, who is above all and through all and in all" (Ephesians 4:6).

God. At death we are forced to let go of all we possess—our material goods, our pets, our work, our friends, our families, our bodies, even our breath—and to let God rise into a radically different kind of aliveness. For those who like to be in control, this prospect can be frightening. Thankfully, we can bolster our confidence in God's resurrection power before our last day arrives. As we learn to "let go and let God," we discover for ourselves how God constantly acts through a process of death and resurrection to give us greater wholeness of life. Against the background of his own dying-rising, Jesus underlines this gospel pattern when he says: "Very truly, I tell you, unless a grain of wheat falls into the earth and dies, it remains just a single grain; but if it dies, it bears much fruit" (John 12:24).

Throughout our lives there occur numerous minor deaths in which we can rehearse the art of letting go and letting God. These dying episodes could be the ending of a significant relationship, the giving up of a destructive habit or thought pattern, the removing of our false masks, children growing up and leaving home, the failure of an important project, the loss of a job, the limitations that come with aging, retirement, and most painful of all, the loss of a loved one. Each of these experiences confronts us with a choice: cling to what was, or let go, believing that God is always acting to transform death into life. The first option imprisons us in the past, blocks us from starting again and prevents us from taking up whatever fuller life God has prepared for us. Daring to let go frees us for the future, enables new beginnings and allows Christ to rise afresh in us. The choice is always ours.

Letting go and letting God seldom happens without grace and grit. Relinquishing what needs to be laid down usually feels like a slow, lingering and painful death. Consequently, we often prefer to

DARING TO LET GO FREES US FOR THE FUTURE, ENABLES NEW BEGINNINGS AND ALLOWS CHRIST TO RISE AFRESH IN US.

cling to the way things have been, even if this choice cancels out possibilities for growth and change. Facing up to this resistance and sharing the struggle to let go with a trusted soul-friend usually prefaces the relinquishment process. What follows are the critical steps of yielding ourselves more deeply to God's Spirit, allowing the old to die and entering into the new. Mary's words, spoken in the midst of her own transitional crisis into motherhood, remind us of the courage and self-surrender it takes to bear the eternal within us: "Here I am, the servant of the Lord; let it be with me according to your word" (Luke 1:38).

Experiment with learning how to open yourself now to heaven. You may decide to take time out on a regular basis to become still, or try to live more consciously in the "sacrament of the present moment," or discover how to "let go and let God" before falling asleep. Choose one that "speaks" most relevantly to your immediate condition. Give yourself between one and three months to build your intention into your everyday life. Monitor your awareness of the Divine Presence with your own spiritual responsiveness during this time. Remind yourself constantly that as you inter-

Holy Experiment

RELINQUISHMENT

The opportunity to practice relinquishment comes around at the end and beginning of each day. Every night, just before falling asleep, lay down all that has happened during the day. Picture yourself giving to Jesus all the day's mistakes, stupidities, tensions, pressures and demands. As you close your eyes, trust the Spirit of God who hovers over you to do within you whatever your soul needs. The following morning becomes a resurrection moment as you, in union with Christ, arise to tackle the responsibilities and tasks that face you. Developing this daily habit will enable you, when it comes to the more painful and difficult dying moments, to "let go and let God" with greater confidence and faith.

act with God in the here and now, experiences of the Holy Divine are intimations of the kingdom to come.

TO LIVE MEANINGFULLY, WE NEED TO KEEP BEFORE OUR HEARTS AND MINDS A VISION OF HEAVEN.

To live meaningfully, we need to keep before our hearts and minds a vision of heaven—not as a place far away, but as an eternal realm of infinite love and goodness which enfolds and penetrates our entire physical world, and which Jesus makes available to us. Let us resolve with Christ to open ourselves to the rich realities and treasures of this kingdom. As we enter into the stillness, live fully in the present moment, and let go and let God within the many "minor" deaths that occur during our lifetime, we provide openings for the life of heaven to touch us where we are. Only then will we be able to say with conviction and assurance that "the best is yet to be."

Following the Signpost Together

1. What is one experience of the Divine Presence that you have had?

2. How do you honestly feel about your own dying?

3. In what one way do the New Testament convictions about the afterlife challenge or confirm your own?

4. What aspect of heaven-life means the most to you?

5. Talk about your personal experience of any one of the three ways in which we can open ourselves to heaven.

6. How do you think you can best prepare for heaven?

16

GROWING INTO CHRISTLIKENESS

The Signpost

TO BE A DISCIPLE OF CHRIST is to put on the nature of Christ and become like him. When we observe the character of Jesus in the Gospels we see that central to his work was an understanding of the value of people. We must learn to look at others through Jesus' eyes and to pray that the divine passion for people will be formed in our hearts. Concrete, Spirit-empowered actions embody this passion for those around us.

Holy Experiment

Hospitality

Praying for our enemies

Reading

From beginning to end the actions and sayings of Jesus are characterized by a profound and passionate concern for people. Trace the footsteps of Jesus through the Gospels. Listen to him teach as he unpacks the meaning of kingdom living. Observe him carefully in his ministry encounters with everyday women and men. People matter more than anything else. Jesus recognized the image of God in every human being. With uncanny double vision he sees people as they are, and as they can become. Seeing people through these kinds of eyes, he both enfleshes the heart of the Holy One and demonstrates the intended outcome of his transforming work in our lives.

Understanding this supreme gospel value signposts our way forward toward the goal of the Christ-following life: *to be a disciple of Jesus is to grow into Christlikeness.*

From God's perspective there is nothing more valuable than the human being. Right from the outset of the biblical record this is made clear. In the first chapter of the Bible we discover that, of the entire created order, only you and I bear the divine image. A few sentences later we learn that it is into human hands that God entrusts the responsibility for his world. Reflecting on this rather awesome job description, the stargazing psalmist exclaims with wonder that we have been made "a little lower than God, and crowned . . . with glory and honor" (Psalm 8:5). Can we see how much we really matter?

God's attitude toward human life becomes audible and visible in the life and ministry of Jesus. Listen in on his conversation with his disciples as he draws a comparison between people and the birds of the air: "Are not five sparrows sold for two pennies? Yet not one of them is forgotten in God's sight. But even the hairs of your head are all counted. Do not be afraid; you are of more value than many sparrows" (Luke 12:6-7).

Imagine the life-affirming effect these words would have on the lives of these early Christ-followers. Without a shadow of doubt they would have known that they mattered to Jesus and to the One of whom he spoke.

Sayings like these were underlined by the actions of Jesus. Whether it was hugging a little child nagging for attention, touching an outcast leper living on the margins of society, sitting down for a meal with a politically incorrect tax-gatherer or accepting a used and abused prostitute, Jesus acted toward individuals with immeasurable respect and care. He enabled them to realize their sacredness and specialness. He called forth from their depths their very best. People mattered to Jesus more than they would ever fully comprehend, and he would love them—and us—to the end.

This is the heart that Jesus desires to form in us. Recall that gospel invitation extended by Jesus to the two fishermen, Simon and his brother Andrew, as they cast their nets into the Sea of Galilee. "Follow me," says Jesus, "and I will make you fish

FROM GOD'S PERSPECTIVE THERE IS NOTHING MORE VALUABLE THAN THE HUMAN BEING.

for people" (Mark 1:17). For many years I interpreted these words in a strictly evangelical sense. Here, I believed, Jesus was seeking to motivate his disciples into "catching people" for the kingdom. Only after spending a few hours in the company of a committed fisherman did I reconsider my understanding of this text.

Fishermen, I discovered, are passionate people—passionate about fish! They prepare for their fishing adventures with painstaking attention, rise from sleep at unearthly hours, fish throughout night and day with enduring patience and, upon their arrival home, talk incessantly about their triumphs and near triumphs! Their hearts are set on the task of fishing. Knowing this to be true about Simon and Andrew, Jesus in effect says to them: "Come with me and I will replace your passion for fish with an-

PEOPLE MATTERED TO JESUS MORE THAN THEY WOULD EVER FULLY COMPREHEND, AND HE WOULD LOVE THEM—AND US— TO THE END.

other kind. I will form in your heart the divine passion for people. You will learn to see men and women through my eyes."

This transformation in learning to see people differently takes time. Certainly this has been true of my own experience. Over the years the poverty of my own eyesight has revealed itself in a variety of ways: cynicism and resentment toward people's needs, nonresponsiveness in the face of visible suffering, lack of engagement with those "principalities and powers" that have sought to dominate and oppress, and sometimes personal actions and words that I know have brought harm to others. Still today, in spite of really wanting to see people through the eyes of Jesus, these symptoms of dull vision constantly reappear.

THE WAY WE SEE OTHERS DETERMINES THE WAY WE BEHAVE AND RELATE TO ONE ANOTHER.

Regularly checking the eyes of one's heart is therefore a gospel necessity. For this diagnostic exercise you may want to search out your responses to the following questions: With what kind of eyes do I see people? Is my seeing prejudiced by the other person's color or culture? In relation to my neighbor's pain do I have eyes that are aware or blind? Do I see people as mere statistics or, as Archbishop Desmond Tutu once said, "sacraments of God's presence"? Wrestling with questions like these is crucial for the serious Christ-follower. For the way we see others determines the way we behave and relate to one another.

"LORD JESUS," OUR CRY MUST BE, "HELP ME TO SEE THAT PEOPLE MATTER. ENABLE ME TO RECOGNIZE YOUR IMAGE IN ALL MEN AND WOMEN."

A legend from the Middle Ages makes this clear: Two warriors in full armor were riding along in a forest, each thinking they were alone. In a particularly dark and wooded area their paths crossed. Both were frightened, and each interpreted the movements of the other as hostility. Believing their lives were in danger, the knights unbuckled their weapons and began to fight. When the one knight fell to the ground the other rode across to him and drove his lance through his heart. The victor dismounted and walked over to the one he had killed. He pulled back the face mask, and there, to his horror, in the pale moonlight he recognized his own brother. Mistaken seeing had ended in tragedy.

In our blindness we hurt and destroy each other. That is the story of our lives and of our world. Like the blind man of Bethsaida, we desperately need the second touch of Jesus. Remember how, after Jesus had placed saliva on his eyes and touched him, he asked the man, "Can you see anything?" "I can see people, but they look like trees, walking," the man replied. And then Jesus touched the man a second time and he was able to see everyone clearly (Mark 8:24). This blind man symbolizes our common need for a fresh way of seeing. "Lord Jesus," our cry must be, "help me to see that people matter. Enable me to recognize your image in all men and women. Form your divine passion for people in my heart. And may all that I do and say spring from this supreme value of yours."

Integrating this supreme gospel value into the fabric of our inner being requires determined effort. Repeatedly the apostle Paul reminds us that personal transformation will not happen without our wholehearted cooperation. His writings are peppered with phrases inviting us to participate with the Spirit in our ongoing conversion: put away your former way of life (Ephesians 4:22, 24); clothe yourselves with the new self (Colossians 3:9-10); put on the Lord Jesus (Galatians 3:27 KJV); and above all, clothe yourselves with love (Colossians 3:14).

Discerning those behaviors characteristic of Jesus and making them our own is one way of taking these invitations seriously. From my own reflections I propose three "gospel actions" as a starting point.

THE GOSPEL ACTION OF HOSPITALITY

In our Communion liturgy there is a grace-filled moment when, immediately after the bread and wine have been consecrated, the minister turns to the congregation and says: "This is the Lord's Table. Christ is our Host and he invites all to come and feast." There can be no more vivid symbol of the gracious hospitality that God extends to his people. Everyone's name appears on the invitation list for the banquet of the kingdom. There is a place especially reserved for you and me. The testimony of the psalmist becomes our own: "You prepare a table before me" (Psalm 23:5).

Not surprisingly, therefore, both Jesus and his early followers practiced hospitality. You will have gleaned from your own reading of the Gospels that whenever Jesus was at the table, anybody and everybody was welcome. Nobody was sent away. This was the scandal that horrified the religious leaders, challenged prevailing customs but—on the other hand—made the gospel credible for those outsiders and outcasts

who felt they did not matter to society. Later the theme of hospitality would appear in the writings of both Peter and Paul and became, in the expansion of the church, one of the key criteria for holding a position of leadership in the local congregation.

Hospitality gets twisted these days to serve ends that betray its essential nature. Sometimes the outwardly hospitable invitation disguises a multitude of less attractive hidden agendas. Have you ever had the experience where, at the conclusion of an evening shared with your hosts, you wondered why they wanted your company in the first place? Was your presence desired because your hosts honestly cared about you and wanted to get to know you—or was it a calculated effort toward getting what they needed from you? Talking about this kind of abuse of hospitality the other day, a friend made a comment that echoed something of my own suspicions. "Hospitality," he remarked, "has become a subtle and sophisticated form of social engineering."

Nothing could be further from what genuine hospitality is all about. Consider Abraham receiving three strangers at Mamre and giving them water, bread and

---

HOSPITALITY IS A WAY OF SAYING TO ANOTHER, "YOU MATTER. I WELCOME YOU AND WANT TO PROVIDE FOR YOU A SAFE PLACE WHERE YOU CAN BE YOURSELF."

---

meat; the widow of Zarephath offering food and shelter to Elijah; and the two Emmaus pilgrims inviting the stranger home with them to sleep over for the night.[1] From these biblical stories we learn that hospitality is a way of saying to another, "You mat-

Holy Experiment

HOSPITALITY

We extend hospitality by asking friends and those still strangers to come and share a meal. Or when we invite the outsider in our midst into our circle of friends. Or when we accept serenely an interruption by a visitor. How can you offer hospitality today?

ter. I welcome you and want to provide for you a safe place where you can be yourself. If at all possible, I will meet your needs for friendship and refreshment. I have no desire to change you, judge you or get anything from you. Make yourself at home."

Often it is the poor who teach us most about hospitality. Some years ago on a "pilgrimage of pain and hope" a group spent three days sharing the life of a deprived and dispossessed community. Two of the pilgrims, both young women in their early twenties, lived with a family of six in a two-room dwelling. For the duration of their stay the husband and wife insisted on the two pilgrims using their bed while they themselves slept on the floor in the adjoining room with their children. Upon awakening each morning the pilgrims found that water had been heated for them over an open fire and a breakfast cooked. When they left, they were given a small gift to take to their families.

Our next stay was in an exclusive and affluent suburb of a major South African city. The same two pilgrims were placed with a couple living alone in a double-storied home. When they arrived, the young adults were asked if they would use their sleeping bags and sleep on the carpet in the family room. Breakfast was cooked for them by the domestic worker, left on the kitchen table and eaten alone without their hosts. On the last day of their stay you can imagine the shock and surprise for these pilgrims when they discovered upstairs three unused, furnished bedrooms. Their contrasting experience became for us all on that pilgrimage a powerful lesson in generous and costly hospitality.

Hospitality takes place in a variety of ways and on many different levels. Henri Nouwen suggests that parents offer hospitality to their children when they provide a free and friendly space for them in which they can grow and become their own persons.[2] Yesterday it meant for me approaching a stranger in our church parking lot and asking if I could help him in any way. "Yes," he replied, "I have inoperable cancer and need some space to pray." I invited him into our chapel where we sat in the silence together. However it may happen, hospitality is a sign of that great banquet to which all have been invited and where everyone matters.

THE GOSPEL ACTION OF LOVING OUR ENEMIES

Return again to our picture of God provided by Jesus through his words and deeds. In his teaching on the mountainside Jesus articulates for his followers what is self-evident from the world of nature. Clearly the Holy One is not someone who rewards the good with sunshine and rain and punishes the wicked with drought and disaster. Experience teaches us that he "makes his sun rise on the evil and on the good, and sends rain on the righteous and on the unrighteous" (Matthew 5:45). He treats friend and foe alike. The blessedness of the kingdom is made available to anyone, even the enemy of God, who wants to enter.

God's indiscriminate and all-inclusive love embodies itself vividly in the actions of Jesus. The writers of the various Gospels make it obvious that there were many who despised Jesus and wanted to do away with him. Yet at no point throughout his public ministry does he seek their exclusion from the goodness and mercy of the One by whom he had been sent. Even from the agony and anguish of the cross Jesus cries out for the Father's blessing on those who had planned his death. "Forgive them," he prays, "for they do not know what they are doing" (Luke 23:34).

Bringing our lives in sync with this surprising kind of God requires that we relate to our enemies in a similar spirit. There is

> **BRINGING OUR LIVES IN SYNC WITH THIS SURPRISING KIND OF GOD REQUIRES THAT WE RELATE TO OUR ENEMIES IN A SIMILAR SPIRIT.**

no way around this difficult challenge. We are to love our enemies, commands Jesus, because this is what God does. The early church took these words seriously. Indeed, it was this attitude toward the enemy that constituted one of the major ingredients of their radical witness of the gospel. Recall for a moment the prayer that Stephen, the first Christ-following martyr, offers up to God as he is being stoned to death. We can almost hear the Spirit of Jesus speaking through him. "Lord," he cries out on behalf of his persecutors, "do not hold this sin against them" (Acts 7:60).

How on earth do we begin to love the enemy? Acknowledging who they are and our real feelings toward them chalks out the starting line. It is a fact that all of us have enemies. It could be someone within the family, a neighbor across the street, a colleague in the workplace or someone whom we consider as our oppressor or exploiter. Enemies are those toward whom we feel hostile, and who sometimes feel hostile toward us. They are the people we try to avoid, speak negatively about in their absence or just cannot stand. Usually we feel that they have sinned against us in one way or another. Unless we honestly own the truth that there are people against whom we harbor feelings of hostility and vengeance, we shall remain stuck in our relationships with them.

UNLESS WE HONESTLY OWN THE TRUTH THAT THERE ARE PEOPLE AGAINST WHOM WE HARBOR FEELINGS OF HOSTILITY AND VENGEANCE, WE SHALL REMAIN STUCK IN OUR RELATIONSHIPS WITH THEM.

Refusing to retaliate keeps alive the potential for redeeming every relationship. Knowing what such refusal does *not* mean is critical. New Testament scholar Walter Wink, in his careful exploration of the emphasis on nonretaliation in the life of Jesus, insists that it does not suggest submission to evil or passivity in the face of injustice. Loving your enemies sometimes requires tough confrontation. He cites the situation

GOSSIP IS A DEADLY FORM OF VIOLENCE.

of a battered wife whose husband has become the enemy. The most loving thing she might do would be to have her husband arrested. This would bring the issue into the open, put the abuser under a court order that would mean jail if the abuse continued, and potentially begin a process that would not only deliver the woman from being battered but free the man from battering as well.[3]

Through his own responses to those who made themselves his enemies, Jesus discloses the essence of nonretaliation. Turning the left cheek, giving your cloak away and going the second mile implies a refusal to be violent toward your enemies. At its most basic level—and hardest—this involves not speaking negatively or critically about them behind their backs. Gossip is a deadly form of violence—it damages our own spirits, builds a climate of suspicion and mistrust, and injures other people's reputation without their being able to defend themselves. If we do have to speak about another person unkindly, either because of the intensity of our own hurt or the possibilities of further damage being caused to others, this speaking must happen with the person concerned or within the appropriate professional context.

Prayer for one's enemies that results in practical action for their good is a further step toward loving them. Have you not discovered from personal experience that when you pray for someone whom you dislike, you begin to view them in a fresh light? From this new way of seeing there flows a new way of relating.

THE GOSPEL ACTION OF DOING GOOD

Jesus would have had no problem with being called a "do-gooder"! Indeed it was one of the ways in which those who knew him

Holy Experiment

PRAYING FOR OUR ENEMIES

Risk yourself in another experiment: think of someone from whom you are presently estranged. Own your feelings toward the person and offer them honestly to God. Resolve to halt all unkind talk about this person in his or her absence. Hold the person in the light of God's presence and pray for his or her blessing and enrichment. Finally, ask the Spirit to guide you into some practical expression of love on the person's behalf. Observe the effects of the experiment on both your relationship with the Holy One and your relationship with the person concerned.

well interpreted his actions. In his reflections Luke writes that Jesus was "a good man, full of the Holy Spirit and of faith," who "went about doing good" (Acts 11:24; 10:38). Whenever this gospel action has marked the spirituality of his followers, there has been a significant impact on the life texture of the surrounding community.

The transforming effect that those caught up in the great Wesleyan revival exercised upon eighteenth-century England is one prominent example. As John Wesley preached men and women into the kingdom, he simultaneously challenged them

to bring an oppressive and decaying society into conformity with that kingdom. His converts rose to the challenge of the historical moment. Commenting on their efforts, leading South African churchperson Bishop Peter Storey points out: "[The] first co-operatives, the beginnings of social work, the liberation of slaves, the emancipation of labour, popular education, the Trade Union movement; all of these and more were established by the spiritual descendants of Wesley."[4]

The secret underlying their astonishing witness lay in their passionate commitment to this one gospel action: on a weekly basis every member of the Wesleyan movement was enjoined "to avoid evil, to do no harm and *to do all the good* they could for as many as possible."[5]

We overlook the lesson implied in this historical example at our peril. Disorganized good offers weak opposition to organized evil. Personal concerns for good, if they are going to effectively counter institutional evil, must be corporately organized for creative action. During the period of the church's struggle against legalized apartheid, this same lesson was learned by many Christ-followers in South Africa. This highly sophisticated and structured evil necessitated much greater opposition than isolated acts of personal goodness could offer—it required the disciplined commitments of organized intercession, organized protest and organized resistance. With this struggle now thankfully in the past, the task of national reconstruction and development will demand from us a continuous commitment to organized efforts for good.

Alongside this participation in organized movements for good, there is the ever-present challenge of spontaneously filling our everyday encounters with as much personal goodness as possible. Opportunities abound in almost every situation in which we find ourselves. We can stop lying and begin speaking the truth. We can offer practical assistance to others in those seemingly trivial and trifling tasks of daily living. We can respect the rituals of courtesy that are found in every culture. Saying thank you, writing letters of appreciation and answering phone messages are all small actions that affirm the dignity of those with whom we regularly interact.

Archbishop Tutu testifies to the indelible impression left upon his memory when, as a young boy growing up in apartheid South Africa, he witnessed an elderly white priest raising his hat in greeting to his aging mother.[6]

Individual actions for good stand out as bright stars in a dark sky. Their witness value for the kingdom cannot be measured in temporal terms. I realized this again when reading a magazine article describing the frightening levels of violence and immorality in present-day South African society. One incident witnessed by the journalist had kept him from complete cynicism and despair. Taking place amidst a protest march that had erupted into an orgy of public looting and indiscriminate violence, it consisted of a single action by a lone woman marcher. While the angry marchers had begun to smash windows and help themselves to the displayed goods, this woman refused to cooperate. Standing outside the shattered windows of a large department store, she kept shouting, almost crying with frustration: "Stop it comrades. Discipline! Don't give us a bad name!" For a moment, writes Rian Malan, it seemed as if the looters were going to attack her, but she stood her ground, and they melted away. She was left holding a single shoe, some marcher having disappeared with its partner. Then she reached through the shattered window and returned it to its proper place.[7]

I do not know this anonymous and courageous woman. Her action was not headlined in the popular press, filmed for national television or rewarded by public acclaim. But it reached deep into a despairing journalist's heart and, through his written words, shed rays of light and hope on the hearts of many readers, including my own. Her simple deed exemplifies the kind of light-bearing power that accompanies the gospel action of doing good. Imagine, if you will, the transforming effect that thousands of Christ-followers distributed throughout society could have on social and political structures if they, like this lone woman, could be counted on not to cooperate with evil and instead to do what is good.

These three gospel actions, and others like them, embody God's compassionate concern for those close to us and enable them to believe that they really do matter. However, a loud warning bell must be sounded. Embarking on this set of behaviors without the inward guiding and empowering presence of the Spirit will surely result in legalism and burnout. Openness to the spiritual resources and energies of the kingdom is an absolute necessity. And these will only become ours as we engage these gospel actions in loving reliance on the ever-present crucified and risen Christ. "If you love me, you will keep my commandments," he said, "and I will ask the Father, and he will give you another Advocate, to be with you forever" (John 14:15-16).

You and I are called to become like Christ. This goal for the Christ-following life coincides with the desperate needs and challenges of our contemporary world. The times cry out for an unstoppable and sweeping movement of Christlikeness throughout the earth. Nothing else will keep human

> OPENNESS TO THE SPIRITUAL RESOURCES AND ENERGIES OF THE KINGDOM IS AN ABSOLUTE NECESSITY. AND THESE WILL ONLY BECOME OURS AS WE ENGAGE THESE GOSPEL ACTIONS IN LOVING RELIANCE ON THE EVER-PRESENT CRUCIFIED AND RISEN CHRIST.

life sacred. Learning to live our lives as Jesus would if he were living in our place is not simply the most important thing in our lives; it is the *only* thing. May we journey single-mindedly toward this goal.

Following the Signpost Together

1. What motto would you give to the life of Jesus?

2. Share one experience of receiving hospitality that meant a great deal to you.

3. How do you feel about the emphasis on nonretaliation in the teachings of Jesus?

4. "Disorganized good offers weak opposition to organized evil." Discuss.

5. What are your plans to grow into Christlikeness?

CONCLUSION

IN EACH OF THE PRECEDING CHAPTERS, I have briefly outlined one or two activities that could be built into a training program. These experimental activities, or "disciplines of the Spirit" as they are usually described, are all bodily behaviors designed to bring us into dynamic interaction with the spiritual realm. Used by Jesus to nurture his relationship with Abba Father, and time-tested by his followers through the centuries, they represent a practical way of following our Master in his own practices. Unless we learn how to wisely structure our lives around these practices—meditation on Scripture, sharing our hearts with God, being present with those who suffer, fasting from many words, giving generously, studying the teachings of Jesus, and so forth—we will not grow in Christlikeness however much we intend to do so.

These spiritual disciplines are not a way of earning salvation. They do not accumulate for us any heavenly merit or spiritual capital. Our acceptance by God, as we are, rests on grace alone. However, there is nothing automatic about the maturing of our spiritual lives. We become more like Jesus only as we make certain purposeful responses to the freely given grace of God. In addition to our habitual reliance on Christ, the purposeful, strategic use of our bodies represents our essential part in the transformation process. Participation keeps our feet walking along the Pilgrim Way, opens our hearts to receive the divine love, and positions us before God so that the Holy Spirit can work within us.

> SPIRITUAL DISCIPLINES ARE NOT A WAY OF EARNING SALVATION. THEY DO NOT ACCUMULATE FOR US ANY HEAVENLY MERIT OR SPIRITUAL CAPITAL. OUR ACCEPTANCE BY GOD, AS WE ARE, RESTS ON GRACE ALONE.

GUIDELINES FOR TRAINING

How do we begin to put together a suitable training regimen that conforms to the way of Christ? In exploring this question I have found the following guidelines helpful. First, if we desire to follow Jesus into his training practices, *we need to catch a glimpse of how he spent his energy and time when he was "off the spot."*

Reading through the Gospels, and paying particular attention to what Jesus does when he is not in the glare of the public spotlight, gives some idea of his overall way of life. We notice, for example, how he renewed his internal resources for ministry, how he kept in close contact with his friends, how he enjoyed himself at parties and, most especially, how he nurtured his relationship with Abba Father. We cannot copy his first-century Palestine lifestyle, but with a little imagination, we can discern some crucial clues as we train ourselves for godly living. The key question is always: How can I structure my life as Jesus would if he were in my place?

Once we have gained some idea of how Jesus patterned his overall way of life, the next step includes *planning our own personal training program around his practices.*

Spiritual commitments, if they are to prove helpful, need to be translated into specific and concrete terms. Otherwise they remain pious-sounding and abstract concepts that mean little when it comes to the real business of everyday living. For instance, rather than saying, "I'm going to spend more time silently in God's presence," it is wiser to budget fifteen minutes each day for that purpose. Instead of saying, "I'm going to become more compassionate toward others," it is far better to set aside one hour each week to be with someone who is suffering. Formulating a training regimen along these lines gives us the essentials around which we can begin to craft a more Christlike way of life.

> SPIRITUAL COMMITMENTS, IF THEY ARE TO PROVE HELPFUL, NEED TO BE TRANSLATED INTO SPECIFIC AND CONCRETE TERMS. OTHERWISE THEY REMAIN PIOUS-SOUNDING AND ABSTRACT CONCEPTS THAT MEAN LITTLE WHEN IT COMES TO THE REAL BUSINESS OF EVERYDAY LIVING.

When I first began seeking a pattern for my days that would reflect my intention to be Jesus' disciple, I came across the writings and insights of the Quaker Elton Trueblood. His life ministry was permeated by an informed passion for the renewal of the church. As he studied the distinctions of those groups which God had used to breathe fresh vitality into the Christian movement—diverse groups such as the Jesuits and the Wesleyan class meetings—he discerned that they all shared a common denominator: the acceptance of spiritual discipline. Based on his studies, Elton outlined a "minimum" discipline as a starting point for any earnest yokefellow with Christ. His suggested list provided for me the essentials around which I could formulate my first "rule of life." Based on the life of Jesus, and bringing together some of the activities recommended in this book, it went as follows:

1. *The discipline of prayer.* To pray every day, preferably at the beginning of the day.

2. *The discipline of Scripture.* To read reverently and thoughtfully, every day, a portion of Scripture, following a definite plan.

3. *The discipline of worship.* To share, at least once a week, in the public worship of God.

4. *The discipline of money.* To give a definite portion of my annual income to the promotion of Christ's cause.

5. *The discipline of time.* To use my time as a sacred gift, not to be wasted, striving to make my daily work, whatever it may be, a Christian vocation.

6. *The discipline of service.* To try, every day, to lift some burden.

7. *The discipline of study.* To develop my mental powers by careful reading and study.[1]

Crafting a gospel-shaped way of life goes beyond these essentials and usually includes components custom-designed for our unique personalities, personal needs and diverse circumstances. Therefore, a third guideline for the formulation of an adequate training program is that we *regularly review and revise our regimen in the light of our always-changing life experience.*

A life-giving rule, while founded on certain basic and time-tested essentials, is seldom rigid, mechanical or unchanging. Were it to be so, there is the great danger that our spiritual disciplines would become ends in themselves, rather than offering us a solid basis upon which we can grow up into Christ. Margaret Guenther, a seasoned spiritual mentor who has experienced herself in many roles, ranging from wife and mother to that of Anglican priest, emphasizes this need for creative flexibility when she writes: "A good rule can set us free to be our true and best selves. It is a working document, a kind of spiritual budget, not carved in stone but subject to regular review and revision. It should support us, but never constrict us."[2]

I recall one painful phase of my own faith pilgrimage when, for the sake of a more balanced life with God, I needed to rethink my entire way of life. Occurring during a time of extreme spiritual weariness, when I was bordering on the edge of burnout, it meant rearranging the way I lived to include more provision for the enjoyment of God's goodness. Taking my cue from Jesus' own celebrative lifestyle, I deliberately set time aside to celebrate God's goodness within the created order. Although these changes may seem small—changes like giving time to some significant friendships, planning special moments with my wife and family, and doing some "non-churchy" things that I really like—enjoying these activities in conjunction with my faith has brought tremendous benefits. Not only was my vision and energy for the work of the gospel restored, but I also found myself living more consistently with a merry heart.

As you ponder these guidelines, you may sense an internal readiness to formulate and write out a training program for your own development of a greater Christlikeness. Begin by writing down your responses to these questions:

- How do I use my time at present?

- Do I make time for the things I say are important?

- Where in my days can I locate special times for dialogue with God?

- What is the place of corporate worship and the sacraments in my life?

- How am I best renewed in spirit, mind and body? Does time need to be made available for study? exercise? music? solitude? play?

- How can I nurture my most significant relationships?

- How can I give myself (energy, money, influences) in greater service to those who suffer?

- How can I make my daily job the focus of my discipleship life?

Your responses to these questions, and your prayerful reflection on them in reliance upon Christ, will go a long way in helping to craft an overall pattern of life that suits your unique circumstances.

Nothing less than everyday life lived passionately in the Way of Christ can satisfy the unquenched longings of the human soul or relieve the overwhelming needs of our suffering world. May you and I experience the truth of this outrageous gospel promise as we follow the signposts outlined in these pages.

ACKNOWLEDGMENTS

I WAS IMMENSELY ENCOURAGED when Cindy Bunch suggested that IVP bring together my first two books, *Signposts to Spirituality* and *Invitations to Abundant Life,* in a fresh handbook format. Although these two books were written some years ago, both remain close to my heart. They reflect my deepest convictions about what it means to live the Christ-following life as God's Beloved. Cindy then followed up on her suggestion by investing huge amounts of her time, energy and competence in the reshaping of the material into its present form. I am deeply in debt to her and to her team for their colleagueship in this venture.

Through his friendship, personal counsel and writings, Dallas Willard has shaped considerably my understanding of what it means to follow Christ as God's Beloved. Ever since he came to share with us in South Africa over twenty five years ago, he has been a wonderful teacher, mentor and friend along the Way. It is a special honor to have his encouraging and generous words as a foreword to this book.

Books have played an important part in my own spiritual journey. Over the years I have been privileged to spend time in conversation with a number of those authors whose words have greatly influenced my life and discipleship. Thank you to David Benner, Gary Moon, Scot Mcknight, Sister Margaret Magdalene and Gordon MacDonald for both their friendship and their willingness to encourage others to read this book.

Presently I spend most of my time ministering in two very creative congregations—the Northfield Methodist Church in Benoni, and Mosaiek, a predominantly Afrikaans-speaking church in Fairlands, Johannesburg. I am thankful to all those with whom I interact in these two communities, and especially to my colleagues on staff. Much of what I have written in this book gets put to the test in the lives of those who make up these two communities.

I am also in debt to all those involved with the Renovaré movement. It was when speaking at the 2008 annual Renovaré Retreat that I first met Cindy Bunch. The work and ministry of Renovaré, initially under the leadership of Richard Foster and now Chris Webb, is a great gift to the worldwide family of God. Their willingness to associate themselves with this book is much appreciated.

If it had not been for the friendship of Philip Bauser during my high school years, I may never have embarked upon the pilgrimage of faith. Along the Way I have been given the gifts of many good friendships with fellow pilgrims from a wide range of church backgrounds. These friends will know who they are, and I thank them for all that they mean.

My experience with these men and women has taught me that faith and friendship go together.

As always, I am grateful to Lyn Meyer who placed her computer skills at the service of these manuscripts in their original form.

And most importantly, I want to thank Debbie, the woman to whom I am married, and our children Joni and Mark. Their faithful love, thoughtful care and playful companionship mean more than they will ever know. It has been within the daily joys and struggles of marriage, parenthood and home that I have learnt most about myself both as a recovering sinner and as God's Beloved. Often when Debbie cannot go to sleep, she says to me, "Trevor, read me a paragraph from your book so I can fall asleep" I hope this book will keep her awake a little longer!

FURTHER READING

Ignatian Spirituality

If you are interested in exploring the ideas of Ignatius for the present day, I would recommend *Finding God in All Things* by Margaret Hebblethwaite (London: Fount 1994).

Spiritual Disciplines

The two most helpful books that I have found on this subject are *The Celebration of Discipline* by Richard Foster (25th Anniversary ed.; New York: HarperCollins, 2003), and *The Spirit of the Disciplines* by Dallas Willard (San Francisco: HarperSanFrancisco, 1999).

Listening

For a fuller exploration into the activity of listening, I warmly recommend *Listening* by Anne Long (London: Daybreak DLT, 1990). I have also written a booklet on the topic titled *Listening to the Groans: A Spirituality for Ministry and Mission* (Nashville: Upper Room, 2008).

Stewardship

Jacques Ellul, *Money and Power* (Downers Grove, Ill.: InterVarsity Press, 1984).

Richard Foster, *Money, Sex and Power* (London: Hodder and Stoughton, 1985).

Edward Bauman, *Where Your Treasure Is* (Arlington, Va.: Bauman Bible Telecasts, 1980).

NOTES

Chapter 1: Drawing a Picture of God

[1]James Houston, *The Transforming Friendship* (Elgin, Ill.: Lion, 1989), p. 216.

[2]Quoted in John V. Taylor, *The Christlike God* (London: SCM Press,1992), p. 100.

[3]John Powell, *The Christian Vision* (Allen, Tex.: Tabor, 1984), p. 94.

[4]Albert Nolan, *Jesus Before Christianity* (Maryknoll, N.Y.: Orbis, 1978), p. 39.

Chapter 2: Discovering Who We Are

[1]Frederick Buechner, *The Sacred Journey* (San Francisco: Harper & Row, 1982), p. 41, italics mine.

[2]Thomas Smail, *The Forgotten Father* (London: Hodder & Stoughton, 1980), p. 68.

[3]Desmond Tutu, *Hope and Suffering* (London: Fount, 1984), p. 137.

[4]Quoted in Walter J. Burghardt, *Seasons That Laugh or Weep* (New York: Paulist, 1983), p. 3.

[5]Henri Nouwen, *Life of the Beloved* (New York: Crossroad, 1992), p. 26.

[6]Mamphela Ramphele, *A Life* (Cape Town: David Philip Publisher, 1995), p. 196.

[7]Morton Kelsey, *Caring* (New York: Paulist, 1981), p. 150.

Chapter 3: Developing a Christian Memory

[1]Quoted in Walter J. Burghardt, *Seasons That Laugh or Weep* (New York: Paulist 1983).

[2]Joseph Girzone, *Never Alone* (Dublin: Gill and Macmillan, 1994), p. 7.

[3]Henri Nouwen, *The Living Reminder* (Minneapolis: Seabury Press, 1977), p. 22.

[4]If you are interested in exploring the ideas of Ignatius for the present day, I would recommend *Finding God in All Things* by Margaret Hebblethwaite (London: Fount, 1994).

Chapter 4: Receiving the Kingdom

[1]Joseph Girzone, *Never Alone* (Dublin: Gill and Macmillan, 1994), p. 63.

[2]William Temple, *Readings in St John's Gospel* (London: Macmillan, 1963), p. 24.

[3]Donald English, *Why Believe in Jesus?* (London: Epworth, 1986), p. 9.

Chapter 5: Belonging to the Family of God

[1]Interview with Cheryl Carolus in *The Spirit of Hope,* ed. Charles Villa-Vicencio (Johannesburg: Skotaville Publishers, 1993), p. 56.

[2]Interview with Mmutlanyane Mogoba in *The Spirit of Hope,* ed. Charles Villa-Vicencio. (Johannesburg: Skotaville Publishers, 1993), p. 197.

[3]More information can be obtained about gospel-sharing groups and other methods of gospel-sharing from Lumko Institute, PO Box 5058, Delmenville 1403, South Africa.

Chapter 6: Becoming Holy, Becoming Ourselves

[1]Donald McCullough, *Waking from the American Dream* (Downers Grove, Ill.: InterVarsity Press, 1988), p. 101.

[2]The two most helpful books that I have found on this subject are *The Celebration of Discipline* by Richard Foster and *The Spirit of the Disciplines* by Dallas Willard.

[3]Donald Nicholl, *Holiness* (London: Darton, Longman & Todd, 1981), p. 62.

[4]I first came across this story in Henri Boulad's *All Is Grace* (London: SCM Press, 1991).

[5]Kenneth Leech writes of "the culture of false inwardness" in *The Eye of the Storm* (London: Darton, Longman & Todd, 1992), p. 14.

Chapter 7: Loving Those Closest to Us

[1]Elton Trueblood, "Quarterly Yoke Letter," June 1994. (Elton died on December 20, 1994.)

[2]Morton T. Kelsey, *Caring* (Mahwah, N.J.: Paulist, 1981), p. 65.

[3]For a fuller exploration into the activity of listening, I warmly recommend *Listening* by Anne Long (London: Daybreak DLT, 1990).

[4]Dietrich Bonhoeffer, *Life Together* (London: SCM Press, 1954), p. 87.

Chapter 8: Discovering God's Call for Our Lives

[1]I came across this ancient Christian tradition in John Powell's *Through Seasons of the Heart* (London: Fount, 1987), p. 373.

[2]Francis Dewar, *Called or Collared?* (London: SPCK, 1991), p. 6.

Chapter 9: Practicing the Presence of God

[1]Paul Tournier, *Creative Suffering* (London: SCM Press, 1982).

[2]Henri J. M. Nouwen, *Beyond the Mirror* (New York: Crossroad, 1990).

[3]Frank C. Laubach, *Open Windows, Swinging Doors* (Glendale, Calif.: Regal, 1955), p. 17.

[4]John Claypool, *Opening Blind Eyes* (Nashville: Abingdon, 1983), p. 69. (Quoted with the author's permission.)

[5]Brother Lawrence, *The Practice of the Presence of God* (London: Samuel Bagster & Sons, 1908), p. 37.

Chapter 10: Opening Our Hearts to God

[1]Ann and Barry Ulanov, *Primary Speech* (Louisville, Ky.: John Knox Press, 1982), p. 1.

[2]Eugene Peterson, *Psalms—Prayers of the Heart* (London: Scripture Union, 1987), p. 11.

[3]Kathleen Norris, *The Cloister Walk* (New York: Riverhead, 1996), p. 104.

[4]Quoted in Elisabeth O'Connor, *Journey Inward, Journey Outward* (New York: Harper & Row, 1968), p. 21.

[5]Richard Foster, *Prayer* (London: Hodder & Stoughton, 1992), p. 195.

[6]Everett Fulham, *Living the Lord's Prayer* (Lincoln: Chosen, 1980), p. 1.

[7]Interview with Govan Mbeki on SABC TV, 1995.

[8]I learned this way of praying the Lord's Prayer from Morton Kelsey.

Chapter 11: Overcoming Evil Within and Around Us

[1]C. S. Lewis, *The Screwtape Letters* (London: Geoffrey Bles, 1942), p. 9.

[2]Interview with Cedric Mayson in the *Sunday Independent* and a letter by Dr. S. Anton-Stephens to the *Church Times*.

[3]N. T. Wright, *Following Jesus* (London: SPCK, 1994), p. 19.

[4]Morton Kelsey, "Facing Our Inner Evil," in *The Pecos Benedictine* (Pecos, N.M.: March 1994).

[5]Richard Foster, *Prayer* (London: Hodder and Stoughton, 1992), p. 270.

[6]Andrew Walker, "Demonology and the Charismatic Movement," in *The Love of Power or the Power of Love* (Minneapolis: Bethany House, 1994), p. 72.

[7]David Benner, *Healing Emotional Wounds* (Grand Rapids: Baker, 1990), p. 125.

[8]"Special Report on the Truth and Reconciliation Commission," SABC Interview, 1996.

[9]Catherine de Hueck Doherty, *Poustinia* (Notre Dame, Ind.: Ave Maria Press, 1975), p. 69.

[10]Walter Wink, *Engaging the Powers* (Minneapolis: Fortress, 1992), p. 311.

Chapter 12: Witnessing to the Good News

[1]Peter Storey, "Faith and Life," *The Sunday Independent,* 1997.

[2]James Houston, *The Heart's Desire* (Batavia, Ill.: Lion, 1992), p. 160.

[3]See especially the books by Rene Voillaume.

[4]Elton Trueblood, *A Life of Search* (Richmond, Ind.: Friends United Press, 1996), p. 47.

[5]Eugene Peterson, *Reserved Thunder* (San Francisco: Harper and Row, 1988), p. 106.

[6]I have modeled this questionnaire on a similar one found in Sergio Milandri's book *Yes to Myself* (published by the Institute for Christian Spirituality in Cape Town, 1992).

Chapter 13: Stewarding Faithfully What We Possess

[1]See, for example, Jacques Ellul, *Money and Power* (Downers Grove, Ill.: InterVarsity Press, 1984); Richard Foster, *Money, Sex and Power* (London: Hodder and Stoughton, 1985); and Edward Bauman, *Where Your Treasure Is* (Arlington, Va.: Bauman Bible Telecasts, 1980).

[2]Ellul, *Money and Power,* p. 76.

[3]Foster, *Money, Sex and Power,* p. 28.

[4]Morton Kelsey, *Reaching* (San Francisco: Harper & Row, 1989), p. 49.

[5]Ellul, *Money and Power,* p. 110.

[6]Elizabeth O'Connor, *Letters to Scattered Pilgrims* (San Francisco: Harper & Row, 1979), p.

[7]Dallas Willard, *The Spirit of the Disciplines* (San Francisco: Harper & Row, 1988), p. 217.

Chapter 14: Speaking Words of Life and Power

[1]Walter J. Burghardt, *Preaching—The Art and the Craft* (New York: Paulist, 1987), p. 6.

[2]Winnie Graham, "Proud Songs Sung Again," a newspaper article taken from *The Star* (date unknown).

[3]Joseph Telushkin, *Words That Hurt, Words That Heal* (New York: William Morrow, 1996), p. 3. (I am in debt to Bishop George Irvine, who drew my attention to this book and kindly loaned me his own.)

[4]Ibid., p. xviii.

[5]Henri Nouwen, *Life of the Beloved* (New York: Crossroad, 1992), pp. 57-59.

[6]Andrew Miles, "Called to Bless," *The Pecos (New Mexico) Benedictine,* January 1990.

[7]Richard Foster, *Prayer* (London: Hodder and Stoughton, 1992), p. 243.

Chapter 15: Looking to the Life Beyond

[1]Taken from John Wesley's sermon titled "The Spirit of Man."

[2]I first came across this analogy in David Winter's excellent book *Hereafter* (London: A. R. Mowbray, 1981).

[3]This story comes from Henri Nouwen's book *Our Greatest Gift* (London: Hodder and Stoughton, 1994).

[4]Morton Kelsey, *What Is Heaven Like?* (New York: New City Press, 1997), p. 13.

[5]Ian Cowley, *A People of Hope* (Godalming, U.K.: Highland Books, 1993), p. 82.

[6]Thomas Kelly, *A Testament of Devotion* (New York: Harper & Row, 1941), p. 29.

[7]Sue Monk Kidd, *When the Heart Waits* (New York: HarperCollins, 1990), p. 193.

Chapter 16: Growing into Christlikeness

[1]See Genesis 18:1-15; 1 Kings 17:9-24; Luke 24:13-35.

[2]Henri Nouwen, *Reaching Out* (New York: Doubleday, 1975), p. 57.

[3]Walter Wink, *Engaging the Powers* (Minneapolis: Augsburg Fortress, 1992), p. 189.

[4]Peter Storey, *Our Methodist Roots* (Cape Town: Methodist Publishing House), p. 13.

[5]Part of the *Methodist Rule of Life* (emphasis added).

[6]Quoted in John Allen, *Rabble-Rouser for Peace* (New York: Random House, 2008).

[7]Rian Malan, "Confessions of a White South African," *Style*, May 1994.

Conclusion

[1]This rule of life is taken from the Yokefellow Movement started by Elton Trueblood.

[2]Margaret Guenther, *Toward Holy Ground* (London: Darton, Longman & Todd, 1996), p. 66.

What is Renováre?

Renováre USA is a nonprofit Christian organization that models, resources, and advocates fullness of life with God experienced, by grace, through the spiritual practices of Jesus and of the historical Church. We imagine a world in which people's lives flourish as they increasingly become like Jesus.

Through personal relationships, conferences and retreats, written and web-based resources, church consultations, and other means, Renováre USA pursues these core ideas:

- *Life with God* - The aim of God in history is the creation of an all-inclusive community of loving persons with God himself at the center of this community as its prime Sustainer and most glorious Inhabitant.

- *The Availability of God's Kingdom* - Salvation is life in the kingdom of God through Jesus Christ. We can experience genuine, substantive life in this kingdom, beginning now and continuing through all eternity.

- *The Necessity of Grace* - We are utterly dependent upon Jesus Christ, our ever-living Savior, Teacher, Lord, and Friend for genuine spiritual transformation.

- *The Means of Grace* - Amongst the variety of ways God has given for us to be open to his transforming grace, we recognize the crucial importance of intentional spiritual practices and disciplines (such as prayer, service, or fasting).

- *A Balanced Vision of Life in Christ* - We seek to embrace the abundant life of Jesus in all its fullness: contemplative, holiness, charismatic, social justice, evangelical, and incarnational.

- *A Practical Strategy for Spiritual Formation* - Spiritual friendship is an essential part of our growth in Christlikeness. We encourage the creation of Spiritual Formation Groups as a solid foundation for mutual support and nurture.

- *The Centrality of Scripture* - We immerse ourselves in the Bible: it is the great revelation of God's purposes in history, a sure guide for growth into Christlikeness, and an ever rich resource for our spiritual formation.

- *The Value of the Christian Tradition* - We are engaged in the historical "Great Conversation" on spiritual formation developed from Scripture by the Church's classical spiritual writings.

Christian in commitment, ecumenical in breadth, and international in scope, Renováre USA helps us in becoming like Jesus. The Renováre Covenant succinctly communicates our hope for all those who look to him for life:

> In utter dependence upon Jesus Christ as my ever-living
> Savior, Teacher, Lord, and Friend,
> I will seek continual renewal through:
> • spiritual exercises • spiritual gifts • acts of service

RENOVARÉ

Renováre USA
8 Inverness Drive East, Suite 102 • Englewood, CO, 80112 USA • 303-792-0152
www.renovare.us